MW01273783

'The Diplomat'

Major Robert Charles Scanlan

M. F. A.

1st WORLD PUBLISHING

'The Diplomat'

Major Robert Charles Scanlan, M. F. A.

© Robert Charles Scanlan 2006

Published by 1stWorld Publishing
1100 North 4th St., Fairfield, Iowa 52556
tel: 641-209-5000 • fax: 641-209-3001
web: www.1stworldpublishing.com

First Edition

LCCN: 2006940382
SoftCover ISBN: 978-1-4218-9904-6
HardCover ISBN: 978-1-4218-9905-3
eBook ISBN: 978-1-4218-9906-0

This material has been written and published solely for educational purposes. The author and the publisher shall have neither liability nor responsibility to any person or entity with respect to any loss, damage or injury caused or alleged to be caused directly or indirectly by the information contained in this book.

The characters and events described in this text are intended to entertain and teach rather than present an exact factual history of real people or events.

Introduction

When a person writes their own life stories it's not necessary that the writer to be famous, many entertaining and successful novels have been written by undistinguished people. My book is a true recording of history, in terms of what it was like for me in the early years, my home life, school life, career, relationships even my taste and habits. How technology, political and cultural reform affected the people and the environment I grew up in.

Reliving the high and lows, l will endeavour to acquaint you with the individuals who I was fortunate, or not so fortunate to have met. With this in mind, I have been indecisive about publishing for some time now, mainly because of the controversy it will cause. Perhaps some might say boarding on slanderous. For those reason some of the characters names have been deliberately changed.

The irony of the story is some respected members of society have gone to their graves as heroes, when the truth is they were not and never should have been. Couple this with the fact suppressed memories and old stories, which others would rather keep buried, will now resurrect themselves.

Although encouragingly my Mammy once said, 'I have been blessed with an investigative mind, acquiring considerable talent for finding out about hidden issues, having the capability of analyzing things in depth', so I dedicate this book to my Mammy.

Chapter One

There was this young man sitting on a wooden-bench, his radio blasting out the Who's all time classic 'Who are you.' It sounded absolutely brilliant an echoed all around the little quadrangle in stereo. He was well into it, nodding his head backwards and forwards in time with the music and was totally oblivious to the entire human race. Standing there for a moment or so I remember saying to the Paramedic 'I'll have some of whatever he's on' jokingly he replied 'I think I'll join you Bob.' He rang the doorbell and I saw a nurse appear through the windows of the short magnolia hallway. This was a secured locked unit and she opened the door with an infrared electronic key strapped to her uniform. Pushing it open with a big broad smile she said 'Welcome Robert, I've been expecting you; I'm Matron Vera the hospital ward manager, please to meet.' The paramedic passed my notes over to 'Matron Vera' we shook hands and I recall commenting 'have a nice life Man' he returned the complement we shook hands and parted waves.

I admit that Monday morning I was a little nervous hearing all these rumours and old stories, things like, 'once you're in there you never get out, straight jackets and padded cell and all that old codswallop.' An old proverb sprung to mind 'the men in the white coats have come to take you away ha-ha', or is that a song? At any rate, glancing around my new surroundings I couldn't help noticing that some of the men were unshaven and tramp looking, whilst the women had tattoos and smelled of body odour, having lost all interest in their appearances. Not everyone was like that though and those who couldn't bathe themselves were helped each morning by the dedicated nurses, so there was no excuse for looking bedraggled.

Further along my eye caught sight of this old man who constantly walked backwards and forwards. He was wearing a personal stereo and was unaware that his training shoes squeaked loudly as he paced out time. Stained over the years from nicotine and coffee his moustache had now gone that brownie colour around his mouth. I pondered how long he'd been here and wondered how long I would also be confined. Then it dawned on me, nobody knew actually knew I was here. I remember mentioning this to Matron Vera and she told me not to worry 'as the Police had already informed my next of kin'. An hour or so later I was seen by not one but three Psychiatric Consultants, asking me all sorts of questions and what has brought me to all this, especially in this time of life. They were really sympathetic and not judge-mental and during them initial hours, I must have relived and visited most of my entire life. It was like I was in a scene from a movie, a spectator looking on as part of the audience, having these sort of mad slow motion flash backs. Then one of them asked 'Has anyone ever tried to kill you Bob?' Their expressions changed and took on a sinister tone when I told them I was a 'Diplomat' in the United Nations with the rank of Major and how in the early eighties worked with the CIA on secret missions spying against the Israelis, nearly getting shot dead on one of my missions. Furthermore I was certain the Israeli Secret Service 'Mossad' would come after me if I told anyone what really happened, as they have been known to 'shoot first and ask questions later'. I'm not sure if they believed me or not but their final question was, 'Have you ever smoked Cannabis Bob?' I remember thinking 'what's that got to do with it?' shrugging my shoulders replying 'Yeah, vast amounts, but that was years ago when I was a free loading hippie in the eighties.' They sent me out the room to wait whilst they discussed my case and made a diagnosis. After a fidgety ten minutes or so I was called back into the room. They said I was a Paranoid schizophrenic', properly brought on by smoking the pot. Or, if I was telling the truth suffering 'Post Traumatic Stress Disorder' basically an unconscious acting out of something that happened years ago, either way they couldn't make their minds up and sectioned me under the Mental Health Act, actually I felt relived. Although they did suggest it could be therapeutic for me to write about my life experiences in some sort of dairy. They went on to explain this would act as a double-edge sword. For once I could get it off my chest, so to speak, and secondly they could make an appropriate Diagnosis. I agreed and was given medication a pen and paper and sent back to the ward and started laying the foundation stones for this book. I did think, 'you may be disappointed if you fail, but you are doomed if you don't try' so here we go!

It was 1960 an as Big Ben struck precisely eight o'clock one sunny evening in London and whilst Elvis was still shaking all over, I was somewhat launched into this unpredictable universe, landing here on this planet we call Earth! Subconsciously, subliminally, sub-everything, I was having a ball, floating and spinning off in this warm gravitation void. Agonizingly struggling all the way, they had to drag me out head first with this shiny alien object, the forceps! Then if that wasn't enough, they turned me upside down and slapped me across my bum; they called this the shock treatment! Plainly it must have been touch and go for or a while, weighing in more like a baby elephant than a baby boy, almost just becoming another mortality static, hats off to the good old British National Health Service.

Actually just being born brought certain attributes sometimes I would be keen not to have. Firstly being the second son of the second son going back generations, I inherited the name Robert. The 'Scanlan' family fiercely protected this old Irish naming tradition, honouring the custom. I suppose it is our way of protecting the family tree. Perchance this may have caused a little light rivalry as my grand father had fourteen children of his own and maybe they all favoured to use the name 'Robert.' Up until that time my Mammy Josie, Dad and my older Brother Tony were all born and lived in the Republic of Ireland. Officially, I am informed we were all on a fortnight's holiday in England, Mammy went into labour and I was born.

One reason why they might have come on holiday at such a crucial time was, Mammy had already experienced life-threatening problems with Tony. Unfortunately the Irish health service was still stranded in the forties, significantly under-funded and in absolute chaos. However that same public hospital in Dublin is now reputed to be one of the finest in the world. Without any doubt I appreciate the care factor was there, but the service was way over-subscribed—especially the materni-ty unit - with the infant mother mortality rate sharply increasing. This may have been compounded by the fact traditionally the Irish people always had large families, anything up to ten and over was quite normal and still is. You also have to consider this, the situation was probably made worse because of the Roman Catholic Church's decision refusing to accept Birth control, which was making sweeping reform throughout the western world, with the newly named 'wonder pill'. The pill was 99 point something effective and almost over night long held sexual restraints could be thrown aside, altitudes were changing and a sexual revolution was under way—well everywhere except Ireland that is. Collecting society's thoughts, they may have suppressed the mood for cultural change because of changes itself; some resist even if it is better for society as a whole. Furthermore, this may have had triggered the mass-migration of Irish people all over the globe? Consequently the Irish and their happy go lucky culture have managed to penetrate every corner of the Earth, very few returning.

Time and circumstance slipped slowly and serenely by and by and engrained in my memory I was coming up to about five and due to go to school, I would have preferred nursery, but this was exclusively for the wealthy Mums and Dads. Work was difficult for Dad to sustain and many factors played a part in this—not only economic ones. Institutionalized racism was rife and the Irish became the butt of jokes relating to his or her intelligence. What a cheek! He was restricted to constructing Britain's new motorway network, along with the rest of the thick Paddies referred to as Navies. Incidentally the word 'Navies' originates from the Victorian times when the Irish men digging the canals were called Navigators, today referred to as Surveyors, so take that. The Navies received their pay at the end of the day calling it 'the lump', now commonly referred to 'Cash in hand', no tax, no national insurance, no pension, no nothing. He wasn't that kind of man, yearn-ing to pay his way and contribute to society, but he couldn't that's how the construction industry was and in some areas still is. We had our own posh house in Kingston London, to be truthful it was a damp ridden bed-sit, extravagantly overcharged and very over-rated, however it seemed like Buckingham Palace to us. If you were lucky you might get a start in the sausage factory processing the meat, this was a grim bloody job but again everyone wanted it, simply because it was legal and on the cards so to speak. Dad even managed to get an interview once. Mammy washed and ironed his wedding suit to make a good impression, the job taking her all day. Her only tools were a tin bath, the heat from the open fire, an old mangle and an aged electrical iron that kept blowing the fuses.

Through the cracked window held together with collotype I was him leave, his necktie flowing in the wind as he punched the sky. Regrettably, through the same pane, I saw him return. His hopes dashed and his fantastic optimism now vanished, replaced with despondency and disillusionment. There was a whiff of Guinness on his breath, he wasn't drunk but had tried to drown his torment of feeling a failure. Fibbing, he confessed 'he starts in the morning', and then the subject was not repeated again that night. Back home in Ireland he was a skilled engineer and followed his father's example in the rail industry. Granddad was the train driver whilst Dad worked as the fireman stoking the boiler, a highly respected profession and a uniform thrown in for good measure! It all must have been quite exciting, perhaps something like an aircraft pilot today. Day after day working on the roads with his fellow compatriots, talking about the old times, he desired to return to his homeland and felt very downcast about our destiny. Relentlessly he continued pursuing these lost dreams, learning the hard way, the streets of London weren't paved in gold.

Things were not all that bad, fortunately as the second child in the family Mammy received family allowance for me. Whoever was in charge, and in his pearl of wisdom, decided only to allow this money to the second child in every family, thus depriving the first child, an old form of British subjugate. However this was later reformed in the late seventies. Make no mistake I was that second child, and held the British passport, receiving £4.10 a week quite a few bob. Amazingly this small amount could feed us for a week with Mammy's dependable house husbandry. For instance on Monday when the payment was due we could have a real banquet, a whole leg of lamb, carrots, peas, gravy and potatoes, followed by a real treat - ice cream and jelly, all washed down with a bottle of red lemonade, yummy. Decimalization hadn't happened yet and the currency was calculated in pounds shilling and pence, funny enough abbreviated to LSD. Citizens of the day bartered in quarter of a penny called a farthing and then half-a-penny followed by a three penny-bit and the sixpence was called a Tanner. The shilling had the same value as twelve pennies and was called a bob. Half a crown was two and half bob; followed by a ten shilling note refereed to as ten bob, and finally a pound note not surprisingly called twenty bob, confused with all these dodgy bobs, well join the club? Ok its like this, for 30 bob you could buy bags of spuds, kilos of sausages, millions of eggs, beans that will make you fart, oh and a good selection of sweets and a packet of cigarettes for Dad, whose name by the way was also Bob, in today's money 'cheap as chips.'

Like any boy, I enjoyed kicking a ball around, becoming engrossed in the World Cup as it unfolded on our portable black and white TV. In that hot summer of 1966 England beat its old adversary Germany in the World Cup final. The match was beamed live around the globe to an estimated audience of 100 million. Whilst inside Wembley stadium the crowd cheered and clapped our heroes on the field, led by the captain Sir Bobby Moore, another Bob, I was there with Tony and Dad. After full time both sides were locked in a two all draw and the nail biting marathon went into extra time, eventually finishing in the final seconds, when Geoff Hurst got his hat trick bringing the score to 4-2. The commentator of the day concluded by saying 'they think its all over, it is now'. England had done the impossible, and on a lap of honour triumphantly carried the solid gold cup around London. Celebrating with them we went to Piccadilly Circus waving and cheering the nation's champions on. What a fantastic day. The Prime Minister 'Harold Wilson' went on the news and declared a public holiday. He needn't have bothered because nobody went to work anyway, and the whole nation came to a complete stand-still.

Luckily for Dad he had an older sister called Laura who moved to London 5 years previously, and invited us over for Sunday Dinner. Her husband Kevin would pick us up in his little white Volkswagen Beetle we nicked named it Herby; sometimes we managed to squeeze seven of us in. Dads' teenage brother Stan had to ride in the boot, which in the

V. W. is in the front not in the back. Leisurely creeping along at a steady thirty miles an hour Stan kept opening the hood, and we all roared with laughter as the whole situation became even more ridiculous. In the early sixties Surrey hadn't been over developed, there weren't many cars on the road and it retained a sort of rural atmosphere to it. It was such a beautiful place to have lived and our hilarious trip took us over Putney Bridge, across the river Thames and into Richmond Park. As you entered the park you are confronted with these two enormous Victorian black cast-iron gates, over 20 ft tall and 30 ft wide. One gets the impression you are maybe entering heaven and passing through the infamous 'St Peters Gates,' peacefully and idyllic. Centuries ago the Royal family hunted here, the deer still roam freely and it is a grand sight to see wild stags rutting, so the place gives you a sense of history, culture and English-ness about it. Auntie Laura lived just outside the park in a little hamlet aptly and simply named Ham. One of the Bachelors Martin lived close by and we went to Mass together, I remember asking for his autograph. Tommy Steel had a huge Mansion nearby and I would often see him as well, so it was quite an affluent neighbourhood. Auntie had a council house with a massive back garden to play in, moreover a little boys' dream come true, not one but two apple trees to pick climb and swing out off. In fact Auntie Laura became like a second mum to me and I stayed at her house most weekends, a part of my life which I will never forget. It was about that time Auntie bought a Sapling Plum tree from Woolworth's; actually she was a member of staff for over thirty years. Anyway, I was given the honour of planting her and I named her 'Bobby' The great river Thames was pollution free and only stones throw away and entrenched in my memories, these were happy and carefree times to have lived, fishing by the bank with my little green net, going for picnics and long walks, slipping as I tried to climb the mossy green banks, I could even smell the sea when the tide came up.

Things were much different then, people actually spoke to each other face to face, and bidding you good day as they walked around with a smile, in fact the only person who had a mobile phone was James Bond, fitted in his Silver Aston Martin. To get a land line was like taking out a second mortgage, even if you were lucky to afford one you couldn't tell anyone, quite simply because you would have endless queues of neighbours wanting to use it and take messages for them. So the other crac, which I still find extremely funny, was at a pre-arranged time; asks the operator for a collect call to a number in Dublin, the swindle being it was just another public telephone box. Anyhow our relatives would be waiting at the box and accept the charge there, naughty but nice. I can only imagine what it must have been like? Absolute mayhem springs to mind, five or six people trying to cram into this little red box. The thing is they were all so desperate and frantic to speak to each other anything up to five conversations could be happening all at once. Moreover, the same hubbub was occurring in the other telephone box, only difference was this was painted green and three hundred miles away, in a different country paying for the call!

Back in real time, I had been in the hospital ward for a couple of weeks and Matron Vera said my blood pressure was still sky high, so she put me on medication to bring it down. Funny enough after a few days I did start to calm down and feel a bit happier. For now my eye has just caught sight of a poster on the wall which read 'Did you know you have a one in fourteen million chance of winning the National Lottery and a one in fourteen chance of Mental illness? Vera was very kind and seemed to take a personnel interest in me, often as we walked the grounds I would read from my manuscript and she would comment and make suggestions. It was her idea not only to describe my past but also my present, equating you the reader with my new home, environment and companions, so at her suggestion here we go!

The wards were split into two half's, the men to the right, the women to the left. They had a strict rule separating the sexes, an invisible line you didn't cross, and know one was allowed plastic bags or razors either. I did think, that's wrong because and I'm being denied one of my fundamental civil rights, which says everyone has the right to a sexual relationship, what do you think reader? The television suite was reminiscent too a doctor's surgery waiting room, with the inevitable out of date life magazines piled up on the small wooden coffee table. It was all neatly decorated in pale blue and nicely contrasted with newly laid laminated wooden flooring. Actually the soft furniture complimented the surroundings and at the back some one had put a personnel touch, displaying a vase of freshly cut flowers on the windowsill. Sitting with an opened newspaper on his lap was a smartly dressed old man watching TV. I remember thinking he didn't fit the stereotype I was expecting. To be honest I wasn't sure what to imagine, perhaps mad gelled up sticking out hair, with red bulging eyes, like Marty Feldman. Although he must have been deaf as a doorknob though, as the TV was on full blast and you couldn't hear yourself think. Undeterred he looked quite comfortable lounging around on one of the easy chairs. Turning his head away from the TV he sort of said in slow motion. 'Hello—my —name—is—Tom'. I just nodded back and said 'Hi I'm Robert, nice here isn't it'. I sat down and felt very comfortable, as if I was intruding on his pace. I stood up and yawned and on leaving the room the fire door accidentally slammed, it made my heart jump like when someone tiptoes up behind you in the dark and says 'Boo'. Walking the corridor I could hear someone singing, it was a young girl's voice and it echoed through the dormitories and bounced back of the narrow walls. It was 'What have you done today to make you feel proud?' Then I heard another door slam and a man shouting in an aggressive cockney accent 'Fecking Lunatics'. Totally ignoring his remark I causally strolled onward and perchance happen to glance out of one of the side windows. Rolling up the small green embankments I couldn't help noticing tens of thousands of fresh buttercups that had now come into bloom. It was like a sea of yellow Blossom and I thought that's nice. Next on the right hand side was the smoking room. Probably one of the last public buildings left in the country where it's not banned. Actually I do think if they tried to stop it there would have been a riot. Sadly before going in one poor soul passed me by, she was around sixty with long grey uncombed witchlike hair. Dressed in her nightclothes her large breasts now seemed to balance somewhere around her midriff and her teeth resembled Stonehenge. She was carrying a toy doll around, continually petting kissing and cuddling it, imagining and visualising it was her real life child, quite moving in fact! Lost within this total despair and hopelessness she even had a blue blanket wrapped round her baby telling me, 'look Sir, my poor darling got nappy rash'. Maybe she lost one of her own and never got over it, no one could find out because she was that ill, poor soul. Entering the smoking room two men looked up to see who had just come in, and in the corner there was a woman who was heavily pregnant. Resting her cup of coffee on her bump she happily puffed away on a cigarette. Tattoo–upped she blew the smoke away in perfectly shaped smoke rings. Vera told her off because it could harm her unborn baby, she didn't stub it out though. Through the plumes of smoke the girl said, 'hi I'm Nicola'. Whilst one of the men bizarrely looked up and rambled on 'I want my rent money, you owe me six weeks and I'm getting really fed up chasing you around, get my drift' He was pointing his finger at me and really meant it. I don't know who he was or didn't have the foggiest what he was talking about. To be honest days drift into night and back into day, time itself no longer mattered and no one really cared what day it actually was.

Hibernating deep in the back of my mind, something was said, I think, it was Dad not getting the job at the sausage factory. In any case I can't put my finger on it, but my next reminiscence was we were back to Ireland very quickly. It was a cold foggy winter's morning in 1968 when we disembarked at Dun Laoghaire Docks and the Irish capital Dublin was waking up to a new day. Noticing the smiles come back, I knew everyone was happy, we were also homeless and penniless but at least we were homestead! Peering through the railings of the Ha'penny Bridge the fog slowly lifted over the river Liffey and the bright sunlight reflected it first rays of the day. Again I smelled the sea and thought about cosmopolitan London and the Thames, pondering if I would ever see them again. The first thing that struck me was most of the women wore headscarves, and the men wore flat-caps and everyone spoke with my parent's accent. The whole shebang was painted green instead of red, the post office, buses and letterboxes; even those phone boxes with all those outstanding charges from London. In the early hours with our suitcases we roamed through the half deserted streets, what else struck me was its oldie-worldly Victorian appeal. There were horses still pulling a variety of delivery carts and proud looking men in suits riding bare-back smoking fags at the same time.

At first we stayed with mammy mum 'nanny Gu-gu,' evidently Gu-gu got her nickname when she was a baby and it stuck to her all her life. Why I'm not sure, maybe it was the first word she ever uttered, although, through my research I have uncovered, it also means the 'Guardian of morals'. Conceivably my ancestors also knew this fact when they named her. Gu-gu was a widow most of her life but not alone, having an older sister called Kitty, they were wise kind old ladies and regarded highly amongst the family. Kitty on the other hand was a spinster; went to mass most days and should have been a nun. The building Nanny lived all her life belonged to the 'Catholic Church' and must have been just as old. The fabric of the house was poorly maintained and hadn't been painted for donkey's years. Stained from coal smog, the external brick walls had now turned black from this acid rain. Inside the whole place smelled of rising damp and dusty old floor-boards. At the top of the winding old staircase lurked a leaking skylight, even with this natural light it always dark and dingy. The banister made a creaking sound and was inclined to move from side to side when you leaned on them and the naked wooden flooring amplified your foot steps through the entire building. This multiple occupancy building hadn't yet been connected to the electric supply yet, so gas lamps were situated outside each of the tenant's front doors. That first night home we had a proper Irish Hooley. Mammy grew up in Francis Street with her sister May and couldn't wait to show off her children to the lady in the corner shop. Uncle 'Con', May's future husband was also there too. Everything was put on 'tick' at the shop and we enjoyed cakes crisps and pop. Guinness flowed freely amongst the adults and Dad was heard singing 'In Dublin's Fair City where the girls are so pretty', you know the one reader! Outside in the coarsely concreted backyard was a pur-pose built brick communal toilet, with three families sharing the same facilities? Some would spend what seemed eternity in there, especially if you wanted to go yourself, studying the racing form I presume. Beside that, was a large white porcelain sink with one hefty brass cold tap? There was an old mangle and a washing line that crossed the yard in a funny zigzag pattern. Water was ferried in buckets; everyone had to take it in turns, up and down the noisy stairs including the deposal of the other. More often than not I saw it go flying out the window a few times, especially when it was raining, a far cry from the leafy suburbs of Surrey. Indecently reader the building is still there, but now it's an Antique shop with a musty smell.

With a box of Swanvesta kept on the mantle piece, Gu-gu would light the gas lamps either side of the fireplace. They gave off a tranquil hissing sound and a ghostly flickering light, which in turn bounced back haunting shadows of every wall. Dad would entertain us by mak-ing shapes with his hands, creating shadows of horses, rabbits and birds against the wall. Gu-gu also seemed to have the biggest brass bed in the Dublin and we all slept snugly together. Except our dad that is, who slept on an inflatable beach li-lo in front of the raging fire. Coal was cheap and plentiful and for an extra penny the coal man would carry it up the stairs, depositing the entire bag on the floor next to the fire for you. It was quite bizarre to wake up and see a huge mountain of shiny black rocks just lying there, and everyone being glad about it. Reliving the milestone, I recall an antiquated gas cooker propped up in the corner, above it hanging from nails on the wall were some blackened pots and pans. The cooker wasn't used much anyway, as the gas was saved for the lamps, a shilling a go in the meter. Anyhow, everyone was accustomed to cooking on the open fire. Next to the window was a large round dinning table. As we sat drinking tea I could see right into the belfry of nearby 'St Patrick's Church' parallel about two hundred yards. Inside were these huge enormous brass bells, complete with the wheels happily swinging away, they tolled in tandem and the sound was quite magnificent. It was especially poignant for me to see and hear this and it evoked some sort of spiritual excitement. Every one went to Mass and we all received Holy Communion and prayed a lot, for what purpose I'm not sure.

After awhile Dad put our names down on the Corporation waiting list, and they moved us into a block of run-down flats called St Teresa Gardens. Soon later another brother was born and we called him Eddie. Now there were five off us in a 2 bedroom flat, in probably the roughest part of Dublin. More for necessity, my plum-in-the-mouth English accent soon faded away, melting quickly in with the rest and Tony I went to school at nearby St Teresa Gardens School. The school was built in a traditional look of stone and granite blocks and must have stood for a millennium of years. Outside on the pavement were black railings, which all the kids and I had great fun on, swinging around like monkeys. Nuns taught me on a black roof slate and stick of white chalk. We had the inevitable wooden lift up desk, with the space for the ink well in the corner; only problem was there was no ink or pens. Exercise books were none existent along with reference books or dictionaries. To me, computers were something to do with Russian space program, which had just put the first man into orbit with Sputnik 8.

Next to the school lived all the Nuns in the Convent; once they even took us in for a look around. Vaguely I remember built out of the same grey stone was a high wall surrounding the entire perimeter. In comparison through my child's eyes it looked like the Great Wall of China, all six thousand and four kilometres of it. Entry was gained through an undersized arched door; if you were tall you had to duck.

We queued up in a straight line, stretching back about a hundred yards and as always I was at the very back, skulking. Definitely no talking, spitting or farting allowed on this one. Poor but happy we must have looked a state; my jumper had been knitted by someone for someone else, having a massive hole on the arm. Tony wasn't much better with a big patch sewn on the bum of his trousers. There was a boy with bright ginger hair and freckles called Malake, whose big toe pointed out of the front of his shoes. Head lice were everywhere, some even had worms, spotting them was easy always fidgeting and scratching their bum. The Sisters patrolled up and down the line, the mannerism and the way they all dressed identically made them look quite fierce. As a real treat each of us was given a red apple to munch on during the guided tour. Contemplating innocently to myself as I passed through the thought gate, this has got to be the 'Garden of Eden'. If that the case I shouldn't eat the apple, starving hungry I ate the core as well. This paradise was skilfully and beautifully balanced, including pure white doves happily flying around symbolizing freedom and peace. There were mature fruit trees dotted around, apples, plums, pears even an allotment growing an array organic vegetables. Some of the Sisters were kneeling down on mats tending the land, whilst others walked around carrying wicker baskets full of fresh produce. They even had a little green house where they grew fresh flowers for our Lord's Altar. Further along the narrow gravel path I smelled lavender and experienced the sight and sound of bumblebees buzzing about. Whereupon we came too a small working farm complete with a brown and white cow called 'Shamrock'. Sister Fiona was sitting on a small stool milking her by hand. It made a funny squeaking noise when it came out of her udders. We all thought it was extremely funny making us all giggle with laughter. On the other bench beside her was a pale of Shamrocks fresh milk. Quietly shuffling past we were allowed a little taste, putting the ladle to my mouth it tasted absolutely gorgeous, rich and creamy. Further on there was a fenced off corral housing a mummy pig and her litter of piglets, one of the sisters fetched a couple for us to cuddle. Being inner city kids this was the highlight of the tour, and little did we know they were soon fattened up ready to be turned into sausages for dinnertime, yummy! At the end of the gravel path set back in a hollowed out rock retreat, was a full life size statue of 'Our Lady Mary', including what looked like a natural water spring trickling over her shoeless feet. Our Lady looked so beautiful, draped over her head her long blue garment matched her pastel coloured eyes. Oddly, able to maintain eye contact from whatever angle you looked at her.

The winding queue of children was then led inside the convent. Entering I was staggered at the high dome shaped ceiling, decorated with a fantastic mural of Jesus and the Apostles at the Last Supper, the colours were bright crisp and clean. The walls however had a dark oak panelling to all sides, and trampled out over the years the wooden stairs now had uncanny low spots in the middle. At the top of the wide staircase was a long landing; through the corridor I heard the sisters singing in harmony, it sounded like Latin. Everything looked so in place including the fresh flowers neatly displayed on the widow sills. We were led hand in hand into their private chapel for our Easter Mass, I thanked Jesus for being alive, Mammy and Dad my two brothers and also could I ask for a little miracle. Firstly, would he fix it so mammy could get a full house on the bingo, not a lot, just enough as not to be greedy? Secondly, as it was Easter could we have proper Easter eggs not the broken bits of chocolate from the Cadburys factory again? Blessing myself I promised to be good, say my prayers and help mammy peeling the potatoes properly. To be honest reader, I had a habit of wasting most of the spud by slicing them into squares, everyone eating the Irish stew new I had helped prepare the meal, simply because they had square shaped potatoes instead of the conventional round ones!

At home time we received a small parcel wrapped in the 'Daily Herald' all tied up neatly with a little piece of string. Sister Naomi told us 'not to open it until we got home, if we did have a sly look, they would find out from God, whom they had direct contact with in Heaven' I suppose that's where the saying put the fear of God into you comes from. Taking no chances, Tony and I ran all the way home as fast as our little legs could carry us. Coming up the street, I saw Mammy looking out from our scullery window and smiling back we waved our surprise bundles. Arriving home Eddie was in the tin bath next to the open fire and scrambled out naked for better look, splashing water all over the lino. Slowly with confident expectation I opened mine, only to discover half a kilo of broken chocolate, 'you're a lucky boy aren't you,' said Mammy. Well I didn't feel very lucky, what about my miracle? And all that time I spent praying, so hard in fact it gave me a splitting headache. Lingering at the back of my mind was the fact that I missed London, and this sense of injustice, the feeling of always being last at the end of the queue, or perhaps it was just me and my unrealistic dreams yet again. In any case, my emotions got the better of me bursting into a flood of tears, running away locking myself in the toilet refusing to come out under any circumstance. Bewildered by my strange reaction Mammy stood dumfounded, whilst Eddie responded by announcing 'if he doesn't want it, I'll have it.' Thinking about him eating my chocolate soon changed my mind and Mammy ultimately managed to coax me out, 'What on earth is the matter Bobby? I tried to speak but my jaw seemed to be locked in the downward position, tear jerking and wobbling around on its own. Blurting, all I got out was 'I hate God, Jesus, Moses all the saints, the twelve apostle and all the holy people in the whole wide world, moreover; 'I'm never going to mass ever again in my life' After my outburst I pretended not to notice a neat little pile of chocolate waiting for me on the table. My brothers were already sitting in front of the fire, watching an old black and white Laurel and Hardy film, happily eating theirs and it didn't take long for me to get into the crac either. Between munching on bigger bits than his mouth Eddie asked 'Why do you hate God so much, what has ever done to you? Finishing me off in his mischievous childish manner by saying, 'Now you'll have to go and wash your mouth out in a bar of soap and holy water, wont you?' Mammy intervened reassuring me God works in very mysterious ways, in the meantime say another prayer and go to confession, and we all sat down quietly filling our faces engrossed in the film.

Although it was a two bedroom flat our only heating was coal fires and during the night the fire would naturally burn out. Not only for comfort, but to counteract the cold we all slept together tightly in the one double room at the back. Remarkably, that Easter morning when I awoke 'Gu-gu' was already there and a roaring flame was just taking hold. Scratching the sleep sand from my eyes I saw mammy was busy as usual and had already started breakfast, hot toast and freshly smoked kippers from Dublin harbour. After breakfast mammy washed us all in carbolic soap, deloused and dressed Tony and I identically in the hand knitted cardigans knitted by Gu-gu and Kitty, our Eddie had a funny looking hair cut. Along with matching socks my grey trouser was neither long nor short and dangled somewhere around my knees; all we had to do now was wait for Kitty to bring our Easter eggs and new shoes. Write on time I saw Kitty get of the bus and Dad went down to help the old girl with her bulging carrier bags. Waiting by the front door all the kids hovered around her in anticipation. Entering Kitty beggared us on for the crac by saying 'Oh-no-oh-no' carrying on 'sit down around the table and you will get your turn, now calm down children' Tearing the neatly wrapped paper to pieces I discovered to my amazement, a pair of new shoes a cowboy hat and a complete unbroken Easter egg. My faith in God was instantaneously restored; nothing now seemed out of my grasp, as long as I did all that praying bit. Listening to the Bachelors 'I remember you' on the radio the grownups finished off their fish, had a cup tea and smoked a Players cigarette. Then all prepared we set off to the Chapel for 11 o'clock mass. Dressed as new pins we held our heads high and followed the immaculately turned out procession, all heading in the same direction. After mass we caught the number 57 bus into Dublin city centre. To capture this moment in time for all eternity Kitty had made an appointment at a high-class photography studio in Parnell Street and we sat on long leather table for a group picture. Gu-gu was there too, guaranteeing if we good and smiled a lot we could have a 'Melon-Colin-Baby.' What a real treat, vanilla ice-cream full of granulated chocolate, exotic fruits and bits of coconut, all mixed up with cold lemonade served in a tall skinny glass, they even gave me a really long skinny spoon to fetch it out with, mouth-watering!

At the time it was all the rage to go to Saturday morning pictures so for the crac we did just that. Topping the bill at the Lenster was the 'Lone Ranger as the sheriff' his horse was called Silver and the trio was made up with a Red Indian scout Tonto. They were the goodies always getting their man dead or alive. They were my real life heroes and I wanted to be just like them, going to the Wild West, ridding stallions, leading the posse and having gun fights at the 'Last Chance Saloon' Before the matinee begun, I got a bottle of lemonade and a bag of popcorn to see me through. The place was absolutely packed and there must have been five hundred screaming kids, I was sitting near the back and had a good view of the screen and all the action taking place in the audience. As soon as the curtains opened and the light dimmed the place erupted and we became thespians ourselves, playing our own part in the film. The noise was absolutely deafening, beginning with the stamping of feet, accompanied by the sound of someone banging and rattling the seat behind you. If you could whistle loudly then you did, failing that you shouted 'Gedie-up high ho silver' at the top of your voice, it was a great crac. Each Saturday was a follow on soap opera from the week before and this week was a special; the lone Ranger and Tonto were fighting for their lives, left for dead, tied up in a snake invested dissuade gold mine, locally know as the 'Widow Maker.' The rainy season was due which made it even more harrowing, as the unusually high water was about to flood the mineshaft. Their only chance was to call 'Hi-ho Silver' and wait for the hero horse to rescue them. Silver had been stolen and dragged away by some strangers called the 'Mexican bum-bandits', and had to escape first before he could help anyone. Cleverly he managed this by chewing through the rope tied around his neck and then sneaking away during the middle of the night, when nobody was looking. He had super hearing and could hear his master calling him from any where, to me this was reality TV and live, hi- ho silver was the crac. Galloping faster than the speed of light he made it to the 'Widow maker,' just as the water rushed down the Grand Canyon. Unbelievably at this crucial point of the film the projector packed up the curtains closed and all the lights came back on. Defiantly all the kids started booing and whistling, sitting firmly throwing popcorn reaped-ally chanting 'we want our money back, we want our money back' this was an even better crac than the film. After a few minutes the picture returned, but we were missing the vital section were Silver was doing his heroic rescue bit, any way know one really cared, now we had been switched to a wild west gun battle. The Lone Ranger and his deputy Tonto had all the gear on, hats, leather waistcoats, spurs, wearing Levi's packing a pair of smith and western guns. I had the cowboy hat I been wearing all day, some of the other kids had the lot, dressed like real cowboys. Our heroes tracked the bum-bandits all over California and the wild planes of Arizona to a small deserted ranching town called 'The Bullocks'. Cautiously they trotted down Gun-ho Main Street, the horses hoofs kicked up the dry dust and the sun glistened on their shiny sheriff badges. Women and children ran for their lives, closing doors and shutters behind themselves. The small undertaker in a tall black hat was making himself busy running round with a tape measure. All was quite as the dynamic due tied and watered their horses outside the 'Last chance saloon'. The music whipped the audience into an absolute frenzy, everyone was screaming and shouting and in my newfound Irish accent, I couldn't help blaring out 'look behind you, look behind you.' At one point Tonto did look round and I actually thought he heard me. Slowly they dismounted glancing from side to side eventually fixing their eyes on the swinging doors of the saloon bar. Inside came the sound of an unturned piano and the laughter of men and women. Casually they strolled in, the music came to an abrupt end when the sheriff said, 'One-Ball-Ted from Texas you're wanted for murder and bank robbery in six states and I'm taking you in, dead or alive'. One ball and his gang were playing cards and had their backs to goodies, it all came to a standstill before One-ball started laughing hysterically, suddenly he turned round in his swinging chair and fired the first shot and the gun fight was on. Our heroes drew their pistols and fired a volley of bullets into the mob, killing all of them one by one, stone-dead. Before dying One-ball fired a few last desperate shots that hopelessly missed, smashing the huge mirror behind the bar, bullets were riddling everywhere; I could almost smell the gunpowder and feel the hits myself. All the bum-bandits died slowly in agony wriggling about on the floor. One ball took about ten hits to the body, taking the longest to die, eventually crashing through the first floor banister onto a table which in turn shattered into smithereens, finally lying motionless with blood dripping from the corner of his mouth. Following the shootout the bar tender popped his head up from behind the counter and pored himself a large whisky then another one, dead bodies lay all over the place which made the undertaker very happy in fact almost ecstatic. The lights came back on and everyone cheered, the Lone-ranger and Tonto were safe, at least until next week that is.

Nothing much happened for a short while until we had a little sister; we named her 'Olive' after one of my great- great ancestors. Six of us crammed in the small flat like a tin of sardines, nice! Luckily Dad had returned to his profession as a engineer and I think I was 8 or so when I had my first business, selling kinder-wood in small bundles lighting the people's coal fires. My firm was the cheapest on the estate, buying all the off cuts from the local wood factory for a penny, and then reselling them for two penny's. My assets included a Donkey called Dougal and an old pram which acted as my cart. Everyone knew us, and all the kids would give me chips or sweets, just to have a ride on him. We were very happy successful entrepreneurs, working together as a team, building up a client base and all. Any profit paid for Saturday morning pictures and the little that was left over went back into looking after Dougal. I really did love him, getting him the best carrots Brussels sprouts and oats; particularly fond of hot toast, which I willing cooked on the nightly bonfire. Fundamentally, if he got sick I prayed a lot, when there is no help I learned to help myself. Astonishingly I learnt about homemade potions, remedies and old fashion medicines, things like how to make a poetess out of boiling hot milk and bread. This worked wonders on infected wounds, literally soaking up the entire puss. However the only draw back from this method was it must have been extremely painful for him. Another good one was if he had a chest infection rub mustard and honey together and then smooth it in all over his chest, this made him stink and unpopular for a while but it was very potent. Sadly some ponies were often poorly treated and the majority where on there last lap, ready for the knackers yard. In the evenings kids raced these haggard looking animals. We called it Jockeying, no one had saddles stirrups or reins, holding on by the seat of my pants I grabbed Dougal's ears, he didn't much like it and repeatedly kept turning round to bite me. At a drop of a hat the race was on, kicking my heels into him too gallop, but Dougal had ideas of he's own and refused to start. The rest of the field had made a couple yards on us, when suddenly he must have had an adrenaline rush deciding to burst into action, or it could have been them Brussels sprouts. Flat out I must have been doing no more than 10 miles an hour, but I didn't care at least I was moving, bouncing and tossing around like the bucking bronco, 'yahoo.' Half-a-ton of animal under your belt made me a man, riding around Dublin like a real cowboy, proud to be part of the posse, Yahoo! Needless to say I came last in that race and every other one too, but what a crac they were. As well, the on course betting meant a lot could be riding on the winner, maybe even a bag of chips!

Dougal had been a working pony all his life, I managed to swap him with for an old bike with some kid at school, in Donkey years he must have been well over a hundred and looked it! With the limited resources to hand, I looked after him the best I could, his green canvas coat kept him dry in the winter and his nose bag was always filled with whatever I could afford. He was also tied up with the rest of the poor animals under the Concur tree behind the back of Mr. Slattery's shop. We had just finished work one night when he started being very sick, lowering his head to the floor he began making a peculiar noise. It was like a sad groaning sound which emanated from deep within him. Knowing he might die rite here and now in front of my eyes on the cold street, I had to do act quickly. Whipping the tears from my eyes, I slowly lead him down the dimly lit cobbled street to the horse doctor—Mr. Saturday. He was a very kind old Gentleman and said he could cure him with his magical powers. He also knew I didn't have two brass farthings to rub together, so suggested I paid him back in kindness. All I had was the few bundles left in my old pram but promised if he would cure him, I in return would give him free fire-wood for the rest of his life. Sure enough that morning when I returned Dougal was well. Eventually I lent Dougal to the gypsies one night; they could give him a better life in the west. Roaming the mountains where he could walk in the green-green grass of home. Saying goodbye though, I looked straight into brown eyes, parting his grey mane I kissed his brow for very last time, I gave him one bigger cuddle wrapping my arms round and said 'love you'.

My pet donkey became a distant fond memory and my attention soon turned to another crac, uncle Con and his red Honda moped, the same ones they use to deliver pizzas. He was like an older brother, teaching me how to ride the bike an all. Helmets weren't compulsory, so as cool as you like we roared around Dublin like a pair of lunatics. On Sunday's afternoons we would ride the bike to the coast, diving off a cliff called the 'Forty-foot'. This was an exclusively all male beach and tradition has it you made the dive naked, nothing perverted it was just accepted as the crac! The sheer vertical drop from the cliff edge was literally forty foot straight down. The dive could only be made when it was a high tide and timed with the incoming swell, quite a dangerous stunt if it all went wrong. Con was brave enough to attempt a full head-first dive; fortunately everything went well and he surfaced a few moments later and shouted 'your go Bob.' On the other hand I wasn't that brave, blessing myself I just ran off the edge naked with my eyes closed, actually it gave me a great thrill and I couldn't wait for another go.

When the tide was too rough the pair of us would go and check out Dublin City Docks. As the boats landed sailors threw ropes shore side whilst others dropped anchor. There were super-tankers, steamships, ferries and a fleet of small fishing boats. Amazed at these vessels, and lost in thought wondering were they came from and were they were going to next. It was a hive of activity, men where busy hauling goods away on pony and trap. I saw boys on peculiar looking delivery bicycles, having a small wheel on the front allowing for a deeper wicker basket. Scooting onward we passed two or three enormous steel cranes, vigorously unloading cargo from the bowls of these great freighters. By the jetty fisherman in leather aprons sharpened knifes, preparing the days catch throwing the waste back into the sea. There was the distinct smell of fish and flapping above hoards of screeching seagulls, diving in now and again to pick up a free meal. Women and children set up shop on the side of the road selling a selection of fresh fish, all wrapped in yesterday's newspapers. I recall noticing a naval war ship in the dry dock being painted battleship grey. Longer than a football pitch, she looked awesome as her big guns swung towards the horizon. On board young men in uniform patrolled up and down the decks. This was the stuff dreams are made out of, and I was one of the biggest dreamers of them all, still am actually! Grouped together on the dock mothers and sweethearts eagerly waited for the loved ones to disembark. My imaginary career path commuted from a cowboy riding the prairies, to a sailor foot louse and fancy free sailing the seven seas. We could spend all morning messing about there, returning home with the fresh fish Mammy had put on her list, and my true fantastic tale of the day.

West of the city are the Dublin Mountains and on occasions Con I would set off for long weekends, camping in the woods next to the lakes. It was grand to escape city life for a while and my time was occupied doing things little boys did best, climbing trees, swimming and fishing for our evening supper. We went hiking and I remember one morning we stumbled on an old pathway. Obviously abandoned years ago the weeds and stinging nettles had taken it over and we became intrigued with this discovery so eagerly followed it to its very end. Twentieth century man had now added barbed wire and on the rise of the hill was a gypsy camp, the smoke pluming from the campfire. Beyond that we came to small woodland and I picked up a nice long stick to help me beat back the overgrown jungle. Prodding and jabbing the scrub as I went, looking for rut holes or illegal traps. There were signs of rabbits and deer, and I had already noticed a few empty gun shot cartages lying around so knew the travellers had been out hunting for their evening dinner. The trees got higher and higher and the sunlight beamed through the dense bottle green canopy in curved narrow rays, oh, it was so lovely calm and surreal. I felt like a real explorer and thought Con and I must have been the only human ever to tread this path. Beating the undergrowth back we made it into the very middle and could hear the wood pigeons cooing in the background. This was a secret place and as I looked up into the canopy I watched the adult sparrows bringing food for their chicks in the nest. We were totally isolated from society and sat down on an old fallen oak tree for a rest. Listening to our little portable radio Con rolled another cigarette, it was someone playing the flute and the sound echoed all over the little forest and seemed to bounce of the tress in harmony. Not long after a pair of friendly Robins perched on a branch close by. I took one of my bread and jam sandwiches from my lunch box and sat patiently holding it out with my hand. Sure enough they couldn't resist and came as close as I am to you now reader, eventually they let me hand feed them both. This harmony and tranquillity was only broken by a scurry of noise and a rustling of dried leaves coming from behind me. The little birds flew away, and as I turned round happened to glimpse a baby rabbit bouncing and hopping along its merry way. When nightfall came we sat around the campfire frying the fresh trout and boiling our fresh duck eggs, yummy! Above us the sky was crystal clear and I studied the universe with his Con's home-made brass telescope. We liked things like that, contemplating the vast cosmic expanse far out.

We were in the late sixties and unearthly extraordinary things were happening in the cradle of humanity. The space age era had already started and the public remained fixated on space exploration. The Apollo 11 mission was launched and Con and I watched the granny black and white images along with the rest of the billions of earthlings. Neil was Captain and for the crac brought two of his mates along with him Mick and Buzz. Their futuristic star ship 'Columbia' blasted off from the launch pad reaching earth's orbit within a staggering eleven minutes. Transfixed I couldn't believe my eyes when the man said they had reached a phenomenal speed of 18000 miles an hour, heading on the 980000-mile trip. When they got there Mick remained on board whilst the other two unlocked the lunar module called 'Eagle' and slowly descended to the unknown alien planet surface and the final frontier. It was all very exciting and I did wish I was one of them; I even remember running out the back yard trying to spot them through the telescope, the things you do when you are a child! Anyway as the module made a perfect touch down Neil said, 'The Eagle has landed' and cheer rang out across the world. Buzz couldn't wait and was first down the ladder, saying the now infamous words, 'one small step for man one giant leap for mankind.' The urban space men spent their time floating and spinning off in the gravitational void, taking photos, collecting lunar rocks and setting up these mad experiments. Rendering everyone speechless Present Nixon phoned them up on the first mobile in the world, congratulating them on such an outstanding achievement. Later on in the hospital I thought what music which might fit the bill, and came up with 'Ground Control to Major Tom' by David Bowie. Remarkably the foot prints they left behind will last for infinity, out living any man made structure including the Great Wall of China, simply because there is no solar wind to blow them away. Unlike the flag which is still abode of attention, apparently it got knocked over when the Eagle jettisoned from the extraterrestrial surface. It appears that section of the original film is missing; adding to the conspiracy theory and the rest is history.

After that moments in time vanished so quickly and another year or so slipped serenely by and by. Mammy had her fifth child, a boy our Francis. Now there were seven of us all crammed into the small cold flat. The housing problems in Ireland were worsening; the waiting list was as long as your arm and didn't hold out much hope either, another five years at least. The estate was a depressing dismal place, political gravity was everywhere and the territory was breading ground for the 'Irish Republican Army', commonly known as the former 'I. R. A.' The troubles in Northern Ireland had flared up again and the 'British Army' had to be called in to protect the Catholics from the Protestants. Faced with the depravity of the situation Dad was under pressure to stay put and wait it out, or alternatively go back go back to England. Things were somewhat taken out of his hands when the environment we lived started taking it toils on his beloved children. Eddie was the first on the hit list, falling down the communal concrete stairs breaking his arm, bashing his head and fracturing his ribs, he really did look like a wounded solider on his crutches. Everything went from bad to worse to catastrophic, while he was still in plaster I fell on a rusty old nail getting a nasty leg infection, needing surgery and stitches. Meanwhile whilst Eddie and looked like the walking wounded, our Francis caught Pneumonia.

That morning our Olive curiously asked why our Francis had suddenly gone very quiet and wouldn't wake up for his morning feed. Mammy told us he was just having a nap and washed and dressed him as usual, wrapping him in his favourite blue and white blanket. Dad had already gone to work and couldn't be reached, so we all accompanied Mammy pushing the squeaking old Silver Cross pram to the clinic. I remember it was early morning, no was around and it had just started to snow. Olive managed to squeeze in next to Francis and cuddled him to keep him warm; Eddie was lying down underneath in the shopping trolley bit, whilst I hobbled along side holding Tony's hand. It seemed to take forever to get there and at one point I thought the wheel was going to fall off the pram. Thank god it didn't and we eventually made it to the clinic.

Inside the white tiled reception area was a queue of people patiently sitting on wooden stools, waiting their turn? I can recall the distinct smell of disinfectant and the sound of another baby crying in the background. Then, still motionless in the pram mammy showed her lifeless baby to one of the nurses, and the atmosphere in the surgery suddenly took on a sinister tone. Tony and I were put in charge of the little ones, whilst Francis and Mammy were hurriedly led away, shutting the door behind themselves. There was an old lady watching the drama unfold and kindly came over and sat with us until mammy came back. At a snail's pace five or ten minutes ticked slowly past until mammy returned from where she had been, this time without my little brother. Frantically looking behind her I asked 'where's our Francis mammy' she couldn't control her grief, her harrowing floods of tears said it all to me. Eddie or Olive were too young and couldn't comprehend what was happening, standing up innocently asking, 'who hurt you mammy'? That was the straw that broke the camel's back, and the last I saw of him, and a few days later he was taken away and buried in a little white coffin. Emotional scars like this are hard to see and even harder to heal, although they mend over time, but the whys and the wherefores are never forgotten. About a week or so later dad sold all his worldly goods, raising the boat fare back to England, leaving our troubles behind we started again.

Although, as I grew I tried to visualise what Frances would have looked like. Asking myself, has he grown up to be a man like me in Heaven or will he always be a Baby. I tried to find his little grave, but to no avail, I bought some flowers anyway and laid them next to a tree, saying a prayer by 'St Francis'.

Lord, make me an instrument of thy peace, where there is hatred, let me sow love.

Where there is injury, pardon. Where there is discord, vision.

Where there is despair, hope. Where there is darkness, light.

Where there is sadness, Joy.

Weeks had now turned into months and as part of my therapy 'Matron Vera' gave me a task to write at least one page a day, it reminded me when I read the book 'The Hobbit'. In the meantime they had a rehabilitation programme called 'Occupational Therapy', where the patients could attend educational classes within the hospital grounds. They also had a small library and I read about mental illness, discovering there are many types of mental ill health. For example did you know we have 'Bipolar Disorder'; symptoms include feelings of omnipotence and power, racing thoughts, extreme mood swings and boundless energy. Through my research I uncovered that American surveys suggest 6% of their population have it. Then we have Schizophrenia, symptoms include illogical thinking, hearing voices, poor concentration, delusions, confused language and unusual behaviour, and withdrawal from family and friends, I admit I did have that and stopped my wife from seeing me. Others include severe anxiety, panic disorder and obsessive compulsive disorder and post traumatic stress disorder. From my observations on the ward the worst was 'Severe Depression'. The main characteristics of this are a feeling of worthlessness, guilt and hopelessness coupled with the lack of concentration and inappropriate emotions or thoughts. I bet you didn't know all these had a mental illness? Winston Churchill, Charles Darwin, Thomas Edison, King George III, Ernest Hemingway, Thomas Jefferson, John Keats, Abraham Lincoln, Michelangelo, Florence Nightingale, Robert Louis Stevenson and Sir Isaac Newton, remember him he discovered gravity because an apple hit him on the head. An old proverb spring to mind that states there is a fine line between madness and genius. Then another door slammed there was a lot of that, and I heard one nurse cry out 'this is getting more like a geriatric ward than psychiatric.' Someone started to laugh hysterically followed by someone else, and then the whole lot joined in.

Robert Charles Scanlan

Chapter Two

The Seventies arrived and even with the wonder pill, there had been upsurge with what they called the baby boom, properly to get the extra child allowance which later changed. Remember the allowance of £4.10 [three dollars] that wasn't payable to the first child, eventually it was improved allowing it to include the first child as well. The Beatles were over and London's social housing policy was also in total reform. The political solution of the day from the Greater London Council [G. L. C] was to build new towns spread across the south of England. Unknown to me back in Ireland and well informed from his siblings on the mainland, Dad had been keeping his ear to the ground about all this post war urban development, secretly hatching a super plan of his own. Lady luck was on his side and remarkably he was offered a choice of one of these new towns, Andover, Basingstoke, Basildon and I think Milton Keynes, so he couldn't have timed it better. Spoilt with choice and smitten with success, all Dad had to do was pick where he wanted to go, sign on the dotted line and bravo the keys were ours. Being fresh of the boat in a manner of speaking, he merely chose 'Andover' because it was first on the alphabetical list, it was simple as that.

On his return back at the bed-sit in London he started opening an ordnance survey map of 'Great Britain.' This was unusual and knowing something was aloft I inquisitively asked 'were we going now Dad,' after studying it for a while pointed with his in deck finger saying 'there, a place called Andover in the south of England', never heard of it was my humorous response.' Mammy immediately blessed herself and started praying to 'St Patrick the patron saint of all Ireland who chased the snakes from the homeland. Gone were the old days of running around with my bum hanging out of my trouser, poverty social exclusion and the feeling of being left behind? An exciting adventurous life lay before me, form a child's eye something like 'follow the yellow brick road.' In vogue was the new idea imported from America called projects, over here called estates, housing up to five thousand in one hit. Slung up as fast as possible and on the cheap, the London over-spill was borne and I was part of it, nice!

Our estate was called 'Cricketers Way' and divided into fifty squares, ten houses to each square, named after famous Cricketers from the fifties and sixties. At first the infrastructure wasn't very good and all you could see was green belt and trees. Gradually over the years the community facilities did develop and we got one newsagent shop, a purpose built community centre and surprisingly a doctor surgery complete with a nurse and dispensary, a triumph of adversary. An old Roman road called 'Smannell' ran parallel to our estate. Along side the brand new school called 'Shepard's spring' was slowly taking shape but not quite finished? In the meantime Mammy tried her best she could to teach me and Dad gave me homework reading the book 'The Hobbit'. My task was to read at least one page a day to him while he eats his dinner after work. Afternoons were great and I spent most of my free time educating my-self, exploring my new rustic environment, and camping out live in 'Hearwood forest.' Angling in the river Anton for fresh rainbow trout, climbing and swinging about like Tarzan in the trees, making secret dens or just paddling in the near by stream. The stream was even better than the forty foot as it was fresh with no salt so it didn't sting my eyes anymore. Andover was also equipped with an out side public bathing pool. For the equivalent of one shilling [a dime] I could swim and dive, cram five gob-s topers don't my throat, a can of coke and sunbathe all day, what a summer pure unabated luxury!

Setback in the Test valley, Andover in Hampshire was originally a small rural town, full of farmers, local yokels and what the Overspill kids called 'Carrot Crunchers' indecently in Ireland we used to call them Red-necks, in America I think they call them Hillbillies. When they spoke everything ended in 'Uh-Are', spotting them was dead easy, always having a long piece of straw hanging between their teeth and generally sat on a wooden fence wearing green Wellington boots and a ridicules looking floppy hat. Although fare dues they did had a sense of humour, the carrot cruncher's that is, releasing a record called 'I can't read and I can't write but I can drive a tractor' amazingly it managed to reach the top ten in the hit parade and was even on top of the pops. For a laugh we all bought it, mainly to take the Mickey keeping it in the charts as long as possible.

Anyways, after having so much time off school I was keen to attend and kick start my academic career, I suppose 'reader' you could say I had enough of all that larking around. Over the months, week by week, and day-by-day, I watched it rise upwards from the ground, the new school that is. Looking on as all the posh equipment was being delivered. On my first day there was an air of optimism running throughout the entire school, personally I felt I was making history itself. Subconsciously saying to myself 'remember this day for the rest of your life', and now I no why. My thoughts were one of the first, pondering on that moment 'how many thousands or possibly millions more to come'. Many mums worked as dinner ladies or classroom assistants, and a sense of community spirit and determination had overcome the colossal obstacles and problems in building my new school, it must have been a Herculean task. In comparison too 'St Teresa Gardens' this was state of the art, ultra modern well equipped, they even had a colour TV. The whole place was freshly decorated, not a mark on the walls or a bit of childish graffiti anywhere to be seen and the children looked neatly turned out in what ever there parents could afford. It was all brand new and smelled so fresh; the highly polished wooden parka flooring was literally squeaky clean as we sat crossed legs for our first assembly. The new Head master wasn't at all nervous as he introduced himself and his staff to what he described as 'The rest of his now extended family'. Our first hymn was 'Morning has broken like the first morning,' there was even someone playing a piano. Our prayer was one of the Psalms by Luke it read, 'Love your enemies, Do good to those who hate you, bless those who curse you, pray for those who ill treat you Amen'. Indecently, I'm not the sort of person to hold grudges, but throughout my entire life I found this commandment the most difficult to live out. After we finished the prayer all the teachers started clapping so we all joined in, it was great fun. I just couldn't believe how the English schools were so superior to the Irish ones and on top of that everything was free, including a little bottle of milk which Maggie later scrapped, a cooked dinner and even a pudding, unheard of back in Ireland, yummy!

Having never seeing a library before, I was bowled over for six with the selection colourful books, like soldiers all neatly lined up ready for my inspection. There were books on every topic under the sun and I particularly enjoyed trying to read adventure stories like Robinson Cruso and Sir Francis Drake. Built to take the influx of the overspill kids the majority of kids came from the London and spoke with a cockney accent, again my Irish accent clashed, which unfortunately made me a target for the inevitable Mickey taking. Making a concerted effort to blend in, but every time I went home, everyone spoke with an Irish accent, so I fell straight back into it. Olive's problems were expiated as being younger picked up all three, Cockney, Carrot Crunching and Irish all the same time. She was so funny to listen too; it got so bad though she had to go to a speech therapist. This was my final year at primary school and I already had enough on my plate, years of poor education had taken it toil and I still couldn't read and write properly, but I was determined to make some headway though all this. At that point in time 1970 the 11 plus examination was around the corner and mine was only a year off. The English children already had a head start, preparing for this as young as five. The test it self was also fundamentally flawed, taking no account of the harsh realities of life which divided the children academically socially or geographically. Education became a bit like a game of monopoly, going straight past jail directly to the upper class 'Grammar School'. When you passed this point on the board you automatically received quality education, high grade exams results, more employment opportunities and hopefully a better quality of life. Tony was quite articulate and a lot cleverer than me, trying really hard and even he didn't manage to pass, so fate didn't hold out much luck for me either. His description of his new 'Secondary

Robert Charles Scanlan

Modern' wasn't at all flattering, in fact it sounded like a roughneck place were everyone lagged around smoking cigarettes all day. Luckily for me I wasn't quite there yet, didn't smoke and my teacher was Mr. Love, a good-looking handsome man in his middle thirties, I remember he had thick black hair combed to one side, clean-shaven and always impeccably dressed in a suit and tie. Actually when he wore his black trimmed glasses he resembled the cartoon character: Superman. Mr. Love had permission from the authorities to raise his hand to his pupils, but to his credit, I never once saw him do that, although if you deliberately crossed him you would hear and see another side to him but definitely no violence. However one very fat middle-aged woman called 'Miss Ruttler' had her own method of literally trying to shake the education and knowledge into you. She had the inevitable task to teach me to read and write every afternoon for remedial English work. Truthfully, she must have weighed well over thirty stone and looked like one of those all in 'Chinese's Sumo' resellers, all the kids were petrified of her and her daunting looks, resembling some sort of raging bull bellowing out her orders at you. She even had to have an extra large chair to cater for her massive bum. The bone crushing fat bitch was so overblown she forced the kids help her out if the chair, otherwise she couldn't get up herself, honestly reader it was like some sort of scene from Benny Hill show. Many of the parents complained, Nile Murphy's dad went up the school in a fury after she cut his lads hair, more like hacking it off in greats chunks than what I would actually call styling. He looked a complete Pratt, bright ginger hair sticking out everywhere, furthermore all the kids took the Mickey out of him at play-time so he ran home crying. Anyhow his dad had to be called away from his work and came up straight away in his car. I saw him through the window as he pulled up and parked, I thought this is going to be worthy of note, Bob. He was absolutely fuming and marched in past the school secretary and then in into my classroom. Raging in front of all the kids, pointing his finger at her ranting and raving threatening to kill her if she ever laid a hand on his boy again, the thing is she couldn't get out of her chair and he was demanding she stood up and talk to him, she refused saying 'I will do no such thing' she couldn't anyway. We didn't see him for a while but personally I thought it was a great crac, laughing to myself I couldn't wait to the others at home how funny it all was. However, to her credit she did teach me to read and write and when I was ill with hay fever she was very kind and looked after me like a nurse.

Mr. Love on the other hand was a pure genius, superb in his communication of facts and figures and dynamic in his delivery of them. When he read, he did so with so much expression and character you almost felt you where taking part in the story yourself. On occasions even prepared to make a fool of him self to get his point across, a hallmark of a brilliant teacher. Without ridicule or fear from anyone including the inevitable bully, I actually felt at ease expressing my ideas and thoughts in the literal and oral form. Poetry was a form of escapism, playing and toying with words suddenly became interesting. For example did you know there is no English words which rhyme with orange, purple, silver or month? Curiously the word dreamt is the only English word ending in 'mt.' Amusingly the word 'boycott' comes from 'Charles C. Boycott', who was hired by an Irish earl during the 19th century, to collect rents from tenant farmers in Ireland, who in turn totally ignored him. What a laugh, the English slang being equivalent too 'Sent to Coventry.' Regularly he would be set me mental challenges, once he gave me a whole week to learn how to play the basics of chess. Using this board game to stimulate my mind and certainly managing to do that. Mutually we must have duelled hundreds of games, encouraging me to start my own chess league, organizing after school chess torments, even to this day this is still one of my favourite intellectual pastimes, I suppose it is akin to mental warfare. On my very last day at school there was one final game between Sir and I, and in total anticipation the entire class gathered around the two of us. Watching on they crunched hard-boiled sweets, crisps and all drank gallons of pop, I had been scheduling this match all term and the atmosphere was absolutely electrifying. We blocked out the sunlight by lowering the heavy dark green Venetian blinds on every window. Hyping the cra up even further we played the record '2001 Space Odyssey', Peter Jefferies switched all the lights off, except the one in the middle directly above our heads, funny enough now it reminds me a bit like the tally program 'Mastermind'. The game could now commence, through my expertise and tactical forward planning, and because I had played him so many times before, I started to be able to predict his reactions to my moves. Although this wasn't going to be a walk in the park, he was a brilliant mathematician, very intelligent who super-studied every move and frankly this was going to be mental brinkmanship to its very limits. My super plan from the on sort was to try and fool him, playing in a certain old style, the one he was used to seeing. Hopefully committing him to certain positions and then reel him in like a fish. Passing the half-hour mark things stated to hot-up and became somewhat attention grabbing, but not quite as transparent as he thought. You could have knocked me over with a feather when he took the bait, my heart started beating faster and faster and within five moves I was calling 'check 'and then on the sixth I executed deadly move with the Queen into attack mode, placing her in he white box calling 'checkmate' There was a short pause and all the kids went quiet, he took his eye contact from the board and smiled at the broad grin on my face. He stood up and whilst firmly shaking my hand said 'well done lad'. With his approval, a big cheer came from my fans, running around patting me on my back, in excitement they shouted 'hip-hip-hooray Bobby's won, hip-hip hooray. The sensation of winning was absolutely brilliant and I think he was almost happy I had beat him, it gave him a sense of achievement, as if at least one of his pupils had learnt something, Hip-hip-hooray!

He also lived happily on the estate, everyone knew him and his family and they were one of us as you might say. He was also acquainted with poverty, as a primary school teacher's wage didn't reflect the importance of the job, so he and his family were in the same boat as everyone else. At weekends and in the evening I often saw him walking along the banks of 'Shepherds Spring', his faithful black Labrador gun dog 'Jessie' by his side. Andover's history can be originally traced back to the Romans who brought civilization to the area, making a fort for the tired soldiers, purely because of the fresh sparkling water, hence the name of our school. We proved this point when in 1971 the school took part in an archaeological dig around the stream. Back in the classroom we studied our finds under a microscope. It was really fascinating and we found coins pots and countless jewels.

Day-dreaming out of the classroom window my imagination went wild and I travailed along side the Romans fighting the Anglo-Saxons, my flight of fantasy took over I became a real life 'Roman Legionnaire'. Leading from the front I instinctively counted my paces and every thousand became a new mile. To keep us all well-fed I went out and had the crac hunting wild boar deer and poultry, I even had time for a spot of fishing. I bet you didn't know part of the pay was made in salt, which we called 'Salarium' and that's why wages of today are known as 'Salaries'. In my minds eye, I was there during the opening games at the Coliseum in Rome in 'AD something or other'. Roaring with the rest of the crowd, spec- tatting as the gladiators duelled not only with each other, but with Giraffes, Tigers, Lions, Elks, Hyenas, Hippopotami and even Elephants. Could you imagine deliberately having to pick a fight with one of them? Anyway, enough of all that baloney', Mr. Love sent the artefacts to the 'British Museum' and unbelievably they displayed our finds and we travelled up to London to see them, what a fantastic day.

Sheppard's spring as we called it sourced its water supply directly from an under ground well, a bore pipe was sunk and from the pressure of gravity alone pumped millions of gallons out at extreme pressure, creating a natural fountain 20 ft high, mother nature at it best. Mr Love was also a keen bird watcher and always carried a pair of binoculars, a camera, a tape recorder and a note pad and pen, his flask of tea and sandwiches neatly prepared by his good wife Sally. He was on the ball enough to use these particular notes, pictures and tape recording in his lectures, from these I learnt to identify all manors of species in my new-found rustic environment. One off my favourites was the Kingfisher, this beautiful petite blue and gold bird migrated thousands of miles, navigating only by the stars all the way from Amazon rain forest. With no time to rest the pair of little birds built a nest into the muddy bank to breed, raising there off spring and fishing the tranquil scene at their leisure. We both found this captivating and would regularly spend hours watching her surveying the bottom of the stream. Then she would spot something and dive, simultaneously arching her back pulling her wings tight into her torso, surfacing seconds later with a wriggling stickleback or bullhead. After watching quietly we shared a corned beef sandwich and a cup of hot tea from his flask, when out of the blue he remarked, 'even a fish has confidence' Some what confused I asked what do you mean Sir, 'well you can hear things, see things, smell things, touch things and taste things, these are your senses but having confidence is another sense you just can't see it, a fish needs confidence to swim and the kingfisher has to have confidence to be able to catch it, if I didn't its young would starve, so the moral of the story is 'Trust your instincts in life Bob and be confident with them'

Never once did I bunk his lessons, in fact I think he is probably the only reason why I went to school, in contrast to some teachers I would meet later. Through my research I managed to track down a copy of my end of year school report, Mammy kept that sort of stuff in the sideboard and to summarize. 'Robert brings spirit and innovation into whatever he involves himself in; he has an optimistic nature and a positive attitude to his work. He also has something of a pioneering personality with the ability to add a dash of humour and originality to his rather unusual style, often using intellectual shock tactics to get his point across'. I think he might have been referring to the chess game.

In the evening there could be as many as a hundred kids from the estate happily having the crac in the stream, bathing and splashing under the fountain or hanging out fishing for frogs, bullheads, tadpole's sticklebacks in fact anything that moved was fair game! It was a great crac and often I would see these kids with jam jars absolutely crammed to the brim with little fish or frogspawn. Actually I bet you didn't know the fastest fish in the world is the Barracuda, it can swim at twenty seven miles an hour; a trout on the other hand can only go as fast as four miles an hour, which unbelievable is close to a top of athlete in the Olympics, more useless information, I seem to be full of it! Anyway during the summer it was more like 'Butlins,' families planned their picnics on the grassy banks next to the stream. There was one major problem, the local farmer Mr. Smiles who grassed a herd of black and white freshens cows in the same field, basically because his cows had an endless supply of fresh water to drink and plenty of green grass to munch on all day. More often than not, for a giggle and out of devilment the bigger kids would deliberately wind these heifers right up, blowing whistles stampeding them towards the picnicking now panicking crowds. If you happened to be wearing red panic really set in, literally having to run for your life like some sort of Spanish bull-fighter who had lost his bottle! Actually this business of waving a red flag in front of a bull is a load of bullocks, as all cows are colour blind and everything they see is in black and white like an old TV programme, more useless info!

Christmas came and everyone was flat broke, so Vic the local butcher decided to act like Robin Hood helping himself to the free beef. He planned it with some of the other dads and got a lorry and made off with one of the cows late one night. That year Christmas came early with everyone enjoying organic free beef with their dinners, yummy! 'Rustlers strike again' was the bold headline of the week in the local advertiser. After that

Mr. Smiles lost his patience and temper with all the people and was reported seen waving his stick around, shouting "I'll get the gun, I mean it, I'm not messing about, I will get the gun and shoot the fecking lot of you'. No one took any notice of him and he became a standing joke on the estate with everyone just boycotting him, as if he was the invisible man off the television. That was the case until he returned on afternoon drunk, in a rage waving a loaded shotgun around, blasting both barrels one after the other in the air, effectively removing everyone off his land in one foul stroke.

After that he became public enemy number one and when he wasn't around we would build these big dams out of anything we could find, old beds, wardrobes, tables and chairs nothing was spared, not even the rusty old bicycle frame some one dug up the week before. It could take up to fifty of us all day to build it, then finally we would cover the whole monstrosity in plastic sheeting making it water tight. We tied a rope to the main structure, leaving us the option to pull it apart in one foul swoop. Over night it rained and filled up dangerously high, the pressure behind the makeshift dam became mind-boggling up to five foot in places. Before the deliberate burst everyone had a little swim, using a scaffold plank as a make-shift diving board, jumping as high as possible to see who could make the biggest splash. There was a fat boy called Keith Simmons who always won; not surprisingly as he weighed about fifteen stone. For a giggle he used to fold his arms across his chest, pushing all the fat together, forming what looked like a girl's cleavage, then all the lads would have a good look and perhaps a little feel, it wasn't perverted we were just having a laugh.

In anticipation to the dam bursting we made rafts and makeshift boats ready to ride the wave like some champion surfer from Hawaii. My vessel was an old tin bath her name painted proudly in black bold letters to each side. We had a naming ceremony smashing a bottle of milk which Peter Clearly nicked off someone's doorstep to her hull. Launching her at the foot of the stream an important person announced 'I name this ship 'Gob-Sheit', God bless all those who sail in her'. She really was the pride of the fleet; inside she was lavishly furnished from tip to toe in royal blue carpeting. Other facilities and luxuries included a metal breadbox to keep my sweets dry, a small wooden stool to sit on and a plastic kids life belt, improvising further I used Dad's garden spade as my paddle. Other kids heard about the boat race on the grapevine and turned up with a strange variety of craft. Industrial wooden pallets made into rafts, huge over inflated bulging black lorry inner tubes, bizarrely one even tried to set sail in a black plastic dustbin. Unbelievably my mate Russell Piper built his boat by cutting the wheels off old silver cross babies pram, he was far too big to fit in and had to be crammed in with his legs and arms hanging over the side. Every one was laughing and cheering when the water level became just about ready and the make shift flotilla was set to sail. Chris, Peter's older brother, was the strongest and elected to heave on the main rope, pulling the dam apart thus disintegrating it and smashing into smithereens.

It was grand to see this vast amount of water cascade in a giant tidal wave, gushing and rushing down the small riverbank, bouncing off the muddy embankment taking huge sods of earth with it on its way down. With more luck than judgment I got off to a cracking start, managing to avoid a chest of draws and hitting the top of the wave bang on time. The main bulk of the water was behind me and pushed me faster and faster. Glancing over my shoulder I noticed a couple of kids on rafts crash into each other hit the bank and then capsize. The most spectacular and properly the funniest thing I witnessed was when one of the over inflated lorry inner tubes hit a prickle bush literally exploding. On contact there was this huge bang, sending this small kid hurtling unrestrained into the air, splashing back down into the fast flowing current. It was all so incredibly dangerous, but very funny at thee same time. If he wasn't drowned or killed by the blast, he ran the risk of being hit by the on coming traffic of hurtling furniture. Besides that loads of kids ran along side on the edge, deliberately throwing rocks and bricks at you as we sailed. At that age you didn't bother too consider the consequences of being hit by a house brick; it was all part and parcel of the crac. As the race continued I was in the lead and just round the bend past the Concur tree was an old washing line, strewed from bank to bank symbolizing the finishing line. The curve was coming up too fast; I was now completely out of control with no steering or way of stopping her. Russell was close behind and came up on my starboard and as there were no rules to this game, got in close and keeled me over from the bow, deliberately scuttling me in deep muddy water. The frantic mob of screaming kids thought this was all extremely hilarious, I was laughing so much I nearly drowned swallowing what seemed half a gallon of murky water.

In the late seventies all the green belt land disappeared along with the Roman stream and ancient ruins. What made me really sad was the entire population of kingfisher's vanished, along with the tadpoles, frogs, water moles and countless other aquatic and organic life, gone for ever and all that remains are the memories recorded here? The water board nicked all the water and the little that was left was buried underground in huge concrete pipes, an environmental catastrophe. Then the 'local council' built another massive housing estate on the on top of that piping, having the face to call it 'Roman Way', more than likely because of the Roman fort that I helped to discover. After my hilarious summer holidays I eventually went to the infamous 'Andover Secondary Boys School re-named 'Winton Comprehensive'.

But you will have to wait for that bit, and believe me its worth hanging on for! Back in real time the hospital had a rehabilitation centre where I could go to cookery lessons, painting, and clay-modelling even computer studies. I used the computers quite a lot and typed out my thoughts most mornings. This afternoon though, I was having a crac at the clay modelling and happily walked over to the classrooms escorted by Matron Vera. She commented her favourite story was the one about Dougal, what yours reader? On entering the class room I saw all the other patients sitting down happily working on their mad creations. Matron Vera introduced me to my teacher Mike and the rest of the notable group of students. Mike instructed me to sit down next to this woman who said her name was Patsy. Mike had fuzzy hair, like an Afro style and he reminded me of one of the cartoon characters from the hair Bear Bunch, Bumpy. Patsy was working on a tall flower vase and said 'that Bumpy smelt of cigarettes and she didn't like that; apart from that he was fine, not a sexual pervert'. I raised my eyebrows and whilst smiling said, 'he's not one of the Mexican bum-bandits is he'? She could talk nineteen to the dozen and at one point I lost total track of what she was actually going on about, until she returned to the original conversation, raised her voice slightly and asked, 'Well are you'? I laughed, 'Am

I what'? She stared into my eyes and said 'You know, one of them,' giggling I couldn't resist and repeated 'What a Mexican Bum-bandit? No of course I'm not.' Bumpy fetched a ball of clay from wherever and plonked it down in front of me to start, stating 'off you go then' and guess what I made that old chestnut, an ashtray. I had just finished glazing my masterpiece and tea- time was called over the loud-speaker. Matron Vera came and got me from the classroom and that was the last I saw of my friend Patsy, that's a shame, I liked her.

Anyway back on the ward they wheeled the food in on a stainless steel bam-ire and patiently I queued up alongside the rest of the gang. I was about fifth or sixth in line and the armoire from the trolley made it even more exciting, lovely! What was even better they had a different menu to lunchtime, a surprise! Then all the other patients seem to arrive from nowhere and the queue went to pieces. While standing there scratching my head I noticed the nurses where busy helping out those who couldn't help themselves, whilst I on the other hand, was left wondering what to do or say next. Actually I was more worried there would be none left for me and started to get a bit panicky. In the end it was my turn in the queue to order my banquet, Lamb Chops with new boiled potatoes pees and carrots and for pudding ice cream and raspberry jelly, lip-smacking! The dinner lady wore a green overall and a funny looking straw hat, and her name badge read Barbra. She said 'I've also got toed in the whole; you know' entertainingly I replied 'you want to watch that, it sounds very nasty, maybe even contagious'! She giggled and then and shouted out, 'We'll have to keep an eye on this one; he's thinks he's a stand-up comedian.' I refused to give in and told her one of my jokes, 'Doctor I keep painting myself Gold, Ah it's just a guilt complex', she laughed and handed me up my free grub with a cheeky smile.

It looked really appetizing and I just put it on the table behind me for a moment or so, whilst I fetched a knife and fork and some salt and pepper. My back was only turned for a second or so and when I looked round this complete stranger was consuming mine. The barefaced cheek of it, I just couldn't believe this guy's nerve. I started to feel really envious because he was enjoying it like I should have been and thought, am I ever going to eat, or am I going to starve to death in this God forsaken hell hole. As I stood on dumfounded the nurse made it perfectly clear, 'look Bob, how many times have I told you, don't leave your food unattended, otherwise someone else will just eat it, and that goes for your possessions too, given half the chance round here they will steel the eyeballs from your head and come back for the lashes'.

Luckily for me I was allowed another helping, Barbs, as I called her this time felt sorry for me and mentioned, 'if there was any left over I could have seconds', I did and finished my feast of with rub-bob crumble and big dollops of hot custard, unsurpassed pure luxury, delicious! It all became part of my daily schedule, routine if you like and everyone's life evolved around food times, occupational therapy, medication sleep and then the same boring routine as the day before, in fact it wasn't a life but an existence. After tea-time I went into the television room. Most of the patients sat glaring at the screen watching cartoons motionless sad and unhappy. I did think what the feck I am doing here? Tom the old man watched it from dawn to dusk, any old station would do, furthermore was accused of hiding the remote control. He denied any involvement but they searched his gear and found it anyways, he got in big trouble. Things like that might seem petty but it kicked of a big argument with the rest of the gang and staff going on all day. As a punishment he wasn't allowed out of the ward for two days, this was not only distressing for the other patients but staff as well.

To get away from it all I went into the smoking room, and as usual the air conditioning unit was on full blast. It made a humming sound and rattled every so often producing a sort of clanging and banging noise. One got the impression you were entering an old British Rail waiting room and you were having your last smoke before your train arrived. Nevertheless, even with this working to its full capacity it was still foggy grey and all misty. Most of the gang smoked roll ups and if they didn't have any they just used the dog ends left behind in the ashtrays, know one seemed to mind, routine in fact, not for me though, I drew the line on that one. Anyway I had my sickness benefit and had plenty of cigarettes and newspapers. On evening I was just sitting their having a smoke minding my own business, when out of the blue this guy decided to remove all his clothing and lay on the floor naked as a jay bird, chanting and humming like the Red Indians do? An old lady knitting in the corner covered her face with her hands saying 'Jesus Mary and Joseph someone get the nurse' Honestly reader, this place really was the back of beyond, none of the others didn't even bat an eye lid, carrying on puffing and chatting away as nothing had happened. I just sat there motionless in disbelieve as one of the staff hurriedly told the man off, saying he was very naughty and should be ashamed of himself. He didn't care one iota and stuck his tongue out at the lot of us. They wrapped a blanket around him and forcibly took him back to his bed screaming 'I didn't do it, I didn't do it' The Cockney guy was now wearing a ridicules black leather hat and sun glasses started shouting 'your all fecking lunatics, do you hear me'! In fact that was his only comment he ever made, oh apart from the fact he wanted everyone to know he was Jewish, proving his point having specially prepared kosher meals made by a Rabbi, which I found out cost three times as much as mine, I think he should have paid for that service himself, what do you think reader? As for myself I still kept getting these mood swings, one minute I had no self esteem whatsoever and felt absolutely worthless and the next minute I was happy as Larry and didn't have a care in the world. There was no happy medium, but at least my writing kept me sane and I seemed to be doing something worthwhile in my life and possibly the hand of fate had reached out and given me this opportunity. At my weekly review sessions Matron Vera and the three psychiatrics said this was all part of the illness and this cloud so to speak would eventually pass. Part of my therapy was to read aloud from my manuscript, building up my confidence, they seemed to enjoy it and I enjoyed reading to them. They concluded, I've had to deal with a lot of things many human beings couldn't cope with, and I was like a volcano ready to explode and needed even more time out to relax and drop out of main stream society for a while. They advised me to continue to write about my experiences and learn from them, as they explained, 'There is no better teacher of experience, than life itself'.

Looking back, it was around 1971-72 and as I said my older brother Tony was already a pupil at 'Andover Boys School', renamed 'The Winton Comprehensive'. By the way literally across the busy London road was the girl's school with roughly the same amount of pupils called 'Andover girls.' Historically both schools were separated by the road and built in the late Victorian times to cater for a much less audience, so consequently couldn't cope with the number of 'Over-spill kids'. Tony chaperoned me around for a few days, informing me there was over six hundred and fifty pupils and one hundred and twenty five staff and twenty three prefects. Compared to what I was used to this was a dive, gone were my familiar surroundings and the teaching I became accustomed too, replaced with a cattle market institution, get them in and out as quickly as possible. You didn't have a name you just became another face in the sea of faces and everyone was called lad. They gave me this timetable that looked like it belonged to British rail, when I asked about a map, I was told 'go away quickly you pathetic Moron.' All these new faces, rooms and sub rooms, offices, restricted areas and non-restricted areas, you couldn't fart without asking permission. Resigned to my fate I held on to the fact school leaving age was four-teen, at the time it was optional to stay until sixteen to take exams. So, my attention was totally focused on leaving in 1974, but the road of life has many detours, as I was about to learn.

Like every secondary modern an automatic bell sounded for break times, one in the morning, again at dinnertime afternoon break and finally home time. On the bell and like an army of termites the corri-dors would become a hive of activity, teaming with hundreds of spotty acne-ridden boys appearing from every crevice, even in these hostile conditions life still existed. On the play ground lads hunched in small groups playing concurs, football, marbles or cards. The currency of the day was counted in cigarettes, sexy pictures of girls and a dinner tickets, worth a free meal at the school canteen. On occasions unannounced live boxing would periodically breakout, hundreds of boys would huddle tightly together around the fight in a circle chanting fight, fight, thus denying the Masters access into the middle to stop it, keeping them well on their toes literally looking in. At the back of the old bike sheds was the smokers union, they rarely got caught because lads took it in turn to keep look out. Continuously bribing the prefects with money or sweets from the Tuck-shop, they were all corrupt, especially the head prefect Dave Harris. After the initial settling in period my other school life was more rewarding, particularly enjoying English Litterateur, History and Science, choosing metal work for my practical studies, which later on came in very handy; believe me. Sport was also a big deal amongst the lads and during the winter cross-country running was compulsory. My first lesson on Monday morning at 9 pm was this horrific 7-mile run along 'Ladies Walk'. Come rain snow hail or even thunder and lightning, we still had to do it, having to complete this horrendous task it in twenty minutes or you had to run again.

Much to my pleasure during the summer we didn't have to do this and my week started off with a dip in the outdoor heated swimming pool, a part of my school life I really enjoyed. So much so I went on to pass my 'Life savers gold award.' Anyway, my games master Mr. Williams a Welshman from Cardiff who had thick ginger hair and a beard to match, noticed my natural talent in the water, inspiring me to train for the oncoming inter house school championship, in his taffy accent said 'go on boy-oo, you know you can do it'

The school was divided into four components called 'Houses', mine was called 'Fosbury' named after the famous British athlete who perfected the high jump technique called the 'Fosbury Flop' in the early sixties. The house consisted of one hundred and fifty boys who met every Friday morning in the drama room, collectively planning our winning strategy discussing and selecting our best contenders. Mr. Sharpe, our Housemaster was the best of the lot, taking the time to listen to his boys and not jumping to conclusions, a sign of a good leader. He had the uncanny knack of finding the good in everyone and then building on that, eventually rallying all his lads into a very completive bunch of young men. Beating the opposition was a matter of individual and House pride; you felt you were actually winning for him! That year the general consensus of opinion was we were good enough to win the grand-slam, athletics swimming rugby and the football. Months of planning, training and trails went into our campaign and like a military operation we chose our best athletes. To help myself prepare I gorged on Vic's cheap organic pollution free meat, beefing up my muscles having extra swimming lessons.

The day came and I was utterly stunned my endeavours and hard worked paid off, unbelievably they chose me to represent them in two events, the four hundreds meters dash once around the track and the swimming gala, the final sprint man for a four way relay team, incredible! I felt so pleased with myself, beating off all the in house competition but now I had to win. The games were always held in the last week in June, just before we broke up for our summer holidays. The caretaker Mr Perryman would spend weeks sowing and mowing, preparing the ground, marking out the crispy white lines for the days track events. I suppose the playing field was about one mile square, and in the far left hand corner the javelin and shot-putt was taking place, in the opposite corner was a well stocked clean sand pit ready for the long jump followed by the high jump. The morning started well for Fosbury winning the gold using the Fosbury flop and two silvers in the long jump and shot-putt. It was all worked out on a points system and so far we were triumphant in our accomplishments.

After a light lunch the entire school gathered round the curved track to watch the main field events. This was the highlight of the day and we all sat in our own teams, those who were participating wore PE gear whilst the other stayed in school uniform. Mr. Williams was the official starter and was pleased as punch when he fired the starting pistol for the first time. Such was the seriousness you would have thought we were at the Olympic Games or something. The opening event was one hundred meters dash and with a big cheer and high pitched whistling the first race was off. Fosbury entry wearing a blue sash was my little brother Eddie; he was up against a lanky six foot boy who we nicknamed Lofty. Eddie wasn't the favourite but had the advantage of being on the outside lane next to all his supporters. As expected lofty took the lead and within seconds outflanked the rest of the field. Their was about fifty meters to go and it looked like it was all over, when St Anthony came to the rescue again and our Eddie found incredible speed, overtaking Lofty and literally diving across the line winning by a short head. In conquest his Fosbury supporters ran on the field carrying him back above their heads, we seemed invincible scoring another maximum fifty points.

Later on that afternoon came my go. Kneeling in the start position in bare feet wearing my blue sash I heard the shot ring out and sprang into action. My plan was to keep up with the rest of the field for the first two hundred meters and then try out-sprinting them all the way to the line. The final curve on the track told me when to start sprinting, eventually romping home five seconds before my nearest rival. Mr. Sharpe came up and personally congratulated me; in fact he gave me a great big hug patting me on the back at the same time telling me how proud I had made him. Thriving on my victory and hungry for more success I set my sights for the swimming gala the following morning.

After a good night's sleep and a light breakfast of jam on toast which was yummy, I set off excitedly on my home made bike to school. The pool was enclosed by a 6-ft wooden panel fence, and the water looked

Robert Charles Scanlan

tempting as the morning sun glistened and reflected its rays. Along the edge next to the fence we used low-level wooden benches to sit on. The teachers on the other hand sat together at the far end of the pool, ad-libbing and having the crac with the boys, which in turn gave off a great sense of bravado and fun. The contestants however, sat deadly serious in a group on there own waiting to be called, towels wrapped around themselves keeping warm and for some unknown reason eating oranges.

As the morning progressed Fosbury were doing well with a couple of silvers under her belt, but we still didn't have gold as I stood the podium for the final race. We were the favourites in this event, perfecting the change-over, practicing our diving skills after school over and over again. So it was no surprise when I took off we already had about a ten second lead. The idea was to enter the water as shallow as possible to reduce drag, my dive was as near perfect as you could get, so much so my shorts flew off me on impacting the water. This was unexpected and I am sure the wolf whistles and laughing could be heard all over Andover as I swam naked for gold. My embarrassing situation was made worse when still naked in front of the whole school I had to retrieve my shorts from the bottom of the pool and put them back on before climbing out. I remember having to do a duck dive, showing of my bum, mooning in front of the whole school. This was my encore or lap of honour if you like and I and the rest of the lads were milking this, for all it was worth. When I did eventually haul myself from the pool they continued to whistle and clap, I am not sure if it is because I won or for being such a good sport, although Oscar Wild once wrote "a man actions are not judged in the way he does them, but the spirit of how he acts them out'. Incidentally we made Mr. Sharpe the proudest man in school pulling off the grand-slam.

The school library was abundantly well stocked and I earned the nickname 'book worm Bobby' always engrossed in one story or another. In comparison with today's youngsters this was the computer suite, the books my internet, my eyes the mouse and the pen the printer. We had a Librarian called Mr. Dyer, a fine old Gentleman who was a decorated Sergeant in the Second World War, successfully bringing back three hundred men off the beaches at Dunkirk in 1940, we nicknamed him 'Monty.' Pottering around all day Monty knew every book on the shelves, properly because he ordered and read every word before putting them out. He also had a photographic memory and was the font of all knowledge, guiding me to particular books even paragraphs to get specific information, mutually respecting each other I wanted to learn he wanted to teach. All the boys liked and respected him he was brilliant man and never once raised his hand to his pupils.

Sitting contented in my favourite corner overlooking the school garden; I managed to escape into a world of fantasy and make-believe. Intrigued with exploration and offbeat wild stories one of my favourites was off 'Sir Francis Drake.' Hungry for adventure like me and armed to the teeth, Francis sailed around the world in his flag ship 'The Golden Hind.' The only problem was know one really knew the way and for months all we saw was   blue skies and sea. Our water kegs were running low and some of the men were secretly drinking the sea-water, everyone wanted to turn back, but him. The weather worsened and hailstones swept down upon us nearly blinding everyone. Huge mountainous waves crashed against the hull and we were in serious danger of smashing into the rocks with all hands lost at sea. I could swim but most couldn't and faced certain death if we sank. Months of this went by and I was on deck splicing some rope when I heard the cry from the look out 'land ahoy,' discovering what we named 'Java'.

We were in high spirits and once on land we filled the kegs from the jungle streams and hunted with our muskets for fresh meat and poultry, I even managed to have some mire time for a spot of fishing. It was a good crac and by the beach I climbed a few trees, harvesting Coconuts and Bananas, luscious! After our little rest our ship was ready for its final part of the voyage home, across the 'Indian Ocean' around the 'Cape of Good Hope' and into the Atlantic. On the way round we felt really hard and attacked a few Spanish cities knocking seven bells out of them, blowing up a few of her Galleons for good measure. Unbelievably at a place called 'Nombe de Doris' we struck it incredibly lucky and our haul included thirty tons of silver and two tons of gold along with countless precious jewels, real pirates like 'Long John Silver', absolutely brilliant, even if I say so my self, bordering on some might say criminal!

Anyway we couldn't cope with all this bounty and had to dig this huge hole and bury fifteen tons of it in the ground, apparently it's still out there somewhere undiscovered. On the last lap of our voyage we sailed past the most southern point of South America naming it 'Cape

Horn.' Finally after two years at sea Francis became the first English Captain to have successfully sailed around the world returning alive. Captain Cook had tried it but unfortunately died on the way round, so alas in my book that doesn't count. When we sailed up the River Thames thousands of Londoners lined up along the banks to cheer us on. Queen Elizabeth 1st came on board and Francis knelt on the deck before her. Using my wild and uncultivated imagination I was there when it was hailed 'The greatest raid of all history.' It was absolutely fantastic; Elizabeth tapped his shoulder with a sword saying 'I bid thee raise Sir Francis Drake' and the crowd cried out hip, hip, hooray.

Considering this all happened in the 15th centaury in a wooden boat powered only by the wind and sweat, I think this was quite a breath taking accomplishment and I yearned for the day when I could be like him and travel around the globe, which eventually I did. Other also inspired me and I particularly enjoyed reading William Shakespeare's work. One of my favourite's is 'All the world is a stage and all the men and women merely players. They have their exits and entrances and one man in his lifetime plays many parts'.

Everyone was into building their own pushbike and in the morning lads hung around the bike sheds bartering for parts, swapping this for that and visa-versa. Mine was a bit dodgy, it was what we called a Bit-Sa, a bit of this and a bit that all bolted together to make one. Only last week I swapped a brand new Raleigh frame for a set of racing handlebars and new saddle. It became one of the school pastimes. like nicking a bottle of milk, someone stole your bike so you stole someone else's, I remember seeing bikes re-sprayed up to fifty times, and the whole carryon had become barmy, you might end up bartering for your own parts back. The thing was you couldn't say anything even if I wanted too, simply because all the parts were nicked in the first place.

One Tuesday morning like every Tuesday, we gathered in the main hall for weekly assembly. Through the window I noticed the Police inspecting all the bikes, which were neatly parked up in the bike shed opposite, thoroughly checking them one by one. After looking on his official looking clip-board started dragging out odd ones out and stacking them against the opposite wall, including my Bit-Sa. This continued for about twenty minutes, one bike after another was pulled and stacked. After assembly we were instructed to go and stand next to your own bike, the head master explained they were looking for stolen bikes and parts. Leaving the hall I walked straight past the line of bikes including my Bit-Sa, declaring I haven't got one. Mr. Williams starred at me replying in his taffy accent 'you've got one, I nearly run you over this morning, and, I saw you with my own eyes Scanlan.' Thinking on my feet I replied firmly 'no not me Sir, must have been someone who looks likes me, or one of my brothers, I can't even ride a bike yet, I haven't got the balance you see.' He saw the funny side of my reply and he started to laugh replying 'that's ridicules Scanlan everyone knows how to ride a bike.' Funny thing was thirty bikes mysteriously remained unclaimed that day, and the coopers had to get a van to come and collect them. A report in the local paper the flowing week read 'Three cheers to the anomalous pupils at Andover boys who eagerly handed in thirty stolen bikes', a police spokesman sarcastically added 'he had never seen anything like it.'

Bullying was a widespread occurrence, not only from other boys but the Masters as well; it follows to say it was an endemic part of school life. Indecently throughout my entire life I have despised the bully and on many occasions have intervened, their all cowards anyway. There was a teacher we nicked name 'Ernie', he new what we called him and absolutely loafed his description. An accurate description would be like saying 'a mini little Hitler, well to me anyway.' One of these feckers who thought they knew everything, desperate for power in what ever form and wouldn't listen or take advice. This anus of a man was five foot nothing and wore specially designed platform shoes to raise his height, attaching metal studs to the soles. As he patrolled the corridors you heard him coming by the sound of the 'Blakies' hitting the floor, I suppose it made him feel hard! Resembling a pipe cleaner with hair, he also seemed to wear a lot of grey suits, thinking about that now; he must to have possessed a lot of grey suits because that's all he wore. The majority of the pupils were petrified of him; to be sure this was a complete arrogant narrow-minded pig. At radon boys were caned in his office, any trivial excuse would do, conveniently always at lunchtime when no one was around to witness the spectacle. The other teachers weren't actually involved, although on the same token probably knew exactly what was going on and never said a dickey bird, [word] so in my book they are just as guilty.

Over the years I was caned for having a penthouse magazine in my rucksack and yawning in assembly. Actually in science 2I found out that when you yawn, you actually breathe out enormous amounts of Carbon Monoxide? Cosmic quantities of this gas left in the brain flip an emergency switch, sending a message to your face yawn. looking at someone else yawning automatically triggers the switch, making your muscles react and then you automatically yawn; I was accused of deliberately causing a mass yawn, starting a chain reaction in assembly with six hundred boys and possible some of the Maters as well.

There was a pop group called the Bay City Rollers at number one in the hit parade. The Band started a craze for wearing alumnus bright coloured socks; they even glowed in the dark. We had no school policy concerning the colour of your socks, so in theory you could wear what you'd like. To add insult to injury, it was all the rage to wear your trousers four inches above your ankles to show them off, I must have looked a complete prat, especially radiating in the dark. Nevertheless, Ernie spotted my unconventional addition to my uniform and dragged me in his office by the ear. He started integrating me, poking me hard in the chest, demanding to know 'What's the name of the gang then lad'. Reality was I wasn't in any gangs, so bravely asked what gang he was actually talking about. With that he gave me a slap over the head, shouting 'don't be flippant with me my lad.' Continuing the verbal and physical onslaught by saying 'the socks were sign'! Pleading my case I explained, 'Sir, it was just a fashion statement from the Bay City Rollers, please don't do this Sir' He wasn't having any of it, 'I'm glad you took this opportunity to confess the name of your gang, now you're only going one on each hand'. He was that arrogant and full of himself he didn't even ask my name, we locked eye contact as he slowly walked over to his cupboard were he kept his array of canes, only breaking it for a slight moment as he quickly looked in choosing his weapon of the day. Hold your left hand out boy, whack, then the one right, whack! After that Ernie became public enemy number one and as the saying goes, 'it's not all over till the fat lady sings'

It was getting close to the annual school play, that particular year it was 'Oliver' a major social event in school life, in fact apart from the sports day, that's all there was. Confidently I can say we weren't much of the socially integrative type. Smoking a crafty fag behind the bike sheds with my two mates Russ and Chris we thought about all this, and fashioned a secret conspiracy to vengeance good old Ernie. Choosing to become thespians ourselves and play out our own part in the school Gala performance. Skiving of Mr. Hard-Bottles history lesson we sneaked onto the back of the school stage. Russell was keeping look out, peeping through the slight gap between where the curtains meet in the middle, whilst behind the scenes the action began, excellent! The stage scenery was designed like window blinds, one behind the other, six all rolled up ready for that night's show. Cunningly we had been timing the scene changes in rehearsals, deceitfully choosing the third one in, twenty minutes into the show when everyone was well into it. Apprehensively I pulled on the cord, and with delight a huge canvas sheet with clouds painted on it released slowly to the floor. Chris took out large tin of black spray paint hidden in his rucksack. Lying around at the back I found a set of old stepladders, Chris stood on the bottom run whilst I climbed to the very top. At that juncture I nearly lost my nerve but didn't, reached out and sprayed in big bold unmistakable black capital letters.

"ERNIE IS A MEXICAN BUM BANDIT"

We waited a few minutes or so for the paint to dry, as we didn't want to smuggle the late addition to the social event of the year. With a stupid grin on my face, I just stood there stunned in silence, the size of it was huge and so were the consequences if we got caught. Slowly we pulled the scenery back, making its way up it squeaked like an old pram wheel. Agitated and uneasy home time was about ten minutes away, so we had fidgety long wait. Eventually the bell rang four times which meant we had to execute the second part of the cloak-and-dagger plan, act as cool as cumbers, keep our mouths shut, and mingle in with the rest of the boys leaving.

That night the grand Gala came and they had been selling tickets by the bucket load. Meanwhile I was at home sun bathing on a wooden stripy deck chair, the same ones you get at the seaside for hire. Eddie was sitting apposite me in a relaxed posture also on a stripy deck chair, with his legs crossed trying to read a newspaper. I had just read it, it was about Concorde making its maiden flight and the age of the supersonic passenger jet was bourn. The British one touched down in the Bahrain and history was made that day in more ways than one. Anxiously I kept asking him the time; he became curious and suspicious of my actions demanding to know, "what's going on Bobby?" When it was exactly 7.20, I confessed to the deadly deed. He took a deep breath, opened his mouth widely, paused, and said 'oh Jesus no' and nearly had a heart attack with laughter, so much so I had to run into the house to get him a glass of water.

According to my top spy a prefect called Dave Harris the assembly hall was absolutely packed to the brim; It was a hot evening all the windows were open and whilst air condition units cooled the air, the audience fanned themselves with the evening's program. All the school governors were there, the people with money and good old Ernie. Behind that lot were six hundred eagerly awaiting parents and pupils? Mr. Throw-Bridge the school music teacher and band conductor struck up the orchestra and the play commenced. The curtains opened to the grand applause and the public settled down for an entertaining evening. The play stated bang on time at 7 o'clock and we timed our bit for preciously 7.20. As I said we had been spying on them and monitored when the third scene change was, so we knew!

'Oliver, Oliver' they cheerfully and joyfully sang out, Ernie was happy and was seen singing and clapping along. Of the play, well it all went up the creek, Del boy said 'forget Carnakey Hall and the Royal Albert Hall they ended up 'Sod-all.' The performance was abandoned, having to be postponed until further notice. Apparently one man stood up in the back of the audience applauding, declaring 'it was the best schoolboy prank, he had ever seen in his life', turns out he was an ex-student of Ernie and had a taste of his justice before. According to the grapevine the actors and band were gob-smacked and were also stunned into silence, what's more some of the lads in the audience started hysterical laughter, furthermore rumour has it Mr Williams couldn't stop grinning nearly had a hernia and had to walk out holding his stomach. It seems that the music sort of fizzled out on its own, and one person in the audience fainted collapsing in a big heap, having to be rushed away to hospital in a speeding flashing ambulance, the end, or so we thought!

Over the next few days there were some serous in-house

investigations, the entire school was talking about it and hilarious it all was. Firstly Ernie posted up another declaration, saying if the Culprits didn't come forward within twenty-four hours; boys at random would be caned, I knew that meant six of the best. The pressure on us was extremely intense to say the very least. They wouldn't stop talking about it and how side-splitting it was; even the boys in the play appreciated the crac, all I wanted was for it to go away on its own and forget about it, but that didn't look like that was going to happen. We had an emergency meeting at the back of the old bike sheds of the newly formed thespians and I chaired the meeting. Reluctantly we unanimously agreed to come forward owning up; we just couldn't let our mates take the rap for all this. Unenthusiastically we went to see our house master, he always treated his pupils courteously and when we finally admitted it, he simply said 'I had an inclination it was you lot, but why?' Collectively we made him more aware of what was really going on, I told him about the socks incident and the other two explained similar experiences. He realized there might have been some justification for all of this; in any case it was out of his hands and now going to be literally in hours. Being fair he also made it clear we could refuse the whipping but it would be worse if we got expelled instead. During the early seventies expulsion was rare, seriously effecting your career prospects, especially if you wanted an apprenticeship. Overall his advice was just take your punishment like a man and be done with it, so the cane from Ernie it was. Making our way to Ernie's office he let me borrow another lads blazer to try and make a good impression, mine was worn out a hand me down from Tony. Unhurriedly we walked with our heads down through the long corridors; he did all the talking trying his best to console us and even tried to make me laugh. Querying, I understand most of it but what's the Mexican connection all about Bob? I had no answer to that apart from 'it just a crac Sir from a cowboy film I saw years ago' he just smiled back pointing out we would be heroes for coming forward, and martyrs for taking the punishment. To be honest at the point I was absolutely beside myself with fear and wish I hadn't done it, but it was too late for that.

Russell's was called in first, when he came out he was crying so hard he really alarmed me, 'how many I asked' tearfully replying 'one on each.' Next was Chris, when he came out his face was even more cautioning and had gone completely white and looked like he was about to throw up. 'How many I apprehensive asked?' 'Two on each hand' came back the hushed reply. In there, in front of him, it seemed like time and eternity had stopped still for all the wrong reasons and I was absolutely terrified. Sweat was pouring from forehead and a cold feeling was running down the back of my spine. Ernie was well in practice now, flying his cane into the air like there was no tomorrow. The rotten pig was making sure he didn't hit the suspended light fitting hanging above him with his swing. After completing his training simply said, 'step forward lad and hold your left hand out,' I reluctantly obeyed his command and then he went for it. Honestly reader the sound of the bamboo cane travelling through the air at high speed made it more terrorizing, as you knew what to expect next. Nearly passing out, I refused to cry or in fact show any emotion, we locked eye contact yet again, one, two, three at that point I thought it was all over, until he demanded my other hand, six of the best as history tells it. Sincerely my hands felt like they were been burnt with a blow-torch, instantly going white swelling up as big as a bunch of bananas. Weighing in over twelve-stone and well able to look after myself, I considered grabbing it, giving him a taste of his own medicine, but my hands were on fire! And I surely would be expelled. He hit me that hard I was excused from writing for two days; I couldn't even hold a pen. If he had given us all the same, I could understand and except that, but he didn't.

Hiding my hands from my parents wasn't easy, understandable mammy and dad kept a special eye on us all. Accomplishing this task wasn't easy, obviously my brothers knew and helped me out with the paper round, in any event I didn't feel the need to tell them, I had taken my punishment, wasn't expelled and learnt my lesson, well to some extent anyway. The milestone past and from them on if I saw Ernie or heard him approaching, I would hide and duck down behind other boys, or deliberately scurry along another corridor. The only thing keeping me sane was the fact next year I would be fourteen, my intentions were to scrape through as quietly and discretely as possible, or that's what I thought.

My hands healed but my heart didn't and weekends couldn't come quick enough. About three miles north of the estate was a typically English rural village called Little London and I enjoyed spending my free time riding around exploring on my Bit-Sa. The picturesque scene was complete with a corner shop, the Royal Oak pub a post office and farmhouse bakery. I used to wash the man's windows and in return he gave me free cakes, absolutely gorgeous! It was not unusual to spot cattle being led to the dairy for milking, or riders on horse back tipping their hats as they trotted along the deserted roads and footpaths. Mr. Smiles was the farm manager at the village and not surprisingly trusted no one from the surrounding estates, properly because of what Vic did too one of his cows at Shepard's spring. He was also a very opinionated man and thought everyone who lived on them was a Cockney-Overspill-Kid, a rustler and properly a bank robber thrown in for good measure, actually he was properly rite. On the other hand I had retained my Irish accent and could turn it own at will; therefore in my native Dublin tongue continuously pestered the poor man for work. Summer reaping was in season and I knew he wanted help harvesting his wheat crop; my persistence eventually paying off.

One sunny afternoon I had been out happily blackberry picking, proudly harvesting a whole bucket full ready for mammy to make jam out off, tasty! Eagerly riding home it was quite difficult to balance the bucket on the side of my handlebars, requiring all my attentiveness not to fall off. Whistling contentedly along, when out of the corner of my eye I spotted a man outstanding in his field, anyhow it was Mr. Smiles, he saw me and signalled like a policeman with the palm of his hand to stop. Idiotically I took my hand of the handlebars to wave back. The situation somersaulted completely out of control and so did I, directly into a prickly hedge, followed by my five thousand freshly picked black-berries. To add to my humiliation it was just my luck to land right in a flock of resting black birds, enjoying their afternoon snooze. They weren't too pleased with this unexpected mid air alarm call and made a horrible squalling sound as they dispersed. Some how in that split second, without even opening my mouth or even thinking I had got myself in to trouble again, causing complete pandemonium, what next I thought!

To his credit to Mr. Smiles immediately ran over, shouting franti-cally for me not to move. Immobilized literally hanging upside down it was impossible anyway, snagged by the thorns on my trouser legs and T-shirt. Dazed from my reshuffled upside down position he looked like a demented scarecrow in his green Wellington's boots and straw hat.

Robert Charles Scanlan

One way or another he managed to free me from the prickles turned me up the right way and enquired if I was hurt. My arms and back were scratched from the experience but apart from my pride I felt fine. Bizarrely the farmer then went over to inspect his hedge, I thought I've heard of being an ecologist but this was ridiculous, twisting around on his heels he faced me saying. "You're lucky there is not Deadly Nightshade in there, or you would be stone cold dead by now, this hedgerow is full of it, but luckily not the bit you landed in." He continued "I've got a job for you as a farmers boy, can you start tomorrow, if you're on time and I will give you cash in hand?" Well this was the fortuitous break I had been waiting for, and now I was going to be on the lump like dad. However somewhat stunned he still wanted me, considering the nincompoop I just made of myself, he kindly persisted. "Tomorrow you can join the rest of the crew for a slap up breakfast in the farmhouse, and in the afternoon about two o'clock, the missus will make you a tradition ploughman's lunch for you. Now pick up your berries, go straight home and make sure your mum gets all the thorns out, see you in the morning, how's that Son?' "Yes boss, what ever you want me to do ill do it" was my keen on the spot response.

The old farmhouse must have stood there for centuries, and believe me reader, that very morning I found my vocation in life in more ways than one. Deliberately secluded by tall trees, the cottage was not visible from the road and set back about fifty meters up the tarmac driveway? Either side of the tidy drive way was an orchard, the red apples just right for scrum-pinging. I was tempted to take one, but as it was my first day, thought otherwise. Facing south, the early morning sun was breaking through the clouds in narrow beams and lit up the ivy that camouflaged the front wall of the house in a deep sea of green and indigo. The thatched roof had now gone grey like a man with maturity, as a feature next to the smoking chimney was a thatched model of a pheasant. Amusingly standing at the front door I recall reading the name plaque on the wall which read 'Pleasant-Plucker.' Hesitantly I knocked twice and patiently waited a short while, but there was still no reply. My first response to my dilemma was to stand there mindlessly scratching my head, then through some sort of divine inspiration had a brain wave to take a stroll around the side of the building. Round the back I heard laughter coming from the green stable gate doors that had just come into view, approaching I saw the top half was open and I caught sight of Mr. Smiles who waved me over. All the other labourers where there sitting down enjoying a slap up breakfast off eggs and bacon, sausages tomatoes mushrooms, white bread, brown bread and then washing the whole thing down with extra large mugs of tea. Mr. Smiles had a copy of 'Farmers monthly' in front of him and was engrossed in an article about 'the reproduction organs of bulls,' or is that bullocks! You may think this is a load of bullocks but now its called artificial insemination and cloning, only braking his concentration to say, 'come and sit down over here lad next to me, tuck in and fill your face your going to need it.' Indeed he will, one of them said. There were sniggers of laughter from the rest of the room and I got the distant impression these carrot crunchers knew something I didn't.

After breakfast everyone jumped on their tractors heading off in different directions and Mr. Smiles instructed me to jump on with him. Everything was going great until we entered the farmyard, where there was a horrendous stink of fresh animal manure. From the begging of this job I had a feeling something was in the air, however Mr. Smiles seemed totally oblivious to the stench as it ever increased. Continuing on we came across barns constructed out of corrugated tin sheets covered in Grey asbestos roofing, I spotted a swallow feeding on insects as she flew. He resisted on country proverb that says, 'one swallow does-n't make a summer, it is not until large flocks are seen, that countrymen know to expect the warmer weather'. The barns had huge sliding doors that were open either end; as we drove past I could see what was in them. In the first was a very large grain silo, he mentioned as we went by, 'there's ten thousand tons of wheat stored in there ready for grana-ries', continuing 'all that came from one field'. In the second barn was a crop of potatoes staked up in one corner, in another cubicle were cabbages, beat root, onions and an array of other organic pollution free vegetables, all freshly harvested only yesterday. My first notion was yippee, Mammy wouldn't have to buy any more vegetables! My boss headed for the furthest barn, about two miles away on the brow of the hill and by now the stench was getting increasingly potent and I was heading straight for it. Unrelenting he continued on with his mission, turning right at the top of the hill driving into this open barn. On entering I couldn't believe my eyes and confronting me was the most colossal gigantic pile of Cow's dung you have ever seen in your life, there was even hot steam coming out if the titanic pile; stopping the tractor and trailer to the side of this breathing monster he switched off the engine. Flabbergasted would be a good word, I just sat on the trailer looking at it, then we looked at each other, when he said 'well, it's no good looking at it, and me, that wont get it done, theirs a pitchfork there and I want you to load the trailer for me, ok. Form this point my breakfast had made its way up my wind pipe, almost strangling myself I had to sallow hard and re-consume. My concept of my new job was being a cowboy riding the horses, collecting the crops and branding cows like John Wane, very much now a figment of my bootless imagination.' How could I refuse? Repeatedly I had practically begged for this job, but honestly this must have been the smelliest direst job in the whole wide world! Stranded in the middle of now where he just walked off waving his stick around saying he would be back at dinnertime. When he got to the end of the shed he turned round shouting, 'there is a sandwich and a flask of hot tea in the cab, help yourself'.

As soon as he was out of site, I couldn't resist looking to see what he had left me, sure enough it was all there, along with the keys in the ignition, now I could listen to the radio and might even have time to have a go driving the tractor myself. The pitchfork he left me, had three prongs and looked liked it the Devil himself owned it. Starting on the edge I worked my way in, honestly reader the smell was over bearing, but cleverly I put tissue paper up my nostrils so I couldn't whiff it anymore. The radio wasn't working properly and all I could tune into was a classical station. On full volume I listened to Showfanns flight of the bumblebee, Mozart flute concerto and some fat Italian lady singing opera. The sound echoed all over the vast empty barn, giving an acoustic resonance as if you were at the Royal Albert Hall for 'the Last night of the Proms.' Isolated listing to all this, I soon drifted into a world of my own. My adolescent imagination was working in overtime taking me far away from all this crap. Day dreaming about this particular girl I had seen at the youth club, never having the courage to ask her out on a date. Every time I tried I just went red in the face, made myself look a nitwit and completely clamed up. Her name was Katie, resembling one of the bond girls coming put of the sea, or rather in my flight of fancy I thought she was. All the other boys drooled and fanaticized over this particular girl, but I knew we liked each other and further more, only a matter of time before something happened. Maybe I was in love, conceivably in my tiny little head she was in love with me.

This magical love story was starting to come alive, my thoughts inspired me to work harder, and I soon drifted into what seemed actual reality. I suppose you could say a romantic fool at heart escaping up-to-the-minute life. The crac went like this, we had been out to the cinema watching the smash hit film of the times 'Love Story,' sitting together in the back row holding hands throughout the entire picture, occasionally kissing and pledging life long allegiance to each other. It was absolutely great; my red face had gone along with my inhibitions, as you would throw caution to the wind. After the pictures, we walked hand in hand for a meal together at the local Wimpy bar. Sitting opposite each other, gazing into each other eyes, we talked and we laughed, wondering what the other one was really thinking. When we finished our romantic meal of cheese burgers and milk shakes I got down on one knee and proposed, presenting the engagement ring at the same time. Overwhelmed, crying with happiness she immediately said 'oh yes my darling of course I will'. Now it was official, ring and all and time for me to escort her home via 'Cock-wood followed by Lovers Lane' then to her front door, the rest I leave for your own wild thoughts and imagination to take over.

By now my task was a quarter's way accomplished and it started to look feasible I might actually finish on time. Listening to the symphony in the background it was an odd feeling, alone in the barn with just the wild life to look at and the classical music blasting out in the background. To keep me company there was a pair of Kestrels patrolling the skies from one end of the barn to the other, scanning the ground for a mouse or a tasty airborne bug. The pair seemed to time their pass over with the rhythm of the music, showing off by getting closer and closer to me. After about five minutes of this aerial display I started to throw pieces of bread in the air to see if they would catch it in mid flight. Sure enough they took the feed and started performing spectacular mid air acrobatics, all in time with the symphony. After my break I returned the tissue paper up my nostrils and continued shovelling, by now I must have loaded at least two tons of the crap, but it looked another twenty tons to go, or so it seemed. It was getting close to dinnertime; Mr. Smiles was due back around two, so to make a good impression I turned the radio right down and rubbed saliva on my brow to make it look like been sweating. Dead on time I heard another tractor coming up the lane, pulling up next to me he turned off the engine and smiled the way he did, 'well done lad, over there is a trove of water, go and wash your hands and have your lunch, ill finish this off for you, by the way how old are you' 'Fourteen boss.' As I sat on his tractor eating my plough-man's he continued loading the trailer, telling me many hands make for light work. He was right, by the time I had finished the bread and cheese and pickled onions the job was done, and the trailer was finally loaded. He came over to me and asked, 'have you ever driven a tractor before?' 'Not quite boss, but I've seen it done on the television programme 'Emmerdale Farm,' oh, and by the way, 'I'm a very quick learner' was my eager lying response. He started to laugh but in any case we had two tractors on our hands and only me and him there. It all related to some antiquated law, allowing farm labourers over the age of fourteen to drive the tractors anywhere, even on the public roads, what a crac!

He explained a lever on the steering wheel controlled the speed and the foot pedal operated the brakes and don't worry about the gears, well this all seemed painless enough. Up until now my only experience of was going fast was on 'Dougal' or dicing with death on the stream, but this was the real combustion engine. He told me follow him back down the lane, through the farmyard and turn left, two miles up in the road was a fallow field, which meant every four years the farmer would give the land time to recover and replenish it with organic fertilizers, the bullshit. Everything went well even better I would say, as we drove along we passed a gang of about ten kids from the estate out on an afternoon bike ride. They couldn't believe it, last week a Bit-Sa now a five-ton tractor and trailer. Gob-smacked I saluted them as I passed by; smitten with envy I heard one of them say 'look at Bobby Scanlan driving the big red tractor'. When we eventually reached the field my enthusiasm soon wore off though, literally spreading this crap all afternoon. He drove the tractor whilst I stood on the trailer shovelling away all day; it was really smelly and totally mind-bendingly boring, continually back-wards and forwards. Weak from fatigue covered from head to toe in manure and stinking to the high heavens I finally finishing around 7 o'clock that evening.

Olive opened the front door, took one look at me and roared with laughter, calling the rest of the family to witness this scene. 'Come and look at the state of our Bobby' running from wherever, they just stood there with their mouths open, keeping me standing at the door laughing and jeering me. One of the neighbours came out to see what all the fuss was about and also started pointing at me taking the Mickey. Mammy came running from the scullery to see what all the commotion was all about; joining in the crac amusingly asked 'I don't have to ask what have you been up to all day'? Eddie piped up and joined in adlibbing, 'Bobby's normally in the shit only this time he's really up to his neck in it'. Dad had just got in from work and was sitting down eating his dinner of Irish Stew and jumped up from the table shouting, 'he's a health hazard get him out, get him out,' insisting I strip naked in the garden and dispose of my rank clothes in a black bin bag. Tony out of devilment plugged in the hosepipe saying 'move out of the way while I hose him down like an animal'. In the meantime mammy went upstairs to run me a nice hot bath. After my stew I had the last laugh, proudly presenting my newly earned £5.00 note. The job continued throughout the summer holidays and every weekend for a couple of years. Picking the potatoes were the hardest, bending over all day long. Mr. Smiles didn't mind if I filled my pockets with spuds, just as long as I showed him. He didn't mind one bit. He became quite a good friend and I felt sorry for the way we treated him at Shepard's spring. He taught me to drive all the different machinery, the tractors, hay bailers combines, Lorries and even the Land rover.'

Everything was fine until I got Tony a job with me on the farm. In essence at the age of fourteen with approval from Mr. Smiles and the Government and dad, I became the new farm-driving instructor for my older brother, what a crac! Tony had been begging me to have a go and an opportunity arose in the field one afternoon. Mr. Smiles had left two tractors with us, so for a laugh we decided to have a race; the first past the pigs shed was the winner. There was no one in sight as we lined up for the start, it was a good mile to the finish and I got off to a blinding start. Tony was quick on my heels and rammed his machine into high power. I screamed at him and waved at him to slow down, but I guess he couldn't hear me, and by now had now lost control of this three-ton beast heading straight for the pig shed. At the very last moment before impact, he looked round blessed himself and then jumped off. Simultaneously as he hit the ground, there was deafening crashing noise as the tractor smashed its way through the asbestos sheeting, narrowly missing two hundred feeding pigs and piglets. They went absolutely berserk, squalling and ruining all round the place in sheer panic. The tractor continued on it path of destruction and came out the other side, causing even more noise and demolition. In the midst of this clamour and upheaval, I had to drive in to rescue Tony from the now angry marauding pigs, which were now out to kill him. We just managed to escape with our lives but Mr. Smiles was going to kill us anyway if he could catch us. We formulated a quick plan to rectify some of the damage and retrieve the run away tractor, now rammed against an embankment, engine still running! After parking both machines side by side I locked the gate behind me and we ran all the way home, never looking back or to return. It was good while it lasted, I found the work interesting and liked been outside in the Hampshire countryside, getting paid was a bonus as was the nice sun tan into the bargain. More importantly the money came in handy and now I needed to find a new job that fitted round school time, evenings and weekends.

It was long before finding my new trade, working with Vic in the local butchers shop. In essence a butcher's boy was the general dog's body, washing all the blood up and making the mince-meat and sausages. My hours were after school plus all day Saturday, all for a fiver a week,[seven dollars] Although it did have its perks, firstly I got to look a real professional in my crispy clean white coat and smart pinstripe apron; secondly mammy gave me a meat list as long as your arm and for next to nothing we eat the best quality Scotch beef, tasted the finest West Country hams, and feasted on whole lambs, which proudly I had learnt to cut and pack myself. What was even more gratifying was the fact mammy never had to buy meat for a couple of years and I was the source? I also had a morning paper round and was a regular baby sitter in the evenings for a neighbour Johnny the Scotch man. Looking after two little girls and a small boy while he and his wife Wendy worked a petrol station most evenings, it was ok, they left me out pop and crisp and I could watch any station I wanted on the television. One Saturday I put a tenner on Red Rum to win the Grand National and he did. It was brilliant, sailing home over the fences winning by twenty five lengths, Yee-ha. With my little win and all my modest jobs I was doing alright even managing to open my own personnel saving account at the post office. Each week I took great delight in building up my small fortune, I wasn't really saving for anything in particular, I just liked too see my little nest egg accumulating. Each week the lady at the post office on 'River way' would congratulate me on all my deposits and not one withdraw. All that altered one night after finishing my baby-sitting. When I came home dad said he wanted a seriously talk with me and would I sit down. This sounded all very ominous and I contemplated I must be in some sort of trouble again, or someone has died. Dad put in plain words that Tony had nicked the milkman's money from the milk float and he had been round that night ranting and raving calling Tony a robber, further more if he didn't get his money back tomorrow he was going to the Police, over a £100.00,[two hundred dollars] Tony had already spent the money buying sweets a new bike and a camping tent and stove. Dad didn't have that sort of hard cash and the only person with it was me, so reluctantly had to ask me to hand over my savings.

The very next day mammy had a day of work and we went together to get the money. The lady in the post office said 'Are you going to get your new bike today Robert, you've done very well, you must be so proud of him Mrs. Scanlan, he's a lovely boy'. Subsequently and throughout my entire life I never saved another penny, it just turned me off the whole idea. Tony did swear to pay be back but he never did, he had no money anyway so I put the hole lot down to experience and wrote the entire dept off. Actually you know what they say 'there's no better teacher of experience than life itself'.

It was my last year at school 1974 having one more term to go or so I thought. Then to throw a spanner in the works there was a general election and the new government changed the school leaving age to sixteen over night, becoming law immediately. Effectively, dashing all my hopes of an early escape from this hellhole, this really cheesed me off; resenting the fact I had to stay on I blamed the Government and school for holding up my apprenticeship and my life. Other reforms to radically shake up the education system were happening; they the hierarchy decided to scrap Secondary modern for what they called 'Comprehensive Schools.' Local history was made that summer when work started on a bridge, linking us with the girls school across the main London road, renaming it 'The Winton Comprehensive' When it was finished it was a brute of a construction and looked like one of those steel and concrete motorway bridges. This was all very much different, now, after all these years I could set foot on the other side, which the lads called 'no mans land'. Over the years we had speculated what it must have been like and I am sure the girls must have thought the same. Instead at looking at six hundred hairy bums we now had voluminous buxom girls thrown into the equation, spurring on my adolescent hormones even more. Luckily with this educational gamble went all forms of corporal punishment. Friendship view was, 'well if it's not ok to cane a girl, how can you a boy?' Intervening officially, the government of the day banned all forms of Corporal punishment in state schools, although I am not sure about Public Schools. Officially now it was a criminal act to hit the kids, but old habits die-hard, especially if that was the only control they knew, like Ernie. The majority of masters were only used to teaching their own sex and a lot of the old ones took early retirement or moved to a different profession. The knock on effect was an influx of young new teachers straight from university. After a while things settled down and we got used to seeing the girls around, it was better for us boys now not getting belted at the drop of a hat any more. Concentrating hard on my studies admiring the girls from a distance, I kept my head down and didn't get in any more trouble. Until something strange happened one afternoon in my biology studies, the big lad we nick- named 'The Swede' deliberately started an argument with me during a lesson and I promptly told him where to go in no uncertain terms. The conversation was overheard by the teacher, a Miss Smith, who indecently was fresh out of university and not much older than me. Ant how, later on that day I was summoned to Mr. Sharpe as the young Miss Smith had made a complaint and reported that I swore at her, when in fact it was the Swede I told to 'feck off'. Moreover she just happened to be in ear shot, hiding away in the store room eavesdropping being nosey! As a result Mr Sharpe gave me a serious rollicking, all about morals and behaviour in front of ladies and in addition, I was to go and apologies to her straight away. I thought this was all a bit odd as she had been my teacher for some time now, and I presumed we got on rather well. Normally if she had something to say, she would just say it and be done with it, and not get anyone else involved.

Feeling rather angry deceived and perhaps a little betrayed I reluctantly agreed to his demands and dully went to see Miss at her classroom. Everyone was in lessons as I walked along the lime green painted corridors, so it was much to my surprise to discover Miss had her free period and didn't have a class to teach. I knocked on her door but there was no reply even stranger I thought, what was she playing at

I wondered. Miss had gone to all this trouble and wasn't even three to except my apology. Any case I tried the door handle and it was open, strolling in I apprehensively called out 'hello'. From the stock room at the back I heard her reply, 'Come-in here if you like bob'. There was another door to that room, so I turned the door knob and slowly opened this one. By and large this was a restricted area and I had never been in here before and this was starting to intrigue me. Pauline as she instructed me to call her then, new the rules about being alone with 6th formers in her private room at the back, above all especially when the rest of the school was busy in lessons. Entering she gave me a funny look and instructed me to shut the door behind me. Here was me just sixteen alone with this attractive twenty one year old woman, wearing black silk stockings [her not me] when she said 'what do you think, I would think, if you used that sort of language in front of me, especially if we were going out together.' To be completely frank I was a bit embarrassed by her remarks and went bright red at her oblivious sexual advances, not for a jiffy had I suspected she was like this. I replied 'but we are not going out together are we Pauline?' Naturally my boyish hormones went through the roof. This was something you only read about in one of them mucky magazine and I couldn't believe my luck. Pauline had planned the whole thing, but we both changed our minds at the last minute, but the intent was there. The thing was I went round and told all my mates I had had sex with her and the play ground was a wash with rumours. I believe the powers above got wind of this and transferred her out of the area. Anyway I can't help wondering what my psychiatrist's would make of all this, would he conclude I was sexually abused or not, and if so, was she my abuser, or was this normal behaviour between two people that are attracted to each other? Actually to be honest since the day I've had this fetish for girls in black stockings, or is that also normal, what do you think reader?

Nothing else really changed apart from Ernie remaining on my case, I tried turning the other cheek, rising above it and all that, but Ernie wasn't having any of it, relentlessly hassling me, accusing me of this that and the other and of having a serious attitude problem, well maybe I did after that wiping he gave me. To be honest I don't truthfully know, but I knew I wanted some sort of justice though. However now unable to resort to violence to make his point he started a new campaign of ongoing verbal and mental abuse. It was absolutely terrible and I skived

Robert Charles Scanlan

off as much as I could. I was leaving soon so revenge was now or never. There were four sets of keys to Ernie's office and unless I could get a copy his office was impregnable. Obviously Ernie had his own set; the caretaker Mr. Permian had a set and the school Secretary also had a copy. Mr. Permian was always around doing odd jobs, so I targeted him. The quandary for me was his set hung on a long chain coupled to his belt, never leaving his side. After giving this a great deal of thought I realized there might be a way. Firstly I studied his routine and started hanging around him when he opened doors-spying. Through my surveillance I identified which key opened what door; they all had different coloured plastic tags you see. He was a creature of habits, also observing he skived off work everyday to have a pint at the local pub called 'The Queen Charlotte' and back the horses, returning half cut sleeping it off in the boiler room.

This particular afternoon I put my cunning preparation into action, laying in wait behind the potting sheds for him to return. Guessing he had a win or two, he wobbled back around 3 o'clock half-cut and as anticipated headed straight for the boiler room, where it was nice and warm and wouldn't be caught. Half an hour went by, until I sneaked in after him. There he was on his long leather armchair, the Daily Mirror on his lap, fast asleep. I had seen on the television the film the 'Great Escape' and how they made impression of keys from a bar of soap, so I came prepared with a new bar of Palmolive. To his side dangling over the edge of the armchair was the full set of keys, but I only needed impression of four, which meant I had to go through the whole lot and find the ones I wanted. His old brass alarm clock was ticking away and was set to go off in about five minutes or so just before home time. Kneeling down my knees cracked penetratingly, disturbing him only for a second or so he yawned, turned his head and went back to sleep. We were that close I could smell the nicotine and pale ale on his drunken breath. Each key was colour coded, Purple was for the staff entrance; Green allowed access to the science labs, yellow for the quadrangle and finally the white one which opened Ernie's door. Having found the correct ones I made my perfect impressions; the next step was the school metal workshop.

Previously I bought some blanks of some kid who worked part time in a locksmith. Then when no one was looking gradually filed them to the correct shape, it took me about a month and hay-presto it was that simple, I even used their tools and facilities, now that is called taking full advantage of the situation, or some might even go as far too say extracting the urine. That night the ten o'clock news had just finished. The main bulletin was about the Americans buying London Bridge and shipping it brick by brick back to Arizona. They actually thought they were buying Tower Bridge, but that had already been sold a few times over by the 'Cockney Wide-Boys'. I did think my mission was a piece of cake compared to that one. After supper and saying good night, every one went to bed and I said my nightly prayers. I couldn't sleep, lying awake for hours, 'but again I was thinking I'm bloody innocent' Festering at the back of my mind was he subjected me to five years of absolute grief and heartache and maybe now it was about time he got a taste of his own medicine. I was determined to get him back in some shape form or fashion, so I decided to use my newly forged keys and really wind him up that night.

In the dead of night I silently crept down the stairs and got dressed. This was my first time out on a job, borrowing Dads screwdriver, gloves, black balaclava that my mammy knitted, a small file, the replica keys and finally the torch light. Dressed all in black I felt prepared like James Bond on a secret mission, or the man in the milk tray advert who always gets the girl. It was a full moon and cycling flat out I passed through the deserted playgrounds bypassing by the silent red telephone boxes. Although being quite a big lad it was a feeling of aloneness I never forget, even my own shadow and heavy breathing was stressing me out. Finally I reached my destiny and as planned hid my bike under a bush by the side of the tennis courts. With the security of today I doubt if I would get within fifty yards of the place, but then it was an open shop! Anyway, using my newly forged keys I gained initial entry via the staff entrance. Tensely I turned the key and opened the door, still expecting someone to jump out of the dark and catch me. His office was deliberately situated in the centre of the school, with no exterior windows making it impossible to get to, unless you dug a tunnel or had the keys like me! Actually just thinking about it now makes me sweat. The place was completely silent and still, I never seen it like this before, as if it was haunted by previous pupils and masters and I was been watched by a thousands possibly millions of eyes. My heartbeat was pounding getting faster and faster and at one point I thought it was going to jump rite out of my chest. Sweat was running down my brow into my eyes making them sting, I admit I was bricking it. Running through the corridors the moonlight gave me just enough light to see were I was actually going. Making my way past the Science labs I couldn't help glancing in, like I had done a million times before, only this time I was the uninvited guest. Putting in service my second set I opened the next internal door that gave me access to the quadrangle, no problem so far so good. Ernie's door was next, my hands were shaking so much so I had to stop and take a couple of deep breaths, still trembling I put the heavy duty key into the lock, and unbelievably it didn't work, what now I thought. Undaunted I fiddled about with it for a while, filling it down here and there making a few final adjustments and then trying it again for the last time, I silently heard the lock disengage and bingo it fitted like a glove and I was in. I remember shutting and locking the door behind me and shining my torch around, looking for the light switch, eventually finding it. This wasn't meant to be a robbery but all the school dinner money was there for the taking, so I took it as compensation money. I felt quite relaxed and it all became very amusing sitting on his big leather chair with my feet perched on his desk, sipping tea and treating myself to his fruitcake and cookies. Whilst enjoying myself I had a good look around, his filing cabinet caught my eye first, were he kept as trophies his now illegal canes. Using the screwdriver I managed to pick the lock in seconds, no difficulty opening that either. All his evil torture instruments were there, half a dozen canes lined up ready for use. One by one I put them over my knee and had great satisfaction breaking them up, and my thoughts and heart went out for the rest of the boys that couldn't make it tonight. Next on the agenda was his desk draw, this proved a little more difficult but my faithful screwdriver came to the rescue once again. Sliding it open I hit on a load of top secret documents, all about the other teachers and the kids even the dinner ladies no one was spared. There must have been fifty pages of this stuff, all of it was mine to take away and study at my leisure, which I did. The next item on my shopping list was the detention book, knowing how this would help the rest of the lads, who would now not have to do it. After an hour or so I put everything I wanted in my rucksack including the remainder of the cake and biscuits. To be funny I thought I would leave him a note; it was a quotation by Winston Churchill, 'If you have an important point to make and don't try to be subtle or clever. Use a pile driver. Hit the point once. Then come back and hit it again. Then hit it a third time-with a tremendous whack! To confuse them even further locking up everything as I left, I new then he would have to change all the locks, winding him up even more. Making my way home I cycled through the fields larger than life. Nothing worried me now and knowing that I had got away with such mischief was so exhilarating, moreover I had eventually repaid a debt that was long over due. Home again I hid my loot in the shed, replaced the tools back under the sink and crept back upstairs. Eddie woke up and rubbing the sleep from his eyes asked 'what's going on Bobby?' chuckling to myself I replied smiling from ear to ear. "Just getting a glass of water,"

Breakfast was as usual, cornflakes with hot milk and after I finished my paper round got myself ready for school, where I knew the preverbal was going to hit the fan and it did just that, big time. Can you just imagine the look on his face as he entered his office first thing? Honestly reader it looked like an elephant had gone on a mad rampage, plus on top of that he lost all the school dinner money. That morning it was like a police investigation warehouse, coppers running around everywhere dusting for prints and searching in the shrubbery for clues. Not one, but two plainclothes detectives as well, fame at last I thought! I wasn't quite sure weather I was under suspicion or not, but Ernie and Mr. Sharpe kept giving me funny Look's all day. The police went away empty handed saying 'it was on going and they would be back' they never did. About a week later I stated releasing the stolen secret paper work, which by now had been photocopied hundreds of times. Every were you looked this stuff was fly posted all over the school and even in the bus shelter. As quickly as they pulled them down I was putting them up. This was really damming material all about his opinions on other members of staff and a log of how many times he had used the cane, plus the names of the boys who had got it, including me. Actually, I was surprised not to find any photographs and boys pants. This was the icing on the cake and he was getting all this grief from everywhere and everyone; I dare to think was it was like for him in the staff room at break time. Some of the material I didn't make public and shuffled it direct under the teachers doors, it was that bad, depended if I liked you or not. Ernie was getting it from every angle now even offering a large cash reward for the return of his outstanding paper work with no questions asked. My revenge on this good for nothing bastard was sweet, I am not sure what happened to him in the end and I don't really care.

It was around that time Dad let me go on a week's adventure holiday with three of my school friends. With me was Steven, David, and Kenny and off we set of camping in the countryside. We had been planning it for weeks, and I was really keyed up about my new adventure, actually the night before I couldn't sleep a wink. We had all the gear including an ex-army four-man tent, sleeping bags camping stove and all the other things lads need to go camping. Kenny even managed to smuggle one of his dad's mucky magazines from under the bed. It was a great crac, I felt like I was on an expedition to the arctic North Pole and I was a real explorer. That night we made a small bonfire and sat round it telling jokes, playing cards, drinking beer and smoking Woodbine Cigarettes, goggling at all the pretty girls in the photos. Kenny ripped the centrefold out and hurriedly disappeared in the bushes, properly masturbating all over the Dorset countryside. Anyway he came back with a flushed face, all red and sweating minus the centrefold. The others stayed up most of the night, probably doing the same thing. Not me though, being a good Catholic boy and all! Eventually I went to sleep around 3 o'clock and woke up about midday. We didn't really do a lot, simply because we didn't have much money and basically I spent the remainder of Ernie's dinner money on loads of booze and got absolutely sloshed. Steven told us you could get high if we smoked Nutmeg, you know the stuff mums use in cooking. I bought some from the supermarket and tried it; regrettably all it did was give me a splitting headache, so much so I had to take three tablets to counteract it. To be honest with the mixture of alcohol Nutmeg and Aspirin, I didn't know if I was coming or going. On that Saturday morning it was my fifteenth birthday and for a treat decided to spend what little we had on hiring a boat for the day, sailing down the river. We hired it from some man who had loads of them, and the four of us excitedly set sail. David and Kenny wanted to paddle and we quietly drifted down the river, just smoking fags and taking the scenery in, laying back enjoying myself, running my hands through the water. I suppose, from bank to bank, it was about the same length of a tennis court, it was deep, the current was strong fast and too dangerous too swim. We had been sailing for about fifteen minutes and a bridge was coming up. People were standing on the bridge waving and calling us, I thought that was nice of them and waved back at their gesture. As we got closer though I noticed an alarmed look on their faces and I started to hear what they were actually calling out, 'save the boy, save the boy' As we passed under the bridge they went to the other side and started pointing at a small vessel moored along the bank further on. The boat was a small cruiser about fifteen feet long and was high in the water. David and Kevin fought against the current and steered our little boat in as close as possible, but the current was sweeping us away. Steven caught saw of the little lad first, and said whilst pointing 'look Bob'. By now the little lad was desperately trying to scramble up the side of this boat, but it was impossible, he was just too small and in real danger of drowning. Steven dived in first and then I followed, I didn't really think about my own safety it was just instinctive. Luckily we were both strong swimmers and Steven got to the lad first. Seconds later, I arrived and Steven shouted 'get on the boat Bob, whilst I hold him, fecking hurry up'. Some how I managed to make it to the bank and then clamber on board the deck. Leaning over the side I hauled the lad on board first and could see he had gone a funny colour blue. It all happened so fast and when I looked round now noticed that Steven was now in big trouble himself and reached down and grabbed his right arm. This gave him a few moments to catch his breath and then I grabbed his other hand. He was a lot heavier than I thought and it took all my strength to heave him on board as well. The lad was about ten and lying unconscious on the deck and we didn't know what to do next. Fortunately a man watching from the bridge saw all this and ran down to help, I am sure he said he was a Doctor and we passed over the lifeless boy to him. He laid him on the ground and gave him the kiss of life. Spluttering and coughing, water oozed from his mouth his colour returned to normal and thank God he survived. The ambulance arrived and we hung around for a while, the Police turned up asked us our names and what happened. We left and that was the last I heard about it. Looking back though, I think fate played a big part in all this, what I am trying to say is, if I hadn't gone on holiday at that crucial time he probably would have drowned. Throughout my life I often thought about the lad and what became of him, strangely wondering if he had any children.

After my little holiday, my final day at school felt really weird strange unbelievable and worthy of note. All these restraints been told

Robert Charles Scanlan

what to do and were to go were about to be unleashed and finally I was a free man, like I had escaped from Colditz prisoner of war camp. After my dinner of Shepard's pie and apple crumble and custard, which was like the last supper, I simple went to walk out the front gates not bothering to say good bye to anyone. Contemplating my future and the last five years of nonsense I just went through that's not actually surprising considering all the circumstances. As I was leaving though Mr. Sharp was standing by the flagpole, calling me over we stood under The Union Jack and shook hands, smiling broadly they way he did, said 'Are you off now, son?' Astonishingly he then proceeded to thank me for 'dropping off that document from Ernie, he knew along it was me and wished me all the best for the future, in fact his exact words were 'have a nice life, Bob. I'm very proud of you' A couple of months later I received my exams results and not surprisingly got un-graded in every subject. I didn't really care boycotting the lot, my job was all ready lined up and in my opinion they weren't worth the paper they were written on. It's a funny old world and thinking about it now, everyone left with C. S. E. or G. C. S. E. not me though C. C. J. County Court Judgements, in fact I got all A's for absent in every subject.

Moving on, it was just another day in the hospital and I asked Vera for permission to go outside for a little walk in the private grounds. I had been here nine weeks and was now trusted not to run away or commit suicide, not that I wanted too any way. The grass had just been cut and the morning due was still in the air. I could smell it all fresh green and organic. Lying down on the neatly cut lawn in the hot summer sunshine, my cup of coffee to my side I listened to morning requests on my personnel stereo. It was the English composer—Henry Purcell. Glancing around smoking my cigarette I was constantly impressed with this extreme beauty and tranquillity. Beyond description the fully mature trees had grown tall above the single story buildings and the serenity of the grounds were all inspiring, just what I needed to be creative. Sitting comfortably in the clandestine estate I read about the Hospital and its history. It was really interesting stuff and on top of all that was the hot meals thrust under my nose, I even had a three course menu to choose from, now that cant be bad! Nevertheless it's easier said than done to portray my surroundings and pending fate, but I'll try my best to be fair, descriptive, and accurate so here we go. Runwell Psychiatric Hospital is set in beautiful rural scene of the roaming

Essex countryside and a typical example of the best of 1930's Art Deco. As you drive slowly up the neatly kept tarmac road you can't help but notice football pitches either side and there is always a game to watch every Sunday morning. The church stands out clearly and must have been put together from immovable granite blocks. Mature looking the green ivy had now crept up the sides and around the stain glass windows. At 11 o'clock the single bell rings out the service every Thursday and Sundays, you can't miss it. The boiler-house at the back is an all-imposing edifice, the structure is very gothic looking, sooty grimy and dirty, like a stage set from a horror film quite haunting and old looking. The land to the east is the new dual carriageway and with the additional information gleaned from my walks, I have calculated that most of the hospital is now mothballed, derelict and a shame. The Great Hall is now totally forsaken except for the mice rats and pigeons that have made it their home in all the nooks and crannies. Along time ago this must have been the hive of activity. I imagined staff and patients enjoying ballroom dancing, bingo and the odd occasional wedding. I shut my eyes and tried to visualise and picture the sights and sounds of the day. I don't know why but I thought of grand looking ladies in long gowns and gentlemen in top hat and tails, maybe even men and women in uniform. Conceivably people swapped funny stories, possibly having the crac playing cards, or eagerly awaiting the next raffle, dance, drink or basket of chips. Now however as I gaze through the cobwebs of the dirty broken windows, all I can see are upturned tables and chairs with yesterday's newspapers blowing around in the breeze. The cues and balls are long gone and a thick layer of dust now coverers the once magnificent pool table. It was getting close to dinner time and I had to be back on the ward so I quickly hurried back, another day another storey you might say.

I'm not sure, but I think we saw the start of global warning, as that summer of 1976 was a real Indian scorcher. Making the most of I check out a few rays and got a great sun tan and the few drops of rain we had made the news. At Lords rain stopped the cricket for fifteen minutes and the crowd unbelievably cheered, clapped and danced in the downpour. Honestly reader, all the reservoirs dried up and the clay bottoms looked more like the surface of the moon. The temperatures soared and suddenly it was time for barbecues and bikinis in Hyde Park. I was there queuing up with the rest of the crowds, waiting patiently for my ice cream and cold bottle of Coca Cola. Lounging around on the green I listened to my Radio, Alice Cooper smash hit 'school out for summer' was playing. The news caster of the day reported that fire raged across the country and England was going up in smoke, going on to say that 'the Fireman had to look on impotently as acre upon acre of England's finest burnt to the ground'. The water board had to introduce new draconian penalties. Basically banning you from washing your car or watering your garden and everyone was encouraged to take a shower with a friend. Actually the whole country was at it like rabbits and figures for that period indicate a mini baby boom; The Government of the day warned the public: If consumption was cut by half, rationing would almost certainly be introduced; I presume they were talking about the draught and not the sex. Any way the draught passed and I was thrilled to given my new National insurance number. Which in reality meant I could now legally follow my career path as an apprentice welder in a heavy engineering factory, mass producing lorry fittings and trailers, used for transporting heavy freight, steam engines boats and the like, it was in a place in Anna Valley called Taskers Trailers. In point of fact I wanted to be a journalist and was really interested in current affairs, but my English at the time just wasn't good enough, I hope its up to scratch now though! It was also about then an old favourite of mine fought his last battle, John Wayne. Nicknamed the Duke he died after a long illness at the ripe old age of seventy two. Did you know in real life he was married three times and had seven children, a true-life hero who never shot a man in anger, although rumour has it, he was the one who shot 'Liberty Valance? What do you think reader!

Every morning at the factory gates I and four hundred men dressed in blue boiler suits converged onto the one place, like bees buzzing around the honey pot, franticly running through the entrance, hustling and bustling trying to beat the clocking in system. If you were late more than three minutes, it would show up in red on your clock card and as a punishment a quarter of an hours pay would be docked from your wage packet at the end of the week. At first, I enjoyed my work especially all the masculine bits like wearing my boiler suit and being one of the men, using all the tools, welding and cutting huge steel plates with the acetylene torches, turning on the lathes and hammering home the hot rivets, but the pay just wasn't enough, £21.00 a week, roughly about 30 dollars. Mammy asked me for £7.50 house keeping and my fares to the factory were 3.00 per week which only left me £10.50 per week to live on, about six dollars. Furthermore, if I happened to be late it was even less. What was making it worse I had another five years of this crap before I could get the trade men's rate, bring it up to 1981 and I be twenty one. Actually I felt like I was back at school and the whole issue was making me rather depressed and unhappy. In the intervening time all my mates worked on the building sites on the lump earning a fantastic wage, going out every night, wearing nice clothes, driving fast cars and having no cash flow problems, oh and loads of birds hanging of their arms. I was happier and richer out doors on the farm and on my paper round but factory life made me feel down in the dumps. All this effort day after day banged up in a factory for next to no money just wasn't me, and if I didn't leave rite now, I would properly stay here for the rest of my life, just like Arthur did over there. The job became a thorn in my side, on the one hand I was getting advice from the old boys too finish my apprenticeship first, then you can do what you like, always having a trade to fall back on, but I just wasn't interested in working in the factory, clocking in and out for the rest of my life, waiting for the hooters to sound the end of the day. In point of fact sometimes it felt like the factory clock was actually going backwards, and Friday couldn't come quick enough. So at the age of nineteen and against all rational advice I took the courageous decision to scrap my apprenticeship and start all over again. I remember thinking as I clocked out for the very last time, I hope I don't live to regret this Bob, and thank god I didn't, properly one of the best decisions I made in my life. It was a huge risk but my old friend Johnny the Scotch man gave me a job with him building the new Courage brewery in Reading. We were employed in the construction industry by a national company called Wimpy, did you know their acumen was and still is, We, Employ, More, Paddies, Every Year. It was massive amounts of money some times even embarrassing to talk about; people thought you were showing off making them unintentionally jealous. Money did give me some contentment though, my love life which was a complete catastrophe having a string of failed relationships behind me. Consistently leaving a trail of misery, this isn't something I was particularly proud of and it's not in my nature to deliberately hurt someone, but I seemed more interested in the physical interaction than the emotional or intellectual side of a relationship. Mammy told me off for treating one particular

Robert Charles Scanlan

girl they way I did, and in the end I had to finish it, I'm sorry.

The later years of the seventies were a turning point in British history; The Cold War had escalated and the Americans where given permission to launch their Cruise Missile from U.K soil. The airbase when only ten minutes from Andover in a place called Green-ham Common. Being so close to the weapons made me more mindful of current world affairs, it made me think I could be instantly vaporised at any moment and wouldn't know a thing about it. The "war" took the form of an arms race involving multiple nuclear war heads and conventional weapons, networks of military alliances, economic warfare and trade embargos, propaganda and espionage. The greatest fear was the risk it would escalate into a full blown nuclear exchange with hundreds of millions killed, including me. To stop everyone killing each other both sides developed a deterrence policy they called 'Détente' in theory it prevented problems from escalating out of control. It went on for years and but I found the whole experience a little nerve racking. Thank fully it ended peacefully in 1989 with the dissolution of the Warsaw Pact and later the Soviet Union. On a lighter note we had a TV presenter called 'Sir Jimmy Seville' any way he had a Saturday night programme called 'Jim will Fix it' Everyone watched it and wrote in asking him to fix-it to make there dreams come true. I wrote in once and asked him to fix it for me to do a free-fall parachute jump, and guess what, he fixed it for me. What an experience reader and highly recommended if you ever get the chance. They filmed me in action and unbelievably the following Saturday night I was seen on the TV by two million viewers receiving my Jim-will-fix it badge, thanks mate! Floyd's album 'Another brick in the wall' had been at the top of the hit parade for months and was now banned in all the schools, blaming the music for all the social unrest and upheaval within new youth. Were the sex pistols rocked and Floyd's lyrics echoed out, anarchy ruled the country, across London, Liverpool, Bristol Manchester Glasgow and even my hometown Andover. I read and saw it for myself, plastered all over the front page of the News of the World and flashing across the TV screens. Every front page was the same. We also had the miners strike, Arthur Scargill was leading them and they where having pitch battles with the police on the picket lines. The strike lasted for months causing national power cuts, throwing the country into absolute kayos. People were put on a three day working week, simply because there was no coal for the power stations, and the national grid collapsed. Actually it wasn't long after that we switched to nuclear fuel and all the miners were made redundant any way. Social disharmony was the new crac and revolutionary new-fangled culture change was the new age phenomenon. All this social and political reform was a significant part of my life, furthermore I was not about to let an opportunity like this pass me by. Collective unrest and political change was in the air and the Government of the day was being held responsible. They tried to introduce new 'Public-Order-Acts' which just made things worse, curfews were in place and large gatherings and protesting was frowned upon and I felt my freedom of speech was slowly being eroded. Jim Callaghan was the Prime Minister and set up the 'Special Patrol Group' referred too by the media as thugs in blue. They even arrested Arthur and were alleged to have unofficially bugged his trade union offices, what a cheek. It all came to a head with the Grunwick film processing dispute, when I and 18,000 other trade unionist marched hand in hand down Whitehall, equivalent to one and half army divisions. The special patrol group had to be called in, only this time they got a taste of their own medicine and got a rite hammering. Lord Scarman was asked to make a report, concluding the strikers were fundamentally correct in there demands for fair pay, better working conditions and the rite to strike.

After that Labour got kicked out and Maggie Thatcher had a go, making things even worse. She was only in office five minutes and decided to take the trade unions head on, introducing the secret ballot. Previously decisions were made on a show of hands in the factory car park or on the shop floor, now that was illegal and workers were forced to vote in secret with a ballot paper and pen. Then she outlawed the closed shop system, which meant you didn't have to join the union to get a job, this took away any solidarity within the workers and in my view broke the back of the trade union movement forever. Interment had been introduced in Northern Ireland winding up a lot of the Irish; some never forgave her and tried to blow her up in Brighton, nearly succeeding, a bit like Guy Forks and the fifth of November gun powder plot of 1605. I'm sorry so say five people lost the lives and over thirty were injured. By the way reader, just too clarify things; these are facts of British history and not a political statement. It wasn't just that, other public laws where still trapped in the Victorian times and in need of desperate reform, as they didn't represent the general views of the

Robert Charles Scanlan

general public. One of which was a prohibition law preventing and restricting the sale of alcohol between certain hours. This outdated decree originated from the Second World War and basically was something to do with the industrial economic war effort, in essence to stop everyone going to the factories drunk, but the War had been over for at least thirty five years and no longer applicable. Immeasurable amounts of young people were cheesed off with all of this, and didn't like being told what to do, especially from some haughty nosed white-collar worker based in Whitehall. Eventually the people power won over and this particular law scheme call it what you like had to be abandoned, and the pub could open all day, power to the people.

It wasn't long before I had my first car, actually it was an old post office Morris Minor van painted in its original red, it didn't even have a key and came complete with its own made too measure Philips screwdriver. Being an X post-office van it must have been around-the-clock a few times, but that didn't matter, as long as it started and went that was good enough for me. I didn't need lessons as Mr Smiles taught me on the farm. To fool the Police I used to wear a peak cap when driving; those who didn't know me thought I was a postman on his rounds, what's more it was brilliant cover because I never got stopped. It was a good old van and I gave her a name Cathy; I also got myself a green Mohican and decided to join the wild pack, well for a while anyway. Again, against all rational advice I started knocking around with the infamous Hells Angels. Pillion passenger on a 450 Yamaha speed bike; Mr. X nicked the bike from Brands Hatch during a race when no one was looking. The other Angels loaded it into the back of my post office van; someone then threw a blanket over it and I just drove off wearing my peak cap. The rest of the gang rode a long side in tandem, keeping the police and everyone else away from the stolen cargo. Mr. X took out the engine and fitted it to a new frame, then re-sprayed it electric blue. Next X fitted new number plates and got the road tax and it went like a bat out of hell, no one could catch us for love or money. In our gang we also had a 750 Norton Bonneville, two Harley Davidson's, a Suzuki 500 and about five other machines. Every weekend we lived our lives in the fast lane and ride off where ever the fancy took us. Racing these machines at high speed through the deserted rural roads late at night was execrating. We were the quickest in the gang and our bike was super fast, it felt like I was racing in the Isle of Man T. T. My friend John was my front man and he leaned the bike over so much our heads were literally inches from the ground, deifying gravity and death at the same time. John and I would test the bike to it very limits, we even fitted a faring on the front to reduce wind drag. It was dead cool with the number 21 written in bold white at the front. We learnt how to pull wheelies with me hanging on the back for all my might, nearly falling off on one occasion. At weekends we would have a great crac sleeping in barns and hay-stacks, drinking cider, smoking pot and listening to head banging heavy metal music. It was trendy at the time to wear leather jackets with tassels dangling from the arms, and we didn't bother washing to much, simply because we were always working on the bikes. Between Andover and Salisbury the road is an old Roman road and dead straight. We planned to push the bike to its very limit one Sunday morning when no one was around to interfere. Unbelievably we reached a phenomenal speed of 135 miles an hour. This really was tempting fate, so reluctantly I decide to quit while I still had my life, but what fun it was, I wouldn't do it again though, far too dangerous reader and not to be recommended. It was a good crac but I felt I didn't really fit in, sensing more of an alliance with the Hippy movement, waving white flags smoking pot listening to Sergeant Pepper Lonely Heart Club Band and all that baloney, eventually succeeding.

A very small minority of the Hampshire Constabulary had nothing better to do with their time, hassling all the young people and late night revellers. They had far too much power and frequently abused it and were most definitely as much part of the problem as the solution. They had another law we nicked the 'S. U. S.' Stating; if a policeman suspected you might have or about to commit a criminal offence, he could nick you on the spot! Which in reality meant you didn't even have to do anything wrong in order to be searched or even arrested; his opinion was enough to be able to bang you up all night. Couple all this with mass unemployment, poverty in the inner cities and Maggie's ruthless unyielding social policies, designed to make the rich richer and the poor poorer, I am not surprised it was all kicking off.

A common example of this type of carryon happened in the early hours of one Friday night in 1979. Russell and I had been out celebrating my 19th birthday. We had grown up together and were close as two lads could be, sharing most things except our girl friends, we drew a line under that one. In high spirits suited and booted we left the nightclub called 'The Country Bumpkin' around one in the morning, I remember it was a cold chilly night, the sky was crystal clear, the moon had a face on it and as I spoke my breath vaporized in the midnight air, we were just laughing and joking chatting about the pretty girls we had met that night! Then in some sort of dramatic-all performance akin to the Sweeny flying squad, a car full of coppers screeched to a halt in front of us. Preventing us from getting to our destination the taxi rank, then finally home, that's all. We had done absolutely nothing wrong and just happened to be in the wrong place at the wrong time and now about to be escape goats, properly for the entire country.

The cocky arrogant one sitting in the front passenger seat tried to engage me in some sort of bullshit conversation, questioning me where I had been all night. The point is moments earlier he unmistakably saw me leave the nightclub with Russell. We all knew because I saw him parked up staring at us through his unwound window, so we returned his unwanted gesture back. We continued to boycott the lot of them and just walk off. They weren't having this and instantaneously the atmosphere changed becoming insanely hostile. All four of them jumped out of the squad car and surrounded us in a circle preventing us going home, infringing on our civil liberties and without a doubt playing with fire! Here were theses four guys about the same age as us, obviously abusing the uniform on their back and keen to abuse their powers too, or rather they were about too try too. What they didn't know or bank on was, we didn't get intimidated easy and furthermore neither did we take any bullying from nobody, especially the likes of them. Maybe they just had the problem because it was Friday night and we had been out all night enjoying ourselves dinking and chatting up the birds, or possibly they just needed an arrest to keep Maggie happy, who knows? Anyways they started shouting and been aggressive by poking me hard in the chest, I thought what a cheek, so I poked him back. He didn't like that one bit and backed off drawing his truncheon at the same time shouting 'come on then'. Amongst all of this mayhem I heard Russell say 'Fecking leave him alone' and then one of them call for back up over the radio "urgent assistance required Chantry Street car park over". This was total police harassment and really starting to get on my nerves, considering all we wanted to do was get a taxi home. They continued to question us on our whereabouts and we continued to use our silence as our only weapon, we were cautioned 'anything you say and all that twaddle'. In the background I heard a radio responding for the earlier back up request, 'assistant on way'

Within seconds in a blaze of glory the Calvary arrived, lights flashing, sirens blaring, opening all four doors at once before screeching halt, I thought what the feck is this all about. With nothing better too do the entire shift made them-selves busy? Russell was rugby tackled down onto the cold pavement first, which sent me into an absolute fury. Somehow by this stage they'd handcuffed him from behind and he was on his knees posing no threat. Then witnessing with my own eyes I saw one uniformed officer pull back his right arm, landing one almighty punch straight in the back of my mates head. The thug with a pension in blue and black uniform with silvery buttons, said under his breath "Take that you fecking bastard" Until that point dad had taught me to respect and be polite the police, as he was only a man in a uniform doing a job, but now all that had gone completely out the window, furthermore I was about to be arrested for absolutely nothing. Some how I had managed to break free and defending my mate landed a fantastic right hook rite on this renegade officer's nose, blooding his crispy clean white shirt. The force of the punch was so tremendous it traumatized everyone including me. It was like a scene from a movie but in slow motion, I felt detached as if I was watching on as part of the audience, but I wasn't, in fact I had the staring role. For that split second everyone just looked at each other and I heard Russell say 'Holy shit' and then all hell broke louse with a massive brawl happening on the pavement, fists and boots flying everywhere. Amongst all this mayhem I felt the extreme pain from a blow of a truncheon landing on the top of my legs, he was aiming for my manhood but fortunately for me missed, it was all very raw and violent but try imagine how it was for us, two solvent smartly dressed young men who were the victims here and now going to get even more victimized?

After the street brawl they split us up in different cars and take us to the Police Station for further questioning and even more grief. The journey took about five minutes; as we drove along Bridge Street two officers sat either side of me in the back of the car. Travelling along one of them had me in a headlock whilst the other continued to throw digs into my stomach, handcuffed from behind I presented no threat, to justify himself and his actions he kept asking me 'if I surrender yet'? Of course I did, not having much choice in the matter any way.

Finally arriving at the station Russell was already there and from the cells I could hear him screaming and shouting 'Fecking leave me alone, you wankers'. Hearing all of this and whilst looking directly at one of them I sarcastically asked, What the hell were they doing to him, 'Man.' He face seethed with temper, going all bright red he looked like he was going to have a rupture, disgruntled he said rather abruptly 'Rite bang this one up in number three' They knew exactly what they were doing, properly desperate to try out Magies new training tactics, taking a squad of five officers to control and restrain me. They accomplished this mental task by literally picking me up above their heads; spread-eagled each one of them holding me by the legs arms and head and then frog marched down the corridor to my awaiting cell. Russell continued shouting and hollering, screaming at the top of his voice, all I could make out was the word 'Bastards'. To add to the confusion and out of devilment I shouted back, "Russell, Russell they're trying to kill me, help me," with that one of them tried gagging me with his hand and the others then started shouting at each other "hold him, hold him and fecking hold him." The chorus of disapproval was getting louder and louder and by now we had woken up all the other prisoners who in turn started hollering and bellowing at each other, oh and there was some one singing at the top of his voice, an accurate description would be absolute pandemonium. The custody cells were broken into six separate rooms, Russell was in cell number one and I was some what deposited from a great height in number three. The numbers ran in lines of odds and evens like houses do and that particular night it certainly was a full house. Laying their knackered I remembered staring up at the ceiling and hearing the big cast iron door slamming and the rattle of keys as the lock engaged. Actually for a moment or so I thought this must be another one of my mad dreams, and any minute now I was going to wake up, but it wasn't. Russell was in the cell opposite me, so through the bars we could talk and see each other, for my part I was exhausted a little soar but ok. Although this particular man I shared my cell with seemed very happy to be here, in fact too happy. Whilst clinging to the cell bars he sang 'Oh Danny Boy' at the top of his drunken voice over and over again, his facial expressions conveying every emotion possible. The song it's self isn't that bad, but he couldn't sing anyway and never made it past the second verse and the repetition become seriously irritating, managing to wind the night up even further. Along with his drunken songs; the cheers, banging shouting and the cries of help all I wanted was to put my head down and go to sleep, which know one was going to get unless things settle down, which thank god they eventually did. A couple of hours went by and a girl was brought in and needed her own cell, so they moved Russell into our cell. It was then that we found ourselves being watched by the 'signing man'. Still half-drunk his weary un-shaven face was supported by a dirty red neck scarf representing himself as an Irish pikey. "Charles Haughty, what's yours?" we both understood the friendly Irish man proposal and duly introduced ourselves whilst firmly shaking hands. Actually thinking about it now, he did look a bit like that Irish Prime minister. Anyway, during an interesting conversation of his travels he told us about his life touring all over England and what it is really like to live rough on the streets and the predicament he now found himself in. He went on too explain during the winter he deliberately gets paralytic, just so that he can be nicked and brought back to this hellhole, in order to have some kip and a slap up breakfast, ready for the next binge! Funny thing was he seemed resolute with his dilemma looking on the 'Always looking on the bright side of life' whatever it threw at him. I admit I was a little apprehensive and scared with my pending circumstances but my problems paled into insignificance compared to his, which in a bizarre way gave me a little more confidence for the unknown events to come. In the morning breakfast was brought in, for a laugh more than anything we refused to eat it, protesting saying we were on hunger strike as political prisoners, declaring 'Political Status' and to wind it up even further refusing to wear the bright orange prison uniforms, not they intended to offer us one any way. Can you just visualize it, two hung-over young men in a dirty police station in the middle of nowhere demanding the same the rights as Nelson Mandela, for the crac we even started singing his song 'Free Nelson Mandela'?

Scratching his beard Charles asked 'what da feck ya on hunger strike for, eh?' His Irish accent was as thick as his long grey hair, we smiled as we glanced at each other, and before daring to answer he shrugged his shoulders saying 'I agree with you' and started divulging both ours and his own. For such a small man I was astonished that he managed to finish of six slices of bread, three eggs six rashers of bacon and about a tin of beans, all washed down with a large mug of tea. After finishing his banquette he let out the most vile burp I have ever heard in mt life, rubbing his stomach declared 'Aye, its better when I share a cell, I get a bit of company and sometimes more to eat'. Russell and I were looking at this midget of a man in total amazement; the stare was only broken by a police officer shouting through the bars in the cell door. 'I, Haughty, you're not coming back here tonight, there is another station up the road that will have you, for almost two weeks running you have ended up back ere,' Charles smiled and winked his eye, 'Breakfast's horrible here any way, although better than none though I suppose', some how at that point we all managed to laugh, including the decent policeman who brought in the breakfast who played no part in this fiasco, thanks Roy! To be honest after my cup of tea I regretted being on hunger strike and was absolutely starving, but there was nothing I could do about that now, Charles had seen to that. About an hour or so went by, when the pair of us were charged with suspicion of intending to break into cars, the SUS law as it was commonly known. This apparent crime happened at the same car park where we took the beating, convenient for them if nothing else. Before been taken to the courts we had our fingerprints taken and mug shots snapped. Actually it might seem strange but I was hoping to get charged with the hitting the bully officer but they never even mention it. We all knew, in fact the entire shift new they were on doggy ground to begin with, compounded with the truth that they started all this and the one who was throwing his weight around was know were to be seen, they must have sent him home. Know doubt they weighed up the situation during the night and thought about their jobs, considering the potential hostile evidence we had against them, they could even be nicked and slung in the jail. That May night, they deserved everything that was thrown at them, some might say not enough. Make no mistake about all this, we were prepared to shop the lot off them and plead not guilty, tell the whole truth then take a chance with the jury. At the worst risked facing a long holiday at her Magistracy pleasure, but this whole thing was an elaborate set up; they gave us two options and five minutes to make up our minds. Option one; plead guilty to the trumped up charges, keep your mouth shut about what happened the night before. Then if we agreed to that, they on their part would influence the 'Crown' to recommend a fine and time to pay, and more importantly we would have our liberty back end of story. Options two was, if we pleaded not guilty and made public what happened causing a fuss, they would influence the 'Crown' to go for a custodial sentence, rather than a fine. We would be sent straight back to the cells, and have to spend the next seven days with them, properly getting another hiding into the bargain.

Our choice was quite simple, we were in a no win situation, in fact we had no choice at all but to except this bullshit deal, plead guilty and pay the fine and forget all about it, simply because we wanted out. Nevertheless we were not going to let on what we doing until we were in the Courts, so again used our legal right to silence as our only weapon. The copper came back, desperately wanting to know our decisions. We just said, "We let you know in the court house." Rather perplexed with a distressed look on his face he slammed the cell door and walked off with his tail between his legs, Charlie remarked 'you have got them on the run now boys' From my point of view, I couldn't help feeling this wasn't the first time they used this tactic too get themselves off the hook and properly not the last.

Some time later we were led out of the station hand cuffed from behind, we could hear our new friend shouting from the cell block 'good luck boys, up the Republicans' and across the yard our carriage awaited, a black Maria complete with blacked out windows and a single blue flashing lamp. Two officers were in the front whilst another four sat in the back with us, like pees in a pod all huddle together, nice! Although the Courthouse was only five minutes away the journey seemed to take forever, but now the boot was definitely on the other foot and we were in control of the situation. The closer we got the more the atmosphere intensified, not for us though. You see, they still didn't have a clew how we intended to plead yet. As the van pulled into the Court house car park the one in the front passenger seat lost his nerve, turned round and started talking about his family and his precious job and pension, and the fact he wasn't actually involved. It was like rats leaving the sinking ship. What a cheek, what about my job and the criminal record I was going to get, plus all the grief they had put us through. Once more I defended my rite to silence only communicating by lifting my eyebrows and smiling sarcastically from ear to ear.

Suffering from a bad hangover and lack of sleep that morning at 10 o'clock we were led up from the dock, black and blue, not around the face mind you! It felt like we had been to hell and back and it still wasn't over, all I wanted to do was get the whole shebang over and done with, so I could get back down the pub for the hair of the dog that bit me. [Another drink] We were marched in and they released the hand cuffs and stood both side of us. Unshaven unkempt stinking of drink, we must have looked a pair of right ruffians, my suit jacket was all torn from the scuffle choosing not to wear it, hanging it over my arm. The usher had a black cape and looked like Batman, announced 'Court rise' the Magistrate entered and everyone stood up bowing there heads, except us, getting away with just a slight nod. He instructed us to remain standing whilst the charges were read out. She took one look at us and we were already guilty, even before we opened our mouths. We were definitely not making a very good first impression, especially standing there in front of this sour faced prune, 'Madame Flog-them'.

"Are you Robert Charles Scanlan of Constantine Square Cricketers Andover, born on 8th May 1960 in London?" asked Batman, for a second or so I paused and had a long look around. 'Yes, I am that Man' was my sarcastic reply. "Do you plead guilty, or not guilt, to the charge of suspicion of committing a criminal offence?" This time I really held back my reply I was so angry, so much so Batman said "Well, are you going to plead or not?" I can only speculate what was going through the copper's minds; Russell lent over and whispered 'what the hell was I doing, just fecking plead guilty, as we agreed' 'Guilty' was my eventual reply. They repeated the same palaver to Russ, he pleaded the same and then we instructed to sit down. As we both were pleading guilty none of the coopers had to give evidence, and the town prosecutor stood up to outline the fabricated case against the pair of us.

In the early hours of Saturday morning, these young men where seen by the police trying car door handles, obviously trying to steal one to get home. To their credit they have been well behaved in custody and furthermore not wasted the courts time by denying the charge, therefore I have no objection too a fine and recommend time to pay. The Magistrate asked us if we had anything to say, 'no'. Everyone stood up again for her too retire and consider the verdict. The hard hosed bitch returned fifteen minutes later and demanded we stood up for sentencing. Honestly reader we were up and down more than a bride's nigh-tie! "Have you anything further to say before I pass sentence on you?" she asked in her put on upper-class pretentious posh voice, we didn't reply just shaking our heads, not wanting to rock the boat any further.

"You have been found guilty on the said charge; this sort of conduct will not be tolerated in my town, I realize you were out celebrating a birthday and alcohol paid a role. However, I am going to send out a strong message that anti social behaviour like this will not be tolerated, and will be dealt with seriously. You are both extremely lucky you're not facing a custodial sentence. Had it not been the fact, that you both admitted your guilt and did not resist arrest and by all accounts curtsies whilst in custody, I am prepared to suspend that order for one year. In the meantime both of you will pay a £50.00 fine within 7 days. Don't let me ever see you again in here, case closed." The sickening thing was all the coopers smiled and shook each other's hand; they got a result on our expense. I thought as long as there is breath in my body I will get you back for that, eventually succeeding.

After the hearing we went and told our solicitor Mr. Walker all about it. He was disgusted with this miscarriage of justice and immediately launched an appeal on our behalf and guess what reader, justice prevailed and we won the case. Nothing much really happened for a time and all over the new was the Balcombe Street siege. TV viewers around the world saw thee policemen wearing bullet-proof flak jackets aiming their pistols on every move. A husband and wife were held hostage in thier own house after four IRA gunmen demanded a plane to take them to Ireland. The thing is the Irish didn't want them either and washed their hands of the whole affair, fortunately the siege ended peacefully. Actually it was also that year we saw the collapse of the IRA ceasefire which triggered a wave of massive bombings. They detonated their first of ten devices in five days and killed Ross Mc-Mhirter the co-editor of the Guinness Book of records, after he offered a large cash reward for information leading to their arrest. Then we had the Birmingham six, Hugh Callaghan, Patrick Hill, Gerard Hunter, Richard Mcilkenny, William Power and John Walker. They were sentenced to life imprisonment for two pub bombings in Birmingham that killed twenty one people. Like me they where also fitted up by the police and had their convictions overturned at the 'Old Bailey, Court of Appeal'.

My driving test was booked in a month or so, in any case a pack of wild horse wasn't going to stop me. My van 'Cathy' was too knackered to take my test in so I borrowed Russell's 1967 old ford escort for the day, and surprisingly it was taxed. The test centre was in Winchester and on the way I bought a brand new set of learner plates from a petrol station. This proved to a big blunder as they stuck out like a soar thumb, anyone could see they were brand new, not a speck of dirt on them. Topping that my girl friend had to pretend she was the qualified driver, the thing is she couldn't even drive. At the time they didn't bother asking to see hers, just my provisional and on the day we had them fooled, it's called taking full advantage of the situation, or some might say extracting the urine. The day of my test the weather was absolutely appalling, lashing down with rain thunder and lightning even hail stones as big as your fist thrown in for good measure. Along with all the other candidates I sat in a freezing cold waiting room. In the corner was a small electric bar fire, apprehensively I plugged it in, but that didn't work either. Sitting back I started glancing around and couldn't help noticing how much we stood out from the rest of them. Sitting patently they were obviously with qualified instructors or their dads and here was me with this blonde bombshell. Dressed up looking like she was going to the disco, her cleavage was practically bursting out at the seams. What made it worse she had on stilettos heels on, not the most practical shoes for driving and was continually giggling in the background. All the blokes were pretending not to look encouraging her silly childish behaviour even more. Having enough of all this I stood up yet again to get a Life magazine from the table, by chance I glimpsed through the window at this horrendous weather outside and all the cars displaying learner plates. This was starting to become a comedy of errors, [Shakespeare] going from bad to worse. Russell Escort was all' rite but in comparison to the other motors lined up it looked a right jalopy, especially with the new L plates stuck on over the dirt. My chances of passing seemed to have transformed from slim to remote, to now out of this world. I thought about just driving off and forgetting the whole thing, or I could do the dying swan act suddenly becoming very ill, or be brave and sod the consequences and continue for a laugh if nothing else. At least things couldn't get any worse, or that's what I thought!

On the wall was today's schedule and I was second on the list, about half an hour to wait while this guy took his. When he came back they sat in the car for a while, then the lad got out ripping up his L plates throwing them into the air. The examiner then called me over asking which car was mine. That one there! Pointing and spluttering at this old boiler of a car. Starring back at me through his half-moon glasses said 'your not serious are you' he must have thought I was a gipsy or some sort of lunatic when I replied 'deadly serious mate, why what's the problem? He then asked to see my license and read a number plate from another car parked up the road. The rain hailed down relentlessly as we set off doing a right turn onto a main road. That's when the car started to breakdown, the rain had some how got into the electrics and it all went wrong. The windscreen wipers were first, starting to make funny squeaking noises, becoming quite ineffective against this onslaught. We both ignored it but I thought, any minute now there either going to break completely or at worst fall off. We came to a T-junction and he asked me to do another right turn, stopping at the junction using mirror signal, breaking coming to a standstill and engaging the hand brake. With the problems with the wiper blades and the torrential rain visibility was practically zero from side to side, so much so I had to ask him to open his window so I could see properly. He wasn't at all pleased at my instructions saying 'I don't believe this" but had no choice in the matter anyway, otherwise I couldn't see anything risking both his life and mine. After winding the window down the rain started to pelt into the car, he was getting absolutely soaked, having to wipe the rain from his spectacles and then the indicators packed up. Out of the corner of my eye though, I saw all his paper work was getting wet, so wet the ink had started to run all over the page making it virtually unreadable. We had only gone about one mile when he said 'I've seen and had enough'. Demanding in no uncertain terms I pull over and stop immediately which I did, sarcastically asking him as I pulled up on the lay-by, 'was that my emergency stop then? Shaking from the cold and wet and possibly fright he handed me a pink failure slip with mechanical failure written on it. He then insisted we drove back to the centre as it was still raining very hard. Turning the ignition key, I suddenly stopped, and thought about this fecker saying, 'your making no more demands on me, get out and walk', reaching over him, I opened his door saying 'there's a good boy now, off you go then'. He didn't have far to walk anyway, so I just drove off leaving him standing in the rain gob-smacked. Hurriedly as I sped away I saw in the mirror he was sticking two fingers at me, so I returned his unwanted gesture. My friend was still at the test centre and on my return stupidly asked if I had passed, well if I had, it would have been the quickest test in all history. She wasn't that bright but I didn't think she was that thick. Looking back, I find it all very amusing and find myself speculating how many other people in the country have failed on that, not many I think, possibly another first. In any case it didn't stop me from driving Cathy clocking up another 100000 miles before she burst into flames and abandoned very quickly like some orphan on the M1 motorway.

Back at the ward though everyone was tucking into a light supper, one of the nurses used to make it at home using all her ingredients, how kind. She took great delight seeing everyone tucking into her sandwiches, encouraging every one to sample her cheese bits and marmite dips. After supper we all went into the television room, most of the patients sat glaring at the screen watching cartoons motionless sad and unhappy. Tom the old man watched it from dawn to dusk, any old station would do, furthermore was accused of hiding the remote control. He denied any involvement but they searched his gear and found it anyways, he got in big trouble. Things like that might seem petty but it kicked of a big argument with the rest of the gang and staff going on all day. To get away from it all I went into the smoking room, and as usual the air conditioning unit was on full blast. It made a humming sound and rattled every so often. One got the impression you were entering a silent British Rail waiting room. Nevertheless, even with this working to its full capacity it was still foggy grey and all misty. Most smoked roll ups and if you didn't have any they just used the dog ends left behind in the ashtrays, know one seemed to mind, routine in fact. I had endless supply of cigarettes and use to share them out when I saw that. On one occasion I was just sitting their having a smoke minding my own business, when out of the blue this guy decided to remove all his clothing and lay on the floor naked as a jay bird, chanting and humming like the Red Indians do. An old lady knitting in the corner covered her face with her hands saying 'Jesus Mary and Joseph someone get the Nurse' Honestly reader sometimes this place really was the back of beyond, none of the others didn't even bat an eye lid, carrying on puffing and chatting away as nothing had happened. I just sat there motionless in disbelieve, one of the staff hurriedly told the man off, saying he was very naughty and should be ashamed of himself. He didn't care one iota and stuck his tongue out. They wrapped a blanket around him and forcibly took him back to his bed screaming 'I didn't do it' The Cockney guy was now wearing a ridicules black leather hat and sun glasses started shouting 'your all fecking lunatics, do you hear me'! In fact that was his only comment apart from the fact that he was Jewish, proving his point having specially prepared kosher meals made by a Rabbi, costing three times as much as mine. The thing is he never honoured there Sabbath and never prayed, I think he was lying and should have paid for his own meals if that s what he wanted. What do you think reader?

Robert Charles Scanlan

Chapter Three

Slung amongst the estates and rural villages was an army barracks called 'Tidworth' with five thousands soldiers stationed in the one Barracks, all I needed. The handsome big strapping solders were a big attraction to the young ladies. This rivalry caused a lot of bad feeling in the town between the young male civilian population and the military. The local lads couldn't compete with the uniforms and fat wallets; the only alternative was if you can't beat them join them, a lot did too there own peril and a lot of them were murdered in some back street alley in Belfast. Thinking I had fallen in love I set up home with my new friend and we moved into our new council flat with our new baby daughter Joanne. A month or so went by and I was watching the six o'clock news was on the TV eating my dinner, Cod and chips with a picked egg and buttered roll to be exact, traditional English fare one might say! The correspondent on the TV sadly announced 'John Lennon was shot dead today'. Apparently he was walking back from a recording studio with his wife Yoko, when this nutter shot five rounds into his back. I was watching this story unfold when there was an official sounding knock. Who ever this was meant business and my first instinct was 'oh God I must be in trouble again with the police again'. Nervously opening my front door I was astounded to see a British Army officer confronting me in full uniform, I saw his wing badges and it was apparent he was a Paratrooper. We made eye contact and he brazenly asked if my girl friend was in, as if he was inquiring time of day or something. Glaring at him I immediately stuck two fingers up and slammed the door in his face, remarking 'up yours mate' My adrenalin kicked into what must have been overdrive and was pumping through my veins like rocket fuel or I could have been in shock, I don't know. Without saying another word I walked back into the living room, sat down muttering something about 'those bloody Jehovah witness gain'. Literally before I had time to catch my breath or collect my thoughts the cheeky barstard knocked again, now the penny dropped. Jumping up she ran out the house as quickly as she could, down the concrete communal stairs into an awaiting car and sped away and that was the last I saw of her. To be honest I didn't feel very hungry after that and my daughter and I packed what little we had sleeping in my old room, back at Mammies.

Saturday morning came and Mammy looked after the baby whilst I returned to my flat. It was a nice two bedroom council flat in both our names and I was quite happy. Well the month or so I was actually there, but in any case our bed hadn't been slept in. After making a cup of tea and lighting a cigarette I wondered around in quite thought looking out the window, I felt a terrible sense of betrayal and pondered what I shall do next, actually it was properly one of the lowest points in my life. Although strangely I remembered a poem by Alfred Tennyson which went "It is better to have loved and lost, than never to have loved at all." Didn't cheer me up though and I pottered around having a little tidy up and threw the remains of yesterday's dinner in the bin. Next I picked up the phone and within half an hour my mates turned up with a load of cans from the off licensee. In the newly painted front room we drank the beer smoked some more pot and listened to Mike Old Fields new album 'Tubular Bells'. We had a kangaroo court and everyone kept saying, "You're not leave it to the soldiers are you? After giving this much thought I calmly stood up, bent over the TV and unplugged it at the same time. Puzzled they all looked at each other and then me, next without warning I sent my size 10 Dr Martin boot smashing rite through the screen. It made a terrible crashing sound and smoke came

Robert Charles Scanlan

out the back, Chris started moaning saying 'what did you do that for' as he wanted to watch the football and now he couldn't. Rite up for it now properly high on the pot and beer they wanted to continue the carnage, and if it wasn't for my daughter I would have smashed the entire flat up. They kept harking back that she was no good anyway Bobby and not worth lousing any sleep over; it was quite a struggle stopping them from doing this and I had to promise the beers were on me and we left, however I found out later, one of them sneaked away and urinated all over the bed. Before leaving I wrote a really nasty letter telling her how much I despised her and to pick the baby up from mammy, adios. Indecently I thought a lot about my Joanne over the coming years and when she was sixteen we met, she's got her own baby now called Katelan, so that makes me a granddad. Her mum married the solider and went to live in Germany, ending up getting divorced, told you so.

My sister's wedding was the following week, so nothing else really mattered. Oh, apart from Ronald Reagan was wounded in an assassination attempt; someone shot a load of bullets into him as well, anyway he survived. Months of planning paper work and rehearsals had gone into this and it was timed like some sort of military operation. I had my strict orders, which basically meant no carrying on, getting drunk, telling jokes and strictly no Irish singing or dancing. Reinforcing herself by saying it was always me who showed up the rest of the family, and that's why we never get invited to anywhere. Nanny Gu-Gu bless her heart sadly died where as Kitty, May, Con and all Dad's relatives flew over from Dublin for the celebrations, even Auntie Laura and Uncle Kevin came up from Richmond for the crac. Olive arrived late with dad in the white Rolls-Royce looking radiant, I was so proud of her. Afterwards the reception was held in some posh hotel in Winchester, top and tails for the men. At the reception, Olive took some time to attract my attention, eventually doing so next to the scramble happening at the bar. Then whispered in my ear, 'I don't want this to turn into an Irish hula, with all the men getting drunk before the sit down dinner, look I am telling you, I mean it'! Returning her glare befuddled I asked, 'why are you telling me for? You-made it a free bar not me, tell them yourself'. The reception went on all day and well into the night, when Kitty who I was chaperoning asked if she could sing a little song over the mike. Not having the heart to tell her I was under strict orders I beckoned Tony over, telling him the two of us would be accompanying

Kitty, in what Andy Whorhall once descried as 'everyone is entitled to fifteen minutes of fame.' At least this way I wouldn't be the only one who would get it in the neck, or rather that's what I thought. We waited until Olive had gone to change into her evening wear and wasn't around to interfere. The disc jockey was quite accommodating explaining he had a good selection of Irish party songs. Beginning our repertoire with 'When Irish eyes are shinning' Olive came back half way through the performance looking like a bull dog chewing a wasp and wasn't a bit amused, starring at me as the whole place started joining in with the sing song. To make matters even worse and to add insult to injury I started doing my nutty Irish dancing bit. This was exactly what she didn't want, I suppose she was trying to make a good impression in front of the new in-laws or maybe these songs were not politically correct at the time, She never mentioned a word about all this until the following day back at the house, claiming I had ruined her big day, being the biggest pig under the sun for allowing the whole carry-on to turn into an absolute sham- balls. Well I wasn't standing for any of this telling her Kitty had practically begged me, and on top of that she was the only one moaning, moreover exactly what was her problem. Her brand new husband Andy was as just as amazed as me at this sudden tangent and hadn't seen this side of character before. I suppose you could say it was his baptism of fire, joking Olive. I seemed to be getting it from everywhere now and starting to feel really fed up with everyone and everything. The rush of the wedding and the celebrations were over and everything returned to back to its normal self.

As luck would have it, the hand of fate played an ace. A week or so later Kitty was due to fly back to Ireland but said she was too scared to fly, actually I think the ticket ran out! Her exact words were

'It might give me a heart attack, and my blood pressure would go through the sky'

Sensitizing, this might be an opportunity for me to get away for a while, I was glad when Mammy asked if I could escort Kitty all the way home back to Ireland on the on the boat. I eagerly agreed and travelled back to Ireland carrying her two suitcases and all my worldly possessions, not that I had much anyway. I remember it was a Sunday evening when the pair of us set of from London Euston Railway Station. The train was due to depart at 6 o'clock, but as usual there was a delay. After

Robert Charles Scanlan

a while we were heading north on the overnight express too the Welsh ferry port of Holyhead, catching the night boat to Dublin. The Irish sea conditions were really rough that night, blowing a force five gale and the swell was tossing the Car Ferry around like no one business, I actually thought we were about to sink at any moment and honestly said a few prayers.

Thinking on board I might be able to get a few pints of the black stuff at the bar and have the crac, but I couldn't even hold down the bacon sandwiches I had earlier on the train and Kitty needed all my attention taking her to the toilet and making sure she was al' right. The midnight crossing took longer than normal in fact seven hours of pure hell, a complete nightmare to be precise, desperate to get off the dam thing, honestly reader there was sick every where, even some of the sailors were ill. Eventually we disembarked down the wooden gang plank and sailed through the Irish customs. Mammy had given me the taxi fare too Kitty's flat and that Monday morning at 7.30 we landed.

Kitty put a match to the already prepared fire and we sat down round the table for a cup of tea and piece of bread. Through the 'jar door I saw the biggest double bed in the world, indecently it was Gugus old one. Pretending not to notice I suggested that I sleep at the bottom and her on top! Not surprisingly she replied 'I've never slept with a man in my life and I don't intend starting now', I couldn't help but to laugh and asked, 'well where I am going to go then'. To be honest reader I was absolutely shattered, the long journey and carrying all the gear had just taken it all out of me and all I wanted to do was just put my head down for a few hours to get some much need kip. Kitty went to the airing cupboard which she called the press, pulling out blankets and a pillow and then arranged the cushions from the settee in front of the fire, putting the blankets on top. Without even getting undressed I slipped of my shoes and snuggled in front of the raging fire now taking hold. It must have been sometime in the afternoon when I started to wake up properly around

4 o'clock. The fire had been restocked and turning my head away from the flickering flames I caught sight of these three old ladies, peacefully sitting round the table quietly sipping tea, just looking at me. One of them nudged Kitty saying, 'look Kitty, he's waking up now' and then I remember rubbing my eye's and blinking. The one sitting in the

middle said 'Hello you must be Robert, this is Marie and I am Gwendolyn, would you like your boiled eggs and newspapers now? Lying there in this strange house in front of these women I thought for a moment or so, this must be another one of my mad dreams. Then it all came flooding back, the late train and the boat ride from hell. Kitty went into the scullery and prepared my eggs and Gwendolyn continued saying, 'How good I was in bringing her all the way home'. After my eggs and toast and between drinking more tea I read the paper. The headline read 'Its War', Britain had declared war on Argentina.' It was all Greek to me and the article went on about a place called 'The Falkland Islands' apparently the Argentinean's clamed it was theirs calling it 'Maleness' and invaded. With all respect, I never heard of the place and neither had the rest of the country and thought. Talk in the pub was it was one of the Shetland Islands off the top of Scotland somewhere. Anyway my head started to clear, contemplating what I was going to do now I'm actually here. Kitty then instructed me to open the suitcases that I hauled all the way from England. Going on to say that mammy Josie said in no uncertain terms 'not to open them until I got to her flat'. Therefore in front of the all the others I unzipped the larger of the two, discovering six rolls of wall paper, glue brushes a tape measure and a brand new set of scissors, oh and a note from mammy saying 'fooled you.' Momentary looking around her small flat, it was bluntly obvious it hadn't been decorated for years and that was the real reason I was here. They continued by asking me if I liked the paper and do I think I had enough. I couldn't believe how I had been set up and thought how funny the whole situation had now become. How could I refuse the old girl it just not in my nature, having said all that I had nothing better to do with my time anyway? After getting over the initial shock I started to realize this decorating job wasn't going to be that easy, all the old stuff had to be got off first. What do think someone else asked? No problem was my immediate response, but not today if that's all' right, I fancy a few pints of the black stuff first. Sure that's grand said Kitty shoving 40.00 of English money in my fist. At the time the Irish used there own currency called the Punt and the exchange rate was favourable, virtually half as much again so it was worth about 60 punts, in reality a packet of cigarettes and around 30 pints of Guinness. After having a quick wash and shave in the kitchen sink I put on some clean cloths, heading out but not sure exactly were I was going. They told me

Robert Charles Scanlan

there was a friendly pub in Francis Street called the 'Liberty Bell,' were I would be made more than welcome and they would join me later. I remember walking up the street past the old corner shop where mammy got credit and briefly standing out side Go-Gu's old front door reflecting from when I was a boy. It was an odd feeling and all the old memories came flooding back; I could almost hear my old dad singing in the background. On entering the pub I heard an old favourite of mine on the duke box, it was 'I remember you' by the Bachelors. The barman introduced himself as Shamus and we shook hands. He knew I was a bit shrewd when I said I only had English money, replying 'Ah sure that's not a problem, what would you like then Sir', 'well I need to know what exchange rate you would give me for this English twenty first' He looked at me quoting 130 punts to the pound, that the best I can do. Maybe I could have got more at the bank but I couldn't wait for my first pint so we exchanged. On my own I did feel a little awkward but he soon put that to rest introducing to everyone, including the band which were just tuning up for the evening's performance. Kitty and her friend's weren't long behind me, buying them a bottle of stout each as they entered. Considering they were in their seventies and eighties this was going to be some crac as we all sat down to listen to the musicians. We all loved it and at the end of the night I got absolutely rat-arsed and near an enough had to be carried home by new friends, I have absolutely no idea what they thought of me.

That following morning in front of the raging fire, my whole body felt totally dehydrated. My face had gone bright red from the heat and my lips seemed welded together at the seams, as for the inside of my mouth, well it was dryer than the bottom of a bird's cage. My head or rather what was left of it was even worse, thumping and bumping, It felt numb and every noise or little sound became amplified and some what distorted, it was like playing a record on the wrong speed with everything in slow motion and I thought I was about to die at any moment! Over a very long breakfast and drinking gallons of tea, life returned. I remember reading an interesting feature in the morning paper, it was about Israel invading the Lebanon and it was all kicking off big style in the Middle East. Little did I know decades later I would actually get involved in all that, becoming a real life international spy? Anyway I tell you about that later. About 11 o'clock I managed to make a start removing the old wallpaper. Around four o'clock my other two drinking partners returned sitting down drinking tea and eating fresh cream cakes, they were lovely, personally saying it looked better already, but I don't know how they came to that conclusion because it was just bare pink walls and white undercoat. Gwen as she instructed me to call her again went on for the second time telling me how good I was, and perhaps I should consider becoming a Priest, far out, and if I got time could I do her and Marie a big favour. Not even knowing what I was getting myself into I immediately said yes, I just couldn't say no. We need you to carry the coal up the stairs for the winter time; we just can't manage it with our hands, it's the arthritis you see, she said smiling. That's not a problem at all, anything you want just ask me, and in fact I will be your own personnel slave for a week if you like, how's that? Secretly thinking that's an awful lot of bags plus Kitty will need some as well, but what the hell I didn't care. It took about two weeks to finish the decorating and I must have carried half a ton of coal up the stairs for the old girls. Every time I looked at them they kept giving me English money, kind heartily saying 'they had no need for it anyway'. Eventually I finished the decorating but then realized this had only been a short break from reality, kitty and her friends enjoyed having me around but now it was time to go back to England. Not bothering with the boat I flew back on a cheap standby ticket from Dublin International Airport and Uncle Con gave me a lift on the back of the bike for the very last time, stopping outside a cemetery next to airport. We both loved airplanes, space and things like that, so I wasn't at all surprised when he told me he had saved up and bought his own burial plot, right under the flight path. We got off and preceded walking amongst the tombstones when we came to his plot. Just then one of jets roared over head, we were that close I could smell the aviation fuel in the air and see the people waving at me through the port holes. Waving back I playfully inquired. 'How much did you pay for that; Having a fantastic sense of humour he said, he got a bargain only 300.00 punts, but wasn't in that much of a hurry to occupy it, in jest I replied 'I don't blame you'. Strolling back to the bike he continues to comment, 'he could lie back all day enjoying the planes, and when I fly in and out he would be watching over me'. Much to my sorrow that was the last I saw of him and years later his plane-spotting wish came true, God bless.

Back in England the work fizzled out and there was a recession having to sign on the dole for the first time in my life. There was a pop group called 'UB40' who had a record out that summed up the deal; it was called 'one on ten', statically representing the proportion of how many people where signing on the dole. Living back at mammies wasn't too bad, and I spent a lot of my free time doing the gardening or odd decorating jobs around the house, keeping her happy. Eventually I got a job working on the local public market, on the lump selling a held plastic kitchen slicer. There were three of us on our firm, Postie-Andy my good self and Paddy-C. The plastic hand held machine could cut a multitude of vegetables and was marketed as 'a must have fab thing in the kitchen'. I demonstrated it by cutting chips onions carrots and a multitude of other vegetables. It was a hard sell and I become an expert on how to use the machine and deliver a fifteen-minute sales pitch at the same time. We used loads of sharp marketing tricks to get the sales, including wearing hidden microphones and using loudspeakers to broadcast my voice louder. Looking back, I'm not proud of it, but, we used to hype the crowd up further by placing stooges in the audience called Rick's. Their job was to induce a flurry of excitement and anticipation, by saying things like 'that looks good or that's cheap I'll have two, one for mum and one for Auntie Laura for Christmas.' The Ricks bought two or three at a time, convincing the unsuspecting public this must be a bargain and I better buy one or two whilst stocks last. It was all very convincing and cleverly worked out to perfection, we made thousands from the racket. Other market traders called this type of selling 'The Ram' simply because you literally rammed the sale home. The local trading standards officer's new about it but it was difficult to spot and virtually impossible to prove unless it was filmed, some might say boarding on obtaining by deception. In any case we bribed all the Market inspectors for the best pitches and insider information on the whereabouts of the trading standing officers, they were all corrupt. The cash was good, so was the life style and again I got to work outside in the sunshine meeting new people. Eventually we sold so many of the things we flooded the market. Paddy returned home to Ireland and wasn't coming back. We agreed I would pretend I was him and continue to sign on the unemployment register and we split the money fifty, fifty. We nicknamed the scam 'the big fat green giro'. Each week at the post office I would have great delight in sending his half home to Ireland and I am sure he was just as delighted to receive it. I can't swear to it, but I think Paddy was also signing on dole in Ireland at the same time.

Matron Vera said 'why don't you sit down and take the weight the weight of your feet Bob and watch some TV if you like. Your favourite Thunder Birds is on; oh and by the way help your self to teas and coffee.' Rite that will be grand I said plonking my bum down on one of the arm chairs. Meanwhile all the others patients sat around clapping as the hero puppets went to another weekly rescue. Thunderbird one had just started a dangerous mission to save a stricken village. The volcano above them had been hit by a run away hostile Russian missile, and the whole mountain side was set to explode. That's when thunder bird two and three got into the action, flying in with huge fire extinguishers spraying millions of gallons of foam on the red hot molten Lava, it really was dire straights. Every one was clapping and stamping their feet as the little rural community at the foot of the mountain was saved from oblivion. After the job they called in a film crew to interview the heroes, surveying the damage, it was all very exciting and beamed live around the world by puppet satellite. The reporter from Disney News commented 'It was touch and go for a while but everyone survived', till next week that is. After all the excitement died down I helped myself to another coffee and noticed information board behind me, showing today's menu. I had a brilliant selection to choose from and it all sounded delicious, in fact mouth watering. Beef curry with rice or chips or both, diced chicken with new potatoes peas or carrots with gravy, steak and kidney pudding with mash. Or alternatively a vegetarian dish, amazingly made out if vegetables and for pudding, apple crumble and custard, jelly and ice cream or cheese and biscuits with a red shinny apple. Again I was absolutely starving but it was only ten o'clock and it wasn't ready till noon, so I had a couple of hours of tummy rumbling to wait. Hours later I woke up starving hungry and a nurse called 'Hugie' asked if I was hungry, I think he was from the Caribbean and in his accent continued 'I'll get you a sandwich and Robert and don't worry, just take it easy ok and forget about the rat race for a while; you've got nothing to worry about in here'. Well he was wrong, the clock on the wall said 3 o'clock and I had missed out on my lunch and pudding, On top of that tea wasn't till five o'clock and now all I was going to get was a stale pokey sandwich. Smiling he went away returning a short while later with a cheese and tomato sar-ne and a hot cup of tea. He couldn't cheer me up and with my stomach rumbling and feeling a little glum I pulled back the curtain around my bed for some privacy and started eating my lunch. My thoughts were, I wonder what you would be doing, rite now on the outside. Then it dawn on me, it was happy hour in my local pub, and all my mates were drinking the cheap beer, like I should be, making me even more fed up.

At my weekly sessions the psychiatrist asked how do you feel today Bob? To be honest I felt psychologically numb and wasn't quite sure writing about my experiences was actually beneficial for me. Reliving the highs and the lows made me my feelings jump from one extreme to another, one minute I was happy as Larry and the next moment absolute despair and this feeling of worthlessness, there was no happy medium. It was like being on an emotional roller-coaster. In-fact some times I was finding it difficult to distinguish between the past and the present. We agreed to put the book on hold for a while and I was given mind bending hallucinogenic medication, they even offered me the electric shock treatment, I refused. The thing was I enjoyed my writing, that's all I had and after a couple of days I just couldn't resist and picked up the pen once more.

Back home at mammy's house Eddie came home one Friday with his own redundancy notice and all his pay in lieu. He had a least £500.00 equivalent to over a thousand dollars. Apparently he had already made his mind up he was going to hang around for a miracle to happen and was off too Greece for the summer picking oranges, furthermore would I like to join him for the crac! Well this was the fortuitous break I had been waiting for and gladly took up his generous offer; actually I think he was a bit frightened to go on his own. Dad thought it was a great idea too, even giving me £100.00 too get rid of me as well. Maybe he had enough of me loafing about all day sunning myself in the garden, and made up his own mind, 'it was about time we both flew the nest', poetically killing two birds with one stone. Realistically I couldn't wait to get away and explore, out of work with no money and always bumping into Joanne and her mother. Crying crocodile tears saying sorry and all that, but deep down I knew she would do it again, having the feeling I was just delaying the inevitable if I stayed.

Mammy made us a pack lunch of corn beef and spam sandwiches, two carrier bags to be precise. Along with the rest of the hippy movement we set off on our world wide magical tour. Catching what everyone called 'The Magic Buses' departing every Friday evening from Victoria coach station, packed with people who all had the same initiative. Some of the lads like me had long hair caring guitars and the girls wore long flowery dresses and funny looking floppy hats. I remember asking Eddie do you feel like you're in the Cliff Richards film. The one, were all going on a summer holidays? The hippie culture was mostly composed of adults between the ages of eighteen to thirty five. The typical Hippie inherited a cultural of dissent against established institutions and criticed middle class values, why I don't know! It is said the movement was a black lash against the Vietnam War in the sixties. I knew I wanted to be one because they preferred a gentle and non-doctrinaire political principles that favoured 'peace, love and personnel freedom, with the ultimate aim of creating an international pot smoking free loading communities all over the world, and believe me I wanted some of the action.

Inexpensive airfares were hard to come by, so the magic bus was the people's salvation and cheap and cheerful was it catchy slogan. Hence across Europe I headed, waving white flags, smoking vast amounts of pot, professing free love and all that malarkey, excellent! The trip was supposed to take three days but it felt more like three fecking weeks. The car ferry landed in Belgium and we drove through the Swiss Alps. The weather was typically Swiss; snowing so thick the coach driver had to put chains on the tyres, giving the coach some sort of bite, literally smashing the ice and road up as it went along. Every bone in my body was shaking from the vibration making the journey almost unbearable. Then the heating packed up and everyone sat in their seats freezing cold with their coats on, the cheap bit was rite but not the fecking cheerful bit, I tell you reader, they didn't even have any toilets, but we were alright and had commandeered the back seats making do using on old two litre coca cola bottle, god only knows how the girls managed. One day late, after dicing with death, skidding perilously on the ice, dodging a few Avalanches, narrowly missing a few fiords and smashing up half of Switzerland's road net work, we finally reached Germany. We stopped in Munich for a couple of hours while they fixed the heating and took the chains off. Getting off too stretch my legs I swore as long as I live I would never ever travel like this again, but at least I had a couple of hours to look round. The Olympic stadium stood out clearly on the cities horizon and nearby we found a bar; taking this opportunity to sit down, relax having a pint or two. Unfortunately I remembered this place for all the wrong reasons. It was all over the news in 1972

Robert Charles Scanlan

when the Israeli team were held captive in the Olympic village. Unfortunately eleven athletes where murdered and one German Police officer. The terrorist organisation called 'The Black September' group where responsible and reportedly had links with 'Yasser Arafat' The French got into big trouble with the world for releasing the Palestine leader 'Abu Daoud' a member of the group accused of master mining the attack. I think he was given Diplomatic immunity and was eventually expelled to the Algiers, so if any one wants him that's where he's hiding!

Crossing the border into the Balkans was next, communist Yugoslavia, then known as the iron curtain 'Russia'? At the time this was an extremely dodgy place and you only went there unless you had to. Through the grape vine I became aware car cassette player were worth five times as much in Greece, and one of my suit case was full of them. Another of my friends worked in the car factory and was getting them cheap directly from the warehouse, extremely cheap in fact still in the boxes. At the border the Russian guards were as fierce looking as their reputation, demanding in no uncertain termsevery one get off the coach and stand next to there luggage. Being at the back of the coach I was the very last one off and joined the queue at the very end. Waving their Kalashnikov machine guns around I stood nervously next to my cache. He came to me first and in broken English asked for my passport, he was a lot older than me, wearing a big Russian hat, long grey coat and brown knee high leather brown boots. This was becoming my worst nightmare; if he looks in the bag I properly get dragged off and thrown in the jail for smuggling. I was absolutely bricking it, because this time there is no way out, and I actually felt like I was taking part in the film 'Midnight Express'. He was looking at my passport photograph and had just indicated with his hand for me to remove my sunglasses; at that point one of the other guards noticed three suitcases remained unclaimed in the hold of the bus and called out to the others. Handing it back said ok and then just walked off. They all huddled around the find, eventually opening them one by one, discovering kilos upon Kilos of neatly packed coffee. Apparently this was also on the contraband list and was worth its weight in gold on the black market as well. I wish I known that. The guards were exceedingly happy with what they hit upon confiscating the whole lot. Rumour has it they only got paid pittance and this could be worth over six months wages. Personally I think it was the driver gear, as he wasn't too pleased driving very irately as we left the border. In any case I was glad, at least it took there suspicions off me at that crucial point.

In due course as we headed south and the climate started getting a lot warmer. We had been on the road for three days now and had another twenty four hours to go. Making good time we arrived in Athens in the early hours of Wednesday morning. Setting foot on Greek soil we headed straight for the Acropolis, greeting the city in all its magnificence. The hill it stood on was a bit longer than we anticipated, so we stopped off at this roadside café and sat outside. The waiter said something in Greek; we just looked at each paused and asked 'got any Guinness mate'? Irish boys he replied, Eddie unlike me has an Irish passport, and proudly started flashing his one off. The man went away saying 'that's OK boys no problem, up the Republicans', returning shortly with the two pints. It must have been around nine o'clock in the morning listening to band on the run by Sir Paul McCartney, thinking how great it is to be foot louse and fancy free and what a wonderful world this is.

The hill started to look bigger and bigger and after a few more pints we had to call the whole expedition off, at least we had seen it or rather we could from the bar. We started to get really friendly with the bar man, I showed him one of the car cassettes. Back in England I paid next to nothing for them and I had ten in total. Carlos immediately offered me around forty pounds in Drachmas, bundles of the stuff. I thought that's plenty of beer tokens and we done the deal. We stayed there most of the morning and eventually Carlos flagged down a taxi taking us to the main port Para's, harbouring the ships going to the numerous Greek Islands. On the way managing to sell yet another cassette to the cab driver he recommended and now I was really loaded. Eddie went to the dock and checked out the day's sailings whilst I went for a haircut and shave with a cut-throat razor. It was just before the Aids epidemic and public health wasn't in the limelight, but this guy looked professional enough to me and I had confidence he wouldn't cut me, which he didn't. This was the first time in days I had been clean and I felt absolutely brilliant, ready for whatever life wanted to throw at me including the kitchen sink. The main component or quest if you like was too have no plan what so ever, letting fate and providence take us, and so be it. He came back with the tickets a little while later we were bound for the Island of Create, sailing at 3 o'clock that afternoon. All we had to do was stroll down to the waterfront and find our ship 'Athena' after the Greek Goddess of watchfulness and wisdom. Surprisingly the sailing only took five hours across the Mediterranean but lucky enough for me I slept all the way, excellent. It was like when you go on holiday with your parents, and you keep asking them are we there yet? But I didn't have to do that bit, I just woke up and we had arrived, reaching our destination 'Xhania,' the capital.

Eddie disembarked down the gangplank first followed by me. It was a real Mediterranean scene with lots of people hanging around holding up placards advertising cheap rooms. Others were selling fresh water-melons, neatly cut into slices; they looked delicious and tasted even better. Out of the crowd I noticed this old guy, he wasn't hassling anyone so we chose to speak to him first. Approaching each other we made eye contact and this was the beginning of a new and fantastic life long friendship. His name was 'Taki' and he led us through the narrow back streets to his small hotel, which they called Pensions. Ours was in a street I nick named Snake Street, it was written in Greek and I don't really know what it said but that's what it looked like to me anyway. We didn't have a front door just a gate and opening the latch we entered a small concrete courtyard. He showed me the shower room combined toilet. He explained in broken English when you wipe your bum not to put the paper down the toilet as it blocks the drains. There was a small bin to the side full of the stuff. My first thought was how disgusting but you soon got used to it, besides Taki was kind enough empting it every day. Across the yard in front of me was a door and to the left a fight of external metal stairs leading to another room.   Pointing to the ground floor he led me in opening the door saying 'welcome'. It was a large dormitory sleeping four; there was a curtain at the back separating the room in half, at the other end was a small kitchen sparsely furnished with one table, a couple of fold up deck chairs like before, a sink but no cooker, or was that the other way round. Pulling back the curtain hung on a piece of string he showed us our new residence. It consisted of two single beds either side and a small wooden bedside table in the middle. There were no windows and the light fitting dangled down on a long piece of cable, it didn't even have a shade on it. The floor was bare concrete painted red and the walls were that horrible prison green colour, only broken up with a poster of Bob Marley smoking a joint. Taki told us there were six European people presenting staying, four of them were British girls and two Scandinavian birds. Slinging my luggage on the bed I said rubbing my hands together 'that will do nicely' He then said we would have to go to his shop just down the street to register, also mentioning 'we could work in his shop if we wanted'. Reaching his shop was even more bizarre, he was the local undertaker. His wife a small woman dressed in black was sitting at the desk talking on the phone and smiled at us when we entered. All the coffins were on display with the lids off showing the flash interiors. This was the first time I seen anything like this and thought that they looked quite comfortable with their scarlet silk linings. Eddie and I just looked at each and speculating what we had got ourselves into this time; they even had the price tags on and believe me one was on special offer. His wife finished on the phone and introduced herself as 'Poppy'. We produced our passports and agreed a price equivalent to 2.00 Dramas a day which included electric, water and clean sheets, brilliant cheap as chips. We paid one month in advance and shook hands on the deal and Taki went to the cupboard fetching us some fresh linen, wacky as it may sound that was that. I later learnt the Greek people were especially helpful if you carried a British passport, simply because they thought they owed us a dept of gratitude from the Second World War, when we liberated them from the Germans, they never forgot. Alternately Taki told us under no circumstances whatsoever to bring any German tourist back to the pension; he was one of the freedom fighters and lost his father in the War. At first I declined his offer of work, plus having plenty of money just wanting to find the beach, preferably with a bar on it, hopefully with some good looking topless girls to goggle at. No problems apart from that go down the pub every day sunbathe and go scuba-diving. Over the months Taki and I bonded quite well together and one afternoon he invited me up to his house for a typical Greek lunch. It was great to be accepted into the family and he even introduced me to his two daughters, now that is a privilege in Greek tradition. Poppy had prepared the main meal herself: Baked stuff squid—(calamari) the stuffing is a delicious mixture of rice, garlic, tomato paste, parsley, onion, and wine, it was delicious. After lunch Taxi took me to meet some of his old pals up in the mountains, they were very kind people and I will never forget that day. After a while Eddie met up with a nice girl called

Karen, it was in a bar called Cottas, hitting it off straight away falling in love and she moved in with in with the rest of the motley crew. Eventually they got married moved to Staffordshire and had two girls named Holy Candydice, and a boy they called Robert after me, another Bob! They are all happy and doing very well, owning a florist shop in Stoke on Trent, at least there one happy ending.

The money and car cassettes and everything else soon ran out and so did my luck, having to go to work, I didn't fancy working with Taki handling the unfortunate dead people, so I went back to farming, picking oranges, watermelons, grapes and dates. At the crack of dawn the farmer 'Demetreos' would pick us up in an open red Nissan truck and cheerfully we set of too work in the fields. The sun was rising in the mountains and we where singing 'were all going on a summers holidays' and life couldn't be better. Picking oranges was the best paid, earning £2.00 a box and I could pick 10 boxes a day, if I wasn't hung over from the night before that is. The watermelons were hard work though, bending over all day in the midday sun and you might only earn £10.00 a day. The farmers would feed us though, so we didn't have to worry about eating. Not that we did much of that anyway, not having the time, too busy pushing the pints down me neck as fast as I could. There were plenty of old Roman ruins and sites to explore, but I just couldn't be bothered with all that bollocks, partying was the in crac. Out there in the middle of nowhere, nothing much really mattered and I didn't have a care in the world. We made up a saying to describe the crac, which went like this 'Spinning off into a complete and utter void of nothingness'

I started knocking about with a lad called Cozzie from Manchester. He was a real nice bloke and I felt I had known him all my life so to speak. To keep us going all night we eat the girls slimming tablets, the name on the packet said amusingly 'Ponderers.' The reason behind this madness was not to get slim, but get to the amphetamine in the tablet, its street name was 'Speed' a class A drug and very additive, and not to be recommended reader. It kept me up for days on end and I didn't feel tired. It did have its draw backs though I lost two stone in weight and my eyes looked like two pea holes on the snow from the lack of sleep, all mutant red and swollen up. Another thing was there were no postmen, so everyone picked up their mail from the post office. On producing your passport they would give it to you. On one particular occasion I was so poor I couldn't afford an envelope to write home to my parents begging for money, so I made one up out of a sheet of paper and glued it together posting it on its five thousand mile round trip. It took about two weeks to receive a reply and I was ecstatic when the clerk gave me my letter. I did that fooled them and was already spending the money in my head. It wasn't like an ordinary letter this one was thick and fat and bulging and felt like a loads of money. Ripping it open, I was expecting cash, but my sarcastic sister Olive had written back saying mammy and dad were on holiday in Ireland; she didn't have any money herself but was enclosing a load of envelopes for my next requests, very funny Olive.

If we didn't have any work we dosed about the pension all day drinking, smoking vast amount of pot and, reading day old English news paper and having Bar-Bees, finding crazy foolish things to keep our tiny little minds occupied. Sunning ourselves we did mad things like trying contacting the other side using the Wajieboard, never again. Strange things started happening, Cozzie got a message from his 'Auntie Flow' in Manchester, saying he must go home straight away or the slimming tablets would kill him. I don't know if he had an auntie Flow, in any case he ran out of the dimly lit room shaking and trembling, insisting 'one of you feckers must be pushing the glass.' Tom was told he was going to get VD, which he did and one of the girls all her hair was going to fall out, I don't think happened though. Personally I think Eddie was pushing the glass all the time for the crac, he's got a warped sense of humour like that. We also tried levitation, how we did that was someone sat in a chair and four people would lay the hands on top of the subject's head. Then all the hands would apply intense pressure down wards on the head. The subject sitting would take all this pressure and it would literally start bending their spine downwards. When we released our hands we put them under the subjects arm pits and under the knees and lifted them up with ease, it was the spine retracting back, helping to lift the weight of the person own body. Extremely dangerous because you run the risk of breaking your spine, but we didn't bother considering that fact, properly because we were to busy spinning off into a void of nothingness all the time. Sometimes we would try putting each other into a trance; needless to say we were properly all ready in one due to all the self inflicted body abuse. We also tried hypnotism

Robert Charles Scanlan

and practiced telepathy, I became quite good at that, not everyone can do it but its good fun, I once met a girl who was excellent in telepathic communications, in-fact we could spend hours only using this form of communication, occasionally still to this day we communiqué, you know who you are. I can't help thinking and worrying what Matron Vera and the Psychiatrics are going to make of all this when I tell them, I'll let you know. We would sit in a circle lighting jots sticks, chanting and humming like the Red Indians do, know- body cared if you were gay, lesbian, bi-sexual, tri-sexual than means try anything or just a plain tosses, it didn't mater as long as you didn't hurt or offend anyone. One night I came home from the pub and they were having an orgy upstairs, it sounded like a traditionally Roman or Greek sex Olympics and every one was going for gold, I was invited to join in but was too drunk and fell asleep instead, in a way I was glad about that.

Morning time was the most comical of all; many of us had amnesia and bad hangovers from the night before and couldn't remember a thing. Lazing around in the courtyard we would be drinking beer, just having a normal conversation about girls or football for example, when out of the blue one of us would start laughing hysterically for no apparent reason, obviously they had just remembered something funny from the night before, which in turn then started everyone one else off, as you knew what to expect next, we called it flashback. This happened to me once, and after my laughing bit couldn't wait too enlighten the others what my flashback was. Anyway, Cozzie and I got totally hammered, deciding to streak through the market square, singing that old Chuck Berry number 'the streak'. Three Armed Greek Police Officers spotted us and at gun point ordered us to stop and lay face down on the pavement. Xhania is traditionally a Roman Catholic society and things like that just didn't happen around here. I quickly came up with some cock and bull story that we were the victims of a practical joke and were deliberately stripped naked and left on the side of the road for a laugh. We also said we were English and very sorry, but it wasn't our fault and Taki could vouch for us. They fell for it and put us in the back of the squad car and phoned him up. They said something in Greek and started laughing and the next thing I know we were driving back to the pension, thanks Taki. The thing is, as I was telling my flashback Cozzie remembered it and fell off the chair in manic uncontrollable laughter, rolling around on the floor holding his stomach, saying 'please stop bob, your going to give me a heart attack'

One notable afternoon I was sitting alone in Takis shop when heard the church bells started ringing in the village square, a secret code Taki had told me that signals some has died. I knew I didn't have long and instantly upped all the prices and put new stickers on the whole lot, even the special offer was increased. Within minutes the next of kin arrived, and then I had to pretend I wasn't aware of their loss and acted out a big grief scene for the family. Taki and I had an understanding, he looked after me and I looked after him. The days bonus meant I didn't have to go to work for a few days, so extreme partying from dawn to dusk was the order of the day. After a few days I thought they will be ringing that bell for you soon. I felt really hung over and didn't feel at all well and just wanted to go to sleep. Not having much for days warped all my senses, I started to hallucinate and my mind shut down on its own, parallel to a Duracell battery slowly running out of clout. One of the coffins looked really comfortable and I just couldn't resist it, so I put my head down for my afternoon Siesta. Poppy happen to come back earlier than I anticipated and found me fast asleep in the deluxe model. Like a scene from a Benny Hill she stood above me waving and pointing her finger, mouthing off obscenities in Greek, I only new a few phrases however her body language and facial vocabulary was enough to get the jest of what she was actually saying. I thought this must be another one of my mad far-out dreams, but it wasn't. I didn't know how to get out of the situation so blessed my self, jumped out and ran away laughing. I now realise this was disrespectful and I apologise sincerely for my incomprehensible behaviour and I am really sorry.

Life in the pension continued as normal, if that's what you could call it. One sunny day after another unhurriedly shuffled past me by. On one of these sunlight hours I set off on my own. To hand was my beach lilo, walkman, snorkel and a pair of swimming flippers, exploring deserted beaches and coves, getting the bus to a place I think was called Raytheon? Anyway reader it wasn't that far from Xania about five minutes maybe, check it out if you get a chance. I found a shop and spent what little I had on a bottle of the red wine and freshly cut watermelon and tin of spam. Swimming all morning was great fun and through my snorkel I observed these wonderfully coloured fish. They weren't at all frightened of me and darted in and out of the coral as if it was a game.

I bet you didn't know there are 900,000 different species in the world, which includes 8,700 birds, 700,000 insects and 4,500 mammals, yet more useless information. They seemed to be smiling at me so I smiled back. After a couple of hours of this I had finished of my wine and eat my fruit, and read the book 'Robinson Crusoe'. Laying there I thought it would be a good crac to write a nutty message in my empty wine bottle and watch it float away, The message read 'There was a Young Lady of Dorking, Who bought a large bonnet for walking; But its colour and size, so bedazzled her eyes, that she very soon went back to Dorking' It disappeared on the crest of a wave and I fell asleep, I seemed to do a lot of that. However this was no ordinary sleep but a real subterranean deep one. On top of that my Walkman was blasting out in my ears Message in a bottle by the 'Police.' This was a real spin and my thoughts were really weird. Actually I dreamt the sun was literally exploding and I was directly in its flight path. I wanted to wake up but I seemed transfixed almost riveted on the light and the intense overbearing heat, plus the music was carrying me further into this nightmare inferno. My whole skin felt like it was on fire, but no matter what I still couldn't wake up from this firestorm. Somehow I knew this was a dream and eventually would come out of this, but when? Fortunately for me I felt the incoming tide running up my legs, which in turn sparked me back into life. Stupidly I didn't bother with sun cream and woke up as red as a ripe tomato. I was also in agony and know one could touch me for days on end, additionally my skin pealed off in huge great sheets and I seemed to glow in the dark. I learnt the hard way about over exposing yourself in more ways than one, striking a chord with Noel Cowards classic 'Only mad dogs and English men go out in the midday sun'.

My friends were really kind rubbing cold cream on my back and going to the shops for me, it took me about a week to recover and I stayed in lying on my bunk reading the book 'Mac vicar.' Cozzie took the week of work to look after me and we spent hours in the little courtyard discussing every topic known to man and beast. He was an experienced tourist travelling all around the world, hitch hiking from one country to another, working in bars, hotels any job as long as it kept him alive for that day, that's all that mattered. One particular sunny afternoon we were chatting about Israel and he explained about life living on a Kibbutz. He had just spent the last year working on one and it all seemed very interesting and I thought one day I am definitely going to do that, eventually succeeding.

Day after day drifted into the next and I didn't know or care what day it actually was, it didn't seem to matter or bother any of us, a bit like the Ward. After a while ten months to be exact the novelty began to wear off, furthermore my health was now in serious jeopardy. Number one I was skinny as a bean pole; in fact I have seen more flesh on a racing grey hound. Two, my sleep pattern was non excitant and finally, off all the things I missed the most was my mind, I actually started questioning my own sanity, now that can be seriously dangerous, especially for me. Contemplating all of this I used one of Olive's envelopes and wrote one more final begging letter back home asking for the fare. Seemingly dragging on forever, it took about two weeks to receive the cash and guess what, remember I swore never to travel on the magic bus again; well I had too. This time however coming well prepared with three loafs of bread, 10 tins of Corn-beef, bottles of fresh water and bars of Cadbury's chocolate. The coach was equipped with a toilet this time and the journey was actually quite pleasant. We went back through Yugoslavia into Austria and the place was just how I remembered it, really green and clean with hardly any cars on the road and every where you looked the snow caped mountains spanned the horizon as far as you could see. I don't whether the coach driver was having a laugh, but he played 'The hills are alive with the song of music' by Mary Popins and we all joined in. Every so often we pulled into a motorway service station for some munchies and too freshen up. We made good time and in due course went through Germany and Luxemburg. We embarked as foot passengers on the Car Ferry in Belgium; indecently it was 'The Herald of free Enterprise' which later sunk and unfortunately drowned One hundred and eighteen seven people.

Across the English Channel another coach was waiting for us at Dover and took us back to London. At this point I had no money left and had no way of getting back to Andover sixty miles away. On top of that it was lashing down with rain and I must have looked a complete Pratt. Soaked to the skin dressed in a pair of cut down Levi jeans and a ripped T shirt with the Rolling Stones printed on the front, just wearing a pair of old flip flops on my feet, oh and no luggage. Little did I know Maggie was busy winding everyone up again with the poll tax, and it was just my luck to land in London in the middle of violent protests and organised demonstrations. I did think 'nothing changed, welcome home Bob'. While I was away Thatcherism had been discredited and there was every sign that she had lost control of her cabinet. That day it all came to a head at a large demonstration in Trafalgar Square, which turned into one of the biggest riots ever seen in London. Initially it was peaceful and good-humoured but a small group near the tail end staged a sit down protest outside Downing Street. The police tried to move them on, which in turned provoked violence and mayhem. Shop windows were smashed and many businesses had their contents looted. As the police continued to arrest offenders, placards and cans were thrown and the trouble spread to Charing Cross, Pall Mall, Regent Street and Covent Garden. The riot escalated in size and violence and someone broke into a construction site and set fire to it. I remember seeing a cloud of black smoke hanging over Trafalgar Square. Trying to clear the streets they shut down four of the main tube stations, with much of central London cordoned off, I was trapped. All I wanted to do was get home but somehow managed to get caught up in all this, actually I was luckily I wasn't arrested. Eventually I made it to Waterloo train station and found an old train ticket in the bin. My only way past the guard was to wait until the very last minute, and then scamper past him in a dash waving the bent ticket around saying 'I can't stop now otherwise I miss my train'. On boarding the train I took the third class seat again, in the toilet refusing to come out under any circumstances. The guard kept banging on the door saying, 'if I didn't come out straight away he was going to stop the train and get the Railway Police to come and sort me out'. After all the hell I had just been through, he could go and get Jesus Christ for all cared and believe me I told him this in no uncertain terms. Anyhow he gave up and buggered off somewhere and I managed to bunk the fare all the way back to Andover and phoned Dad up. He came straight away and I just boycotted the final guard walking straight past him declaring, "it was a crap service any way and I shall be writing a letter of complaint to the chef executive demanding my money back and compensation' Driving back dad told me that I had Mammy very worried, apparently she had just seen me on the evening news taking part in the rioting in London. Back in the house Mammy was glad to see me and gave me a big hug. Kindly she had prepared my favourite meal, Fray Bentos steak and kidney pie, you know the one that come in the flat tin. Indecently in 1982 during the Falklands war Maggie binned and boycotted this product for all the good reasons, simply because it was Argentine beef, another bit of UK useless information. I seem to be full it. I had been dreaming about food and missed the ordinary things in life like that. It was gorgeous even wiping the tin clean with hot crusty bread directly from the oven. Then for pudding Mammy had made a home made apple and plum cake which I finished off with big dollops of vanilla ice cream. My stomach couldn't cope, beginning to bulge like I was pregnant, well if I was; it must have been the Immaculate Conception. Although I do believe there is a religion who thinks a man can get pregnant and that's why he has nipples. Actually, why has man got nipples, do you know reader? If so send your answer on a post card to my publisher and I promise to reply. In fact I'm looking forward to it. Mammy fetched me a cold glass of Guinness from the fridge and whilst smoking a cigarette I read the local paper, catching up on all the gossip. My friends were always in it and I wasn't at all surprised to see a write up in the crime page about one of them. It was concerning my old friend Jimmy who had got into a fight with the British Soldiers and had been given bail and run off to join the French Foreign Legion and become a soldier himself. He didn't last though and deserted returning back to Andover. The headline of the week read 'Jimmy takes French leave.' Although when he came back he still had to face the music from you know who,' Madam Flog-them' In any case she eventually threw in Winchester Jail for six months. I used to write to him in prison, when he got out we'd often spend hours playing skittles or cards in 'The Angel Pub'. They had a big open fire in the parlour and during the winter we'd all huddle around it, sinning Irish songs and generally having the crac. After a while he got fed up with Andover and decided against my advice and returned to the Legion, having another try at being a Legionnaire. Only this time as a punishment he was thrown in one of their jails and hosed down with cold water for a week and then deported back to England, told you so mate!

Life in Andover continued churning out its relentless ongoing bull-shit, there was nowhere to go, nothing to do and worse no work either. Somehow I expected it to all to have changed and too be different on my return; I suppose it was unrealistic dreams yet again. After a while I got as job in a tea-blending factory, on the night shift driving the fork lift truck. It was a huge twenty four hour plant employing over four hundred people; it even had its own canteen. It wasn't too bad, I only had to work four nights a week, but the pay was absolutely diabolical. 1.00 an hour. What made it a little bit better was I didn't have a supervisor. I was my own boss, furthermore if I finished my work early I even managed to get my head down for a couple of hour's kip each night. The day shift used to call it the good night shift and I had the run of the entire factory. They used to roast the coffee beans there as well, but this was a restricted area because of the price of coffee. On the black market a pound for a pound in weight was the going rate. Well any way, I was told these restrictions didn't stop my friend Mr X, I don't know if he was lying but years later he told me he managed to make another set of replica keys to fit the blending room. He went on to explain he knew if you got ill during the night they would have to bring you home in one of the company vans, it was there health and safety at work company policy. Mr X was well acquainted with the van driver 'Harold' and on the sly they hatched up a secret plan to nick a load of coffee one night.

It went like this, using the replica keys the mysterious Mr X got into the blending room, sound familiar? By means of a forklift not mine, loaded up an entire pallet of bagged coffee. With the hazard lights flashing unchallenged he just drove the stolen goods too the loading bay. Courteously Harold had left the back doors open on the van and Mr X simply loaded the shipment in the back. This all had to be timed when the security guard was on patrol at the other end of the building, so far so good. Mr X then phoned the Duty Manager at the other end of the factory saying 'I think I have appendicitis and need to go home" I then heard over the public announcement service 'Will Harold please report to the loading bay as someone had been taken ill and needs to be driven home.' All I had to do was continue the dying swan act and get in the front passenger seat. The guard they chose to lay this on was a bit thick and he duly waved them through with a smile on his face and they were home and dry. Even if they did get stopped by the police it didn't matter as they were both still wearing the company's uniform and had official permission to use the van. They drove the haul away and unloaded it in my Uncle Stan's garage, I am told about 5000 pounds worth. Apparently he didn't use much anyway so they knew it was safe there. The management didn't know their arse from their elbows and were totally mystified and so was Stan. One minute it was there and the next minute it was gone. Selling the goods was easy for Mr X, because he knew a lot of men. They became a chain of supply and they made a small fortune out of the racket. The management did eventually work out what happened but by then it was too late as all the evidence had been consumed. I worked there for about six months and didn't get involved and not before time got itchy feet and had to leave rather hastily.

I heard through the worldwide grapevine that the French were looking for grape pickers in the Cote adjure. My friend and I Kevin decided to have a crac at all this boloney and before I new it I was on another expedition sailing to the French port of Calla. We arrived in the middle of the night and everything was closed. Eventually I found shelter under a parked lorry and fell asleep using my rucksack as a pillow. The very next day we bought our tickets to a place called St Trapay on the French Mediterranean. Oh it lovely reader, palm tress blue skies and hot weather. We bought a tent from some French guy and stayed at a camp site next to the beach at a place called Port Grimond. My job which I proudly invented myself was picking up the empty beer and wine bottles off the beach and returning them back to the supermarket in my over loaded trolley for the cash refund. No one battered an eye lid and properly though I worked for the council in my bright orange flap jacket. Some days I could earn over 20 franks all to be spent on me, lovely bubley. Kevin was a trained chef and got a job in one of the local restaurant and used to bring home food from the café, so we didn't have to worry about that for a while either and life was good fun. By the way he was also he was on the run from the British Army, absent without leave officially a deserter, with a false passport that Mr X supplied him with. Did you know the British Army executed three hundred and six men for that in the First World War.? Decades later the British Government admitted it was mistake and all the men that were murdered were given a posthumous pardon, a bit late don't you think! Your properly thinking what happened to the grape picking idea, well we were too early and the season didn't even start for another two months or so. It didn't matter though, life was good fun and again I started that mad spinning off that I do, excellent. I didn't bother thinking about things and just let them happen; it seemed the logical thing to do, in fact the more illogical it was the better. We moved up and

Robert Charles Scanlan

down the coast quite a lot stopping of at Nice, Monaco and at Cannes the film festival was on, and I saw Roger Moore promoting one of the James Bond films, I am not sure which one but I definitely saw him; I thought 'I wouldn't mind having a crac at being a spy one day. Unbelievably, years later my wish came true and I was nearly shot dead on one of my missions, I'll tell you about that later and trust me it's worth waiting for. Hitch hiking everywhere was dead cool and I met some very interesting people. Once on the open road a beach buggy pulled up and offered us a lift, too where we didn't care. They were part of the international hippie movement like me and spoke fluent English. They new we were starving hungry and bought us some hot dogs and chips. Driving along with the roof down with the breeze in my face we listened to Simon and Garfuncle and I didn't have a care in the world. We pulled up next to the beach and after finishing off my meal; we smoked a joint and went for a swim. On another occasion we got a lift through the mountains on an electric Milk float, it took hours and we helped the milkman with his rounds. We sat on the back with our legs dangling over the side singing songs and laughing. The driver was very kind and gave us some French bread cheese ham milk and ten franks each. Eventually we ended up in this place called Dijon in central France and this time our luck really did run out. Apart from what the Milkman gave me I hadn't eaten for days and I started that day dreaming about food again, honestly I was famished and could have eaten a scabby horse. We went past a supermarket and looked in at all the lovely food lined up ready to be eaten. The temptation was too much and coupled with the fact if we didn't eat we might die or rather that's what it felt like, in any case we had no choice but to go and rob some off the stuff. I was on look out whilst Kevin filled his pockets with what ever he could get his hands on. We managed to get away and hid in a nearby forest gorging our self's under a Palm tree. We had been there about five minutes when from the undergrowth, I heard a man shouting in French "Halt surrender put your hands up'. We immediately obeyed his orders and out of the bush popped two French police officers pointing their Smith and Wesson handguns directly at us. Kevin's army training instantaneously kicked in and put his hands in the air shouting 'don't shoot don't shoot.' So I tagged along. This was all becoming very serious; making it worse was I hadn't even finished of the ham and bread yet. Further more if I was going to die God, at least could I have a full stomach? Even a condemned man gets that. They handcuffed us both and threw us in one of there French jails until they found an interpreter. A pretty girl arrived, said she lived in Brighton, spoke fluent French and was on holiday with her parents, asking us what this was all about. We gave her some rubbish about being held captive and robbed at knife-point and all our money was stolen and the fact we hadn't eaten for days, perhaps weeks. She went away smiling to herself, saying we were rascals, and was going to sort this all out for us, but in the interim we would still have to go to court. The police-man was sitting there listening to all this and sent out the other copper for two pizza's and a bottle of water. I couldn't believe it and gladly tucked in to this French hospitality. Later on he even apologised for having to threaten us with their guns.

That afternoon they handcuffed us both together and drove us to the courthouse. That was the scary bit; they put us in with a load of Italian Bank robbers, properly the Mafia. They just sat there staring at us for a couple of hours. Then still handcuffed we were presented before the Town Mayor. He didn't believe a word about us being robbed and all that codswallop, saying he was sick and tired of the English coming over here every summer dosing around and generally making a nuisance of themselves. For a laugh I remember shouting out, 'you didn't say that too my Grand Dad in 1945, when he risked his own life to liber-ate you lot form the Germans, did you'? The court went quite and the interpreter summed up in French, asking for bail. Surprisingly we got it; personally I think they were glad to see the back of us. When we got outside the policeman said whilst pointing his finger 'England is tatter way, go and don't come back here ever' he even gave me 50 franks. We knew the British Embassy was in Marseille and it might be possible to get repatriated, well I could anyway and Kevin would make better time hitch hiking on his own, which he did in fact apparently he was smuggled back by a Irish lorry driver under a load of Spanish onions bound for Dublin, even getting home before me.

Arriving at my Embassy in Marseille I was greeted by the Consulate-General. He was an old boy dressed in a pinstripe suit and balding head, anyway he refused to help me saying 'I could walk', I remember replying 'on your bike mate'; sarcastically he replied 'why have you got a bike then Sir'. The cheek of this guy, I just couldn't

Robert Charles Scanlan

believe this baldy headed twat, so I asked him if he was seriously expecting me to walk about two thousand miles. Well, I wasn't having any of his attitudes and refused to leave the building. He threatened to get the police to throw me in another French jail. Well I challenged this, informing him he better make it an English copper as the French had no jurisdiction here. Furthermore as this was technically British soil I asked 'what offence had I actually committed anyway'? It was a Friday afternoon and he told me to come back on Monday, but I knew it was a bank holiday in England and he too would be on holiday, sussing out his Comanche trick I again refused his demands. It was getting closer to the office closing and this guy was going berserk, shouting and balling about this that and the other, whilst I stood firm demanding my passage home. He phoned my Dad in England asking if he could pay, but I had already thought they might do that and phoned Dad myself, telling him to say he was poor and had no money any way. The office clock had about two minutes to go until five o'clock and I didn't know how all this would turn out. Eventually he came back and gave me a travel warrant stamping on my passport to be retained on entry back in the United Kingdom.

Little did I know the British customs and the Special Branch were waiting for me at Dover Hover point? In my opinion I think the guy at the Embassy had phoned them up, deliberately wind me up, because I had been winding him up about jurisdiction and all that baloney. They took me in a room and stripped searched me, as I stood there naked they made me cross my hands on top of my head and spread my legs apart. There was one male officer and your not going to believe me but also one women officer, how degrading. The man left the room for a short time and while he was gone she started searching me all over. In my ears and then in my hair, humiliating me further she even looked up my anus with a small torch and magnifying glass. What for I don't know, I can only presume for drugs, well if that was the case I must have been the poorest trafficker on this earth, not even able to pay my own fare. The man came back shuffling some paper work and she said to him 'its ok this one clean.' Searching my pockets she did find one thing though, a letter from Kevin to his mum that I had to post back in England, just in case he got caught in France. The letter explained why he had deserted and all that about the false passport. They opened it and read it and then thought I was Kevin with the false Passport. They refused to let me go and held me under the 'Anti Terrorist Act' I was then put in jail while they made further inquiries, as soon as they did that I made them get me something to eat, bacon sandwich and a can of coke, not so yummy. My passport was legal but they wouldn't accept it as proof of identity. They asked me if I had been in trouble with the police before. If so they demanded to know when it was, at what court and what the sentence was. I mentioned the incident on my birthday and they went away and checked at Andover police station and court-house. They came back and I had to describe what the officer looked like, the one who brought our breakfast in, I also remembered his name was Roy, which helped. Presumably they managed to get hold of him and he vouched for me over the phone, thanks again mate I owe you one. Not satisfied with that they kept me in custody for over twenty four hours, questioning me about my mate. I refused to answer any more questions, denying all knowledge of any dodgy dealings using my legal wrights to silence as my only weapon, yet again I thought why me. Before departing though I turned round and gave them a load of verbal abuse, 'if this is how they treat their British subjects when they need help, well I want no part of it' They retained my passport and wouldn't give it back until I repaid them their cash. Even then the Home office kept putting up barriers, so much so my Queens Council Mr Walker got involved and had to sort it all out for me.

As I said Kevin made good time and we met up again before he gave himself up to the British Army. He phoned them up from the Swallow pub and he confessed where he was and could they come and get him. They asked him to get a taxi to the barracks but he refused. Within an hour three big Military Policemen turned up wearing side arms. We saw them through the window as they parked up the staff car. They didn't mess about and came straight in. We all glared at the Red Caps and Kevin slung his arms up in the air declaring, 'it's me you're looking for, I surrender, Sir.' After arresting him and that legal baloney they hand-cuffed him throwing a jacket over his wrists and frog marched him away from the bar. As they led him away we jeered at the Red Caps saying if they laid a hand on him we would find out, which they didn't. He eventually got court marshalled and thrown into the jail yet again. They tried to keep him in the armed forces, but he had enough and went to see the Par-dray, lying he confessed to being a prolific drug user and a rampant homosexual, fancying all the men in the shower room and that was enough to get him discharged on compassionate grounds. Later on in life he told me "it had all done him a great favour as he didn't like the Army any way and for love nor money didn't regret or would change any of our adventure'.

I had just returned from my evening walk with Matron Vera and was having a cigarette in the smoking room when in strolled 'Dartanian' a man around thirty-five, dark hair but going a bit thin on the top with brown eyes, a real thespian of a character. Surprisingly he was well spoken with a full plum in the mouth upper class Oxford accent; you know the one the Americans die for. In fact there where a lot of regional accents on the ward and the illness reflected the cross members of society it effected. He sat opposite me and rolled himself a cigarette and said 'Good evening, I nodded and said 'my name is Robert pleased to meet you I'm sure' he replied 'how peculiar that makes four Roberts on the ward now, I shall have to write and tell my wife and sister all about this. My name is Dartanian, and we shook hands. Oh and by the way he was wearing a long flowery dress, a hat and make up, red lipstick blusher and blue eye shadow with painted nails, a full a cross dresser. He went on to tell me he wore men's clothing in the morning and women's out fits for his evening wear, it made him feel better. There was another women sitting in the corner who remarked his eye shadow looked very nice tonight. He explained he had been trying to get this particular shade for some time now, and did they like it? He even asked me, for the crac I said 'yes, it looks ok.' Strangely he then commented 'You know, Robert; there are those who do, those that can't and those who just talk about it, what are you? Continuing, 'I got it from Boots, they have quite a good selection and the ladies behind the counter are very helpful'. At this point I pondered if he's gay. When he said 'I bet I know what you're thinking, I paused 'why are you telepathic like me then? Banjaxed by my response he paused for a moment and said 'you're wondering if I'm gay aren't you? I nodded 'Well actually I was, but it doesn't matter to me who or what you are, but you better know now I'm 100% heterosexual'. At that point the nurse walked in announcing 'Ok —guys - its medication—time! She sort of broadcasted it as if we were in a quiz show, and this was another stage of the game. Anyway this sparked off a flurry of activity with patients running to the dispensary as fast as there little legs could carry them. Like bees round a honey pot all buzzing around trying to be first in the queue. Some irate guy barged in front of me; the nurse saw this and asked him to queue up. He didn't much like being told what to do and started moaning about fecking new comers and how long he had been here. Basically I just boycotted him, refused to make eye contact and he went away very quickly. Little things like that soon blew up into real life calamites, so it wasn't worth getting involved in. After a little wait in the queue my drugs were administered with a drink of water, I said my prayers and soon fell asleep.

My next chain of events weren't that exciting and things dragged on in Andover without any real meaning purpose or point. We had a laugh though and would meet up every Friday night in the Swallow pub. Everyone smoked huge amounts of pot and we had no problem in getting it either, the stuff was smuggled in from Pakistan and its street name was 'Paki Black.' We even managed to score some opium once. As an experiment I smoked it in a joint to see what it would do to me, a Ginny pig some might. It felt like I was dreaming but awake at the same time, really strange and abnormal, a bit like using your consciousness, subconscious and the subliminal in fact sub-everything all at the same time, all very confusing and not to be recommended reader. The police properly new what was going on but didn't seem to bother any of us. Probably because we kept ourselves to our self's and at the end of the day not a bad set of lads, plus the only ones we were abusing where our self's. In fact we used to call it 'self-inflicted body abuse'. In the early part of this decade if you got caught with pot, say for example the size of a pea you could get three months in the jail, that's what happened to one of my friends Delirium. The bit he had was only the size of a pea and it was for his own personnel use. Thank fully today attitudes have changed and the same offence only carries a caution and in Brixton they don't even bother with that. Actually through my friends in the Police force I've heard a lot of coppers are on and every time they do a drug bust they nick a bit themselves.

Anyway enough of politics, once we planed this mad fancy dress party and hired a van and Driver and then drove to Southampton for the crac. I was dressed all in white as a baker serving up the hash cakes like there was no tomorrow. We also had the incredible hulk, Batman and Robin, Superman, Prince Charles look alike, King Henry the tird even Maggie Thatcher and an array of other characters, about twenty of us in all. After a night of touring the pubs we decided to have a sit down meal at this Indian restaurant I think it was called 'Bombay Sunrise' Anyways inside we all sat round the big table absolutely hammered and ordered what ever we fancied, no one cared. The guy must have thought Christmas had come early and duly served us up the best food and drink money could buy, we even ordered a few Magnums of the finest Champagne thrown into the bargain, oh it was such fun. I ordered fresh Lobster and chips, yummy. After the banquet one by one everyone started to slowly disappear, until there was just me and Neil Murphy left. Neil was dressed as a priest and for the crac got his Rosary beads out and started praying for divine inspiration. As he was too busy praying Raja presenting the entire bill to me; it was as long as your arm in fact a huge colossal amount. What he didn't know was all these other characters had planned this before hand. We just acted dumb and the next step was to deny that we new them, who just happened to be in fancy dress, sitting at the same table as me, laughing and joking with one and other, insisting that we are only paying for what we had actually eaten our self's. He went absolutely mad and started jumping up and down banging his fist on the table and eventually he phoned the police.

They arrived and didn't see the funny side of things having to take description of all these nutters in their bizarre clothing. They said it wouldn't be difficult to trace the incredible hulk and his mad friends and put out an all points bulletin on them. In the mean time we new our legal rights and continued to deny that we new them, insisting it was mere coincidence that they also were in fancy dress sitting on the same table as me. In any case I was definitely not paying for them; I didn't have the money anyway, furthermore my Visa credit card was on the most wanted list, there was even a reward on it. The police had no choice but to agree with us, sending these Indian guys of on a mental one. Neil and I were not refusing to pay for our meal and one magnum furthermore we had not made of without payment, so we had done nothing legally wrong and got let off the hook, although for our own safety we had to be escorted off the premises. The copper once outside suggested we left town immediately and if we came back they would throw the book at us. Back at the van we couldn't get out of the city fast enough and laughed all the way home. This was all quite normal behaviour at the time and at least no one got hurt, moreover it was all done in the spirit of youthfulness and good fun and it wasn't racist, some of my best friends are from ethnic minorities. In any case a week later or so later we sent him the cash and an apology letter.

After that, doing a runner from restaurants became additive to myself and Russell, daring each other on more and more, we must have done loads. I remember another occasion in the Pearl Dragon when we ordered a massive slap up meal for two, including two of the biggest T-Bone steaks you ever seen in your life. We acted if we were gay and wouldn't harm a fly; the waiter even lit the candle, how kind! To finish off my banquet I washed it all down with the finest wine known to humanity and to help me too relax before my scamper ordered hot towels to be put over my face. This was extremely dangerous territory, because if you got caught doing one from there they didn't bother phoning the police, you got a bloody good hiding instead. We only tried it once from there and luckily got away by the skin of our teeth. They chased me up the street waving their machetes around, shouting in Chinese threatening to kill me if they could catch me. I was laughing so much I got out of breath quickly and couldn't run properly nearly getting caught, but it was all worth it and I thoroughly enjoyed the meal and would recommend the experience to anyone, yummy!

Chapter Four

It was coming up to Christmas 1983 and I had been thinking a lot about what Cozzie told me about Israel, working on the Kibbutz and all that crac. My friend Syd helped me out and paid my passage, thanks mate you changed my life! Guess what? I was back on the magic bus returning to Greece for what felt like the millionth time. Although Dad amusingly once said 'Bobby I've must have told you a million times not to exaggerate'. Our plan was to fly direct from Athens too Tel Aviv, as it worked out a lot cheaper than flying direct from London. Everything went to plan until we reached the Israeli Customs check point. The officer questioned me 'how long I intended to stay?' and 'how much money I had?' If I had any lying through my back teeth said 'I was only staying for a couple of weeks and I had over a thousand US dollars'. Fooling him even further by pointing to a money belt strapped to my waist, actually it was full envelopes making it look fat and bulging like money, thanks for that Olive. The truth of the matter was, I had one English tenner left and intended to stay for a six months at least, which I did. They could have asked to see the money but lady luck was on my side and he just said 'Enjoy your holiday sir' and let me go. I suppose they could have deported me there and then, or thrown me in the jail for lying about my non-excitant money, properly involving the British Embassy again, but they wouldn't have helped any way, as you can only get repatriated once in a lifetime. I don't really know what would have come to pass and to be honest at that point in my life didn't actually care and let fate run its own course; you could have thrown the kitchen sink at me for all I cared. Actually I did stretch my luck that day and kept thinking about what Mr Love said by the stream, 'Trust your instincts in life Bob and be confident with them'

Cozzie had written down on the back of an old cigarette packet the address where you enrolled; it was in Vincent Van Goff Street, Tel-Aviv. At the signing inn office I was shown what looked like a holiday broachers from Butlins, all in colour and written in English. Explaining where the Kibbutz's were and what was expected of you when you arrived. Amazingly some had heated in door swimming pools whilst others boasted out door canoeing, horse riding and rock climbing. One caught my eye straight away; it had its own pub called the Red Lion, excellent. It did have a draw back though, being geographical situated in the Northern part of Israel, where all the fighting was going on and still is. It was called 'Kibbutz Beit Zera' based in the Jordan valley. In Hebrew it meant the seed or in biblical terms they told me it supposed to be "the garden of Eden" The Great Rift Valley instigates from there and the River Jordan ran through the Kibbutz and extended south to the Dead Sea, then into the lowest point in the world the Red Sea, continuing on into Eastern Africa. They made us aware of the dangers and the war, but also mentioned they place was heavily guarded with armed soldiers patrolling, which there was. That was enough to convince me to take the chance and just go for the crac. They gave me a warrant and a special pass to travel to the Northern Province, but first we had to take a trip to the main bus station in Jerusalem; unfortunately it had been in the news a lot and still is, terrorist had been active and the place was full of armed soldiers just waiting for the next explosion. Additionally it was close to Christmas and this really was 'Gun ho main street," and I couldn't wait to get out of the dive quick enough. Sadly two days later I read in the paper there was a massive car bomb and I'm sorry to say a lot of people lost their lives, including children. I heard through the world wide grapevine, that the suicide bombers family got ten thousand

US dollars from 'Cadaffe,' all queuing up to be so called martyrs in the name of Allah. Regrettably years later in 1998 my suspicions were proved right, when he admitted two of his Libyan Diplomats planted the bomb that exploded on Pan Am Flight 103, killing 270 people over Lockerbie in Scotland.

The journey took about five hours and as we got closer to the Lebanese boarder we were accompanied by two Israeli soldiers, armed to the teeth with their Uzi sub machine guns, grenades and a personnel firearm holstered to their waist, and before sitting down them self's they walked the length of the bus scanning everyone's faces. Surprisingly for me no one took any real notice of them carrying their own personnel armoury. Going about their business as normal, reading news papers, talking, even mums breast feeding the babies. All very strange to take in at first but believe me you got used to it after a while. Furthermore If you didn't look right they would not let you travel on the same buses as them, actually I am not surprised considering some one kept blowing them up all the time and still is. Basically the majority of the Arabs had to travel on blue buses and the Israeli travelled on the red ones. It reminded me a bit of what was happening in South Africa with the black people and Nelson Mandela.

Life can be so simple when you let it so I did just that, not bothering to question too much, arriving late around 8 o'clock that evening. Walking up the tarmac drive to my left was a field growing Green Avocadoes, on my right was a Banana plantation and behind me was the Sea of Gallery. In front of me was the settlement and this was the Jordan Valley, perceived to be the most fertile land in the world, where anything grows, again I wasn't at all surprised. An Italian guy called 'Felvio' noticed we were new volunteers calling us over to one of the huts. The huts were a bit like the ones you see in the old black and white prisoner of war films, each room was separated sleeping four. He asked if we were hungry and I thought that was nice of him. Going on to explain the dining room didn't close until 9 pm and he would bring me over.

I just couldn't believe my luck and this was like a breath of fresh air, topping that lot it was all free. Just as well I was absolutely pot-less using the last of my money to buy some cigarettes and a bit food for the rest of the journey. The restaurant was massive about the size of a football pitch and everyone queued up in a neat line. Walking past this food they took what ever they fancied, it was all laid out in front of them, free! Hot dishes like curries and stews were kept warm in the glass bay-mares and fresh fruit was neatly displayed in baskets on the top. Tucking in I helped myself to freshly roast chicken with new potatoes and other tasty organic pollution free vegetables, yum-yum. Reliving the milestone I remember at least five hundred people sitting on long collapsible tables, quietly talking whilst eating there meals. Then it dawn on me, this is how they eat, not at home around the table but here in the canteen. Sitting on the same table as me was a guy from New Zealand who introduced himself as Phil. He struck me as a bit odd but kind at the same time, a man after my own heart. He was about six foot tall, jet black curly hair and a gouty beard resembling a Wizard, so I asked him if I could nick name him that. He thought it was a great idea, eventually everyone called him "The Wizard" and we soon became great buddies. Indecently he was a qualified School Teacher, having his year off maths and geography I think. After I finished off my meal I noticed everyone putting the dinner plates on a conveyor belt straight into an industrial dishwasher, how cool is that.

Leaving the dinning area I went over to one of the huts converted into an office and the official register, finding out the people in Vincent Van Goff Street had phoned them, so they were expecting us and already knew our names, I was impressed. A lady called Judy from New York introduced herself, saying in her unmistakable accent she was the Volunteer Leader and it was her job to take care of all the new recruits. Continuing 'I would have to go to work' suggesting in the Banana plan-tation, but I didn't really fancy that, so thinking on my feet quickly asked were there any snakes in there, she came back with 'yes, a few but they wont hurt you if you leave them alone'. I started doing my dying swan act, professing I had a life long phobia about snakes and under no circumstances what so ever could I go in there. To be frank I had enough of climbing trees and all that nonsense in Greece and all I want-ed to do was skive off as much as possible, something easy and relaxing! Moreover the only time I had ever seen any snakes was in a 'Tarzan film' where he saves Jane from the marauding Ashanti tribe. There was a boy and his pet monkey called Cheater and an elephant who were also involved. Any ways enough of all the baloney, Judy asked 'what would you like to do then Bob', replying 'I like working with children,' she

Robert Charles Scanlan

responded by saying 'I'll see what I could do, but in the meantime she was looking for a new barman and had I got any experience'. I couldn't believe my destiny and thanked God for this fortuitous break; busting at the-seams now I was thinking free beer as well, what's next, lucky old you?   Not to let an opportunity like this pass me by I immediately said 'Well, I have worked behind the bar before, but I am A Roman Catholic and don't actually touch the stuff myself, except for communion wine on Sundays at Mass, is that O.K'. Judy smiled. This was music to her ears and whispered in my ear 'that will do nicely, oh, there is just one rule Bob, you are not allowed to go to the border'. Secretly thinking, what border sounds all very interesting, winking at Syd replied 'OK' no problem! After filling in the forms I was shown my hut, I was sharing with a guy called Geoff and the Wizard. We went to the pub and Geoff the other barman put in the picture he was a deserter from the Royal Marines. He new I didn't have any money and gave me the free drink and cigarettes all night and every other night from then on. Actually and I gave loads a way as well, especially if I liked you.

The pub didn't open until 12 o'clock, which gave me lots of free time to explore my new abode. It was fine sunny morning the birds were singing and the sky was that pale blue colour, anyways I jumped on one of the push bikes propped against the wall, helping myself I just rode off on it, a bit like the Dutch do. The settlement resembled a small compact village, things like the schools and baby units were deliberately positioned geographically in the very middle and heavily patrolled. These were a strategically situated like this because a couple of Kibbutz's had been attacked and the raiders killed all the children first. How awful that must have been for them poor parents, I suppose that's what happens sometimes in war zones, the children always get hurt. Although God once said 'All the little ones have automatic wrights direct into Heaven.' On my jaunt I also discovered they had fish farm and in the nursery salmon and trout were being raised. They also had a diary farm producing all the fresh milk and beef they required. There was also factory called 'Ark-ill' mass producing plastic garden chairs for the world wide market, this was there main bread and butter making them a small fortune, oh and of course there was the Banana plantation. Next to the dining hall was a shop selling clothes and general house hold goods like light bulbs and bleach. Further on was a small super-market packed to the brim with all the usual stuff supermarkets have including cold packs of Guinness, just what I wanted excellent. The thing is nobody used money and everyone had a card which was swiped, then the money was taken directly from the personal account held at there own Community Bank. Unbelievably they even gave me one, although after a while they demanded it back as I had ranked up a massive unofficial overdraft. After my little tour I went for dinner noticing all the volunteers sat together and the Kibbutz- nick that's what they called themselves sat on different tables, I thought that's a bit funny. The average age of the volunteers that's us was around twenty-five and there were sixty of us in all. If one of the young Kibbutz-nix spent too much time with the volunteers they got into big trouble. The elders said we might encourage them to move away and become westernised. As they 'the elders' were already struggling to keep the population up in the commune, consequently the average age for them was about forty and declining.

The place was an oasis of serenity and the great 'River Jordan' was rite in my back garden. It was just as how I imagined it would be from the Bible. It looked really deep, bottomless, fast and far too dangerous and risky to go for my little swim. The current would just sweep you away and you would be stone cold dead, I suppose from bank to bank it was about the width of a tennis court, anyway it reminded me of my little stream when as a boy we used too burst the dam, but this was different and looked more like a constant solid wall of water. The other side of the bank was no mans land, the formidable 'Golan Heights' and strictly out of bounds. Not that I could go there anyway because there were no bridges and swimming it was out of the question, unless you had to escape for your life that is. The other lads had been here before coming prepared with their fishing tackle, bait and keep net, oh and a few Tin-ies, that's what my new Aussie friend from Sydney 'Alan' called them anyway. Out of the bulrushes and dense undergrowth they hollowed out a safe place just back off the bank, all cut back nice and neat. We then sat down on the deck chairs which where kindly already left there from the previous day, you know stripy ones like before! Geoff put the beers down on the table and I pulled back the ring on my can of Guinness remarking 'Good health gentleman.'

As we fished I chilled out playing cards and told jokes listening too Prochel Harlem's all time classic 'A whiter shade of pale', it was dead cool and I didn't have a care in the world, what was even better I didn't have any regrets and didn't miss England one bit. Geoff was the best Angler out of the lot of us, the catfish he caught was about as big as a small five-year old child and that's no fisherman tail. It felt great to be part of it all and most of my afternoons were spent down there just dosing about, barbecuing the catch on the nightly bonfire. Christmas was only about two weeks away, but you think it was summer time, the weather was hot and sunny just like an English bank holiday in August you might say. What made it really exciting was the fact all these young people had come from every corner of the globe to have the crac, just like me! There was one guy who claimed to be Jewish and had escaped from 'Russia's Iron curtain' by clambering over the wall. His mate was shot dead in the escape and he was wounded, eventually fleeing to Israeli as genuine political refuge, he said it was caught on camera and beamed all over the world. After the collapse of communism in 1989 I often wondered if he was allowed home to see his family, I suppose he must have been.

Anyway back at the bar it didn't take Geoff long to show me the ropes introducing me to everyone. Too fool Judy, every day I put a pale of fresh milk in the fridge, every time she showed up I would be drinking that, which made her happy. Everyone had a card with their name on and they would deposit money at the bank and then I was supposed to deduct it as they bought the beer, again depending if I kike you or not! The pub wasn't really a pub but an old dormitory transformed into what resembled a pub. Some arty person designed the ceiling as an under water scene. As I looked up I saw a dark wooden hull of a row-ing boat looming out of the corner, there were fishing nets strewn from side to side and a pair of fishermen's Wellington boots dangled down from the side of the boat. Hanging on a piece of rope was red and white life belt with the bottom half of a tailors dummy floating in the middle. We even had plastic fish and the whole shebang was painted that sea green colour, actually when I had been drinking all day I thought I was drowning in a sea of free beer. We had a bar and a sound system which actually was quite good, Bob Marley was a favourite and I sold beer by the can 'Stella Artois' and the spirits by the glass, not bothering using a measure, just pouring it directly from the bottle stop-ping when I felt like it, again depending if I like you or not as the case might be! The pub was open every day from mid-day to around 3 o'clock, and again in the evening to midnight. More often than not the time table was ignored and slung out the window, anyway it was my decision and I was in charge, head honcho if you like!

Christmas was absolutely brilliant; the Banana pickers bless their hearts, had worked their nuts off all year and apparently made over a million US dollars for the Kibbutz. The Israelis wanted to thank the volunteers on a bumper crop and gave us a budget of over three thousand dollars to spend on over Christmas and the New Year, so I couldn't have timed my arrival better, thanks men. Incredibly I asked to use the concrete bomb shelter for our celebrations and it was sanctioned. Geoff and I ordered massive amounts of alcohol all too be consumed free by the lot of us. They gave us a shed to store the booty in and the forklift driver took ages to unload this note-able on the house amount. Rubbing ours hands together Geoff and I spent the rest on our Christmas dinner. They let us use the kitchens and the girls knocked up a splendid meal, plus we all got presents, I asked for a new pair of Levi jeans size 34 waist and I got them. In the evening we were aloud to telephone home free of charge. Wearing my new strides I felt proud and phoned home and spoke to Mammy, I never forget Kitty was there too and in her amusing Dublin accent kept saying 'stop messing about Bobby and come home straight away', I said 'alright Kitty, happy Christmas love you' with sadness that was it and I got a mention in her will, God bless. The Israeli people were really great and a few of them actually joined in our celebrations. It was properly one of the best Christmases I have ever had in my life, and there was more to come, next was the New Year only a few days away.

The New Year celebrations down in the bomb shelter where absolutely mind blowing to say the least, bordering on what any normal person would call totally insane, excellent. All week we had been moving the beer and food in, we even had a proper disco to entertain us. I was the DJ and opened up the night with Diana Ross and the Supremes 'Ain't No mountain high enough'. It was great! That night Geoff I and the Wizard made a big vase of punch, Vodka Gin you name it, every thing went into it and every one was on its case, even fresh fruit from the fields far away! Consequently the punch had not only taken me out of action, but every body else as well, spinning the volunteer's heads rite off into orbit yet again. Actually out there in the Middle East

I found myself in quite a unique and bizarre once in a lifetime situation. The crac was we all came from all over the world and we knew what time it was in our own country. We worked out the time distances from one country to another, aware when it would be midnight in your own homeland. So to be fare I thought we would kick off our new year at 7 o'clock Israeli local time, which was 12 o'clock Greengage mean time, get it. For the next 24 hours we rang in another new year from every corner of the Earth and the whole shebang went on for twenty-four hours. In Orson Well's novel he predicted the world would end in 1984 and for a laugh because we were all so smashed waited for it to happen, he was lying. I remember someone saying don't worry about the world coming to an end, it's already tomorrow in Australia' although if the place did get bombed we would have been the only one saved.

The bunker was close to the dinning area and the Israelis used to sit out side on wooden benches, socializing talking eating and reading newspapers and the like. The volunteers started going back to the huts for a rest, wobbling out arm in arm in front of all these families, unable to speak and virtually unable to walk, coming back later on for more action. Some of us tried to converse with the Israelis but they kept giving us strange looks all day, refusing to speak English. Consequently I didn't have a clue what they thought of us, but believe me I did find out later. Although I did start to learn a few phrases for example, when we say 'Alright' or 'Hi'ya' they say 'Mackera' which means 'what happened' and the other person automatically replies 'Culme' which translate too nothing, 'another bit of useless information' It took me two days to get over the ten day bender, laying on my bunk motionless in the horizontal position, my eyes closed and a cold wet towel covering my forehead. Really my brain felt like it was on a pendulum, swinging around, bumping and thumping, pounding on its very own in side my skull. This was one humdinger of a hang over, even worst than the one at Kitty's; at one point it felt like someone was drilling a hole in my temple and I thought 'oh Jesus I am going to die'. They made some of the Volunteers go to work in the Banana plantation, because the crop was over ripening. Climbing trees and all that carry on, I can only imagine what it must have been like for them, being forced at gun point to do that, I dare to think what they must have felt like. The wizard was quite fit strong and healthy, but he came back after an hour looking half dead, closing the hut door behind himself he didn't say much, just laying on his bunk making strange moaning noises, all I heard from under my wet towel was 'Never again.'

The Israel's couldn't believe it, although fare dues we had been on a bender for ten days now and all the drink and been drunk, and no one had gone to work, it was absolutely brilliant. Judy went mad because she got into big trouble herself, sanctioning all the money from the Community Bank. After our strike she called a meeting in the dinning room, furthermore if you didn't attend you will be immediately escorted of the premises by the armed guards, believe me she wasn't bluffing. Everyone arrived in dribs and drabs eventually starting fifteen minutes late. Arriving last, Geoff, I and the Wizard sat at the back skulking, trying to blend in with the rest of the crowd, keeping a low profile. As we sat down as Judy stood up and chaired the meeting, either side sat two Police officers and the armed Solders were visible at all of the entrance. She was absolutely fuming and abrasively delivered a complaints list as long as your arm. It went on and on especially around the bunker. One of 'South Africans' was seen urinating by a tree, in front of all the people and little ones. They identified him and making an example arrested him on the spot, finally being marched of the premises in hand cuffs at gunpoint. Don't blame them; I never liked him any way, always putting the black people down. In addition to that I had serious problems with one of them later on. The gravest charge was someone had stolen an Israeli 'Major Uniform' off the washing line and they wanted it back immediately, they even put up a large cash reward, no questioned asked, I asked what proof they had to suspect it was one of us, everyone cheered. Another allegation included, someone somehow got into the kitchen larder and eat all the best food, especially kept for the pensioners. The ladder was a huge walk in fridge and locked every night at 10 o'clock and they couldn't work out how we got in, another mystery! Although they never once considered the dinning area adjacent, which was never closed and you could get a glass of milk from the dispenser when ever you wanted, 24 hours a day. To get your free milk you opened a small stainless steel door, about two feet square in diameter. On opening this door was a large cardboard box full of milk, with a plastic tap so you could help yourself; by the side were disposable white cups and on the floor was a bin for the used ones. Mr X was up to his old tricks again and worked out if you pulled the box completely out it left a large hole, big enough too crawl through directly into the ladder, giving access to all the goodies. Alan waited the other side of the wall, whilst this mysterious other person passed out cakes, steaks, hams and a variety of fish it was like a supermarket. Mr X put the box back in the hole where it came from and now they were totally mystified, it was like getting into Fort knocks, but we succeeded, as the saying goes 'were there's a will there's a way'. After that the volunteer's responsible wised up and only took small amounts of goodies at a time and the scam went on and was still going on when I left months later, oh and by the way they searched high and low for the uniform, but never got it back, I'd seen to that.

There was an English girl called Pauline whose job was too help Judy looking after the volunteers and next to the pub we had small canteen where she worked. It was pretty chilled out and you could listen to the radio read newspapers and drink tea and coffee. In the morning when everyone was at work she would make my tea and read the newspapers to me. To change our routine she suggested 'don't bother lifting the cup and saucer to your mouth, I will pour the tea straight down your neck for you if you like Bob', I just sat with my hands by my side listening to the BBC world service whilst she poured the delicious hot tea with sugar directly into my throat, I almost thought it was my birthday, pure luxury. Pauline became a nurse and I am sure she was practising her social caring skills on me. We met up years later at a party held in London; it was grand going on to the early hour of the morning. She had a friend called Margaret who was as just as batty, walking past me one day said out of the blue for no apparent reason 'Bob do you no I have big brown nipples? I replied 'that's nice for you Shabbat Shalom' translated means, have a nice Saturday. There was a load of Italian guys from Scilly a contingent of Swedish birds from Oslo, so many Aussie I lost count, Americans the Irish the French South Africans one Canadian another from South America, Germany and I think one guy from even Luxembourg and the list went on and on. It truly was a Multi National Force of young people and I became intrigued with this new concept of friendship. These complete strangers speaking different languages from all over the globe, coming together in the middle of a war zone and bonding, what's life going to throw at me next I thought!

Life was good fun and on Shabbat 'Saturday' nobody worked it was their day of rest like our Sundays. We played five a side football and cricket on the main green, once we even had a sports day and I won the egg and spoon race. I opened the pub all day blasting out the music, a favourite of the Aussie was a band called 'Men at work, Johnny be good.' People sat around smoking, chilled out doing art work laughing and joking, knitting and playing board games, I was the champion chess player. For a giggle my friends used to make me write these mad letters to complete strangers all over the world. They would tell me things and secrets about this person and I would ask questions about them and their character, composing the letter on that information. The idea was to completely flummox the reader and send their heads rite of into orbit on receiving this round the bend correspondence from a complete stranger in a different continuant. To get it bang on we could spend all day just concentrating on this bizarre content.

Once we sent one to Geoff sister Debbie in Bristol England, it was fecking excellent even by my standards. Geoff told me when they were little kids she used to deliberately pinch him on the stairs making him cry. As soon as he started crying she would cuddle him, practising doing her mummy bit I suppose. Making a big deal out of this I told her it had affected him sociology, furthermore he never recovered mentally and that's why he had deserted from the Royal Marines, ruining his career and his life. What's more he was now receiving counselling for this psychological torture that she had put him through and additionally he was under a physiatrist on the Valium. The Doctor Geoff was seeing 'Moshe Dyane' said she was also responsible for his divorce and the string of failed relationship prior to that. Moreover he was never coming back to England in case she did it again. We knew it took exactly one week to arrive and that following Shabbat she got her letter. Putting her out of her misery Geoff phoned her up that evening and she said, 'she had been walking around in bewilderment all day' I must have written to every corner of the earth with these mad barmy stories, some were then even translated into different languages and used over and over again, what a laugh, hundreds went out! They were great crac to do and it kept my imagination occupied for a while at least.

Different individuals came and Left on daily basis and I met an English girl called Tracy from Southend on Sea, who later had a big impact on my life. In fact a few years later in 1986 we got married and had two children Scarlett and Rory, everyone is fine and the children are both studying for a degree, I'm very proud of them all. As I mentioned I kept myself informed as to what was happening from the BBC world service and the Israeli news papers. Being partially interested in what was going on in the Lebanon? The Americans became the main target and massive car bomb in Beirut killed a total of 241 Americans soldiers and Diplomats. At the time in history this was the highest loss of life in a Single day since D Day 1945. The suicide attack changed American presence in Lebanon and they left and basically the United Nations had to be called in to sort out all the trouble. Being so close to the front line made it even more authentic and real, seriously reader I started wondering if they needed any spies. To add to all the action late one night I was awoken with the distant sound of gunfire coming from the Golan Heights behind me, I had to wake Geoff and the Wizard as it got ever closer. Geoff threw a towel over the lamp to dim the light, and we pulled the curtains hovering around the slight gap peeking through where they met' a bit like Russell, spying! It was absolutely astonishing and I heard people running around shouting in Arabic and Hebrew. There was an exchange of gunfire from an automatic weapon and a bright flair was sent up to illuminate the sky. In the morning I asked Judy what all the fuss was about, she tried to fend me off by saying 'it was a training exercise and there was nothing to worry about'; she was lying because near the washrooms I saw them hosing away someone's blood with a hose pipe.

Life settled down and I continued my little hobby fishing on the river Jordan and as I said opposite me were the infamous Golan Heights. One of these lazy afternoons I was out angling quite happily away on my own, relaxed sitting on my stripy deck chair, the same as before! Drinking my cold can of Guinness, my news paper to my side, having a smoke of some Lebanese Gold, just peacefully jotting down a few of my thoughts on paper. Wearing my sunglasses stress-free listening to the BBC world service on the radio 'This is BBC calling the world' the man announced. When like a bat out of hell I heard two rockets whizzing over me at high speed, heading directly for the Kibbutz behind me. I didn't see them, I just heard them, they were that fast. Instinctively I ducked down and dived for cover in the tall undergrowth and bull-rushes. Lying there, I thought this was all extremely dangerous for my health, as I wasn't sure how the Israeli Army would have reacted if they caught me, especially wearing green combat trousers and a white t-shirt, spying with military equipment. Someone told me once they have been known to shoot first and ask question later, especially spying with military equipment. So I resisted the 23rd Psalm and asked God to protect me in my hour of need. The Lord is my Shepard I shall not want; he makes me lie down in green pastures'. From the Kibbutz behind me the air raid sirens started to screech out a deafening howling hum and I thought I bet there all in the bomb shelter, where I should be. Then through Geoff's high-powered binoculars he nicked from the British Army, I focused in as the battle unfolding before my very own eyes; From my concealed position, one mile from the front line I had a good view of all action and felt quite safe camouflaged in the tall reefs and bulrushes. 'He restores my soul and he guides me in paths of righteousness'. The Kibbutz's returned fire hitting the mountains directly in front of me; I saw the shells exploding on impact and one must have hit an ammunition dump, causing one almighty explosion, creating this mushroom shaped fire ball that then went careering into the air. 'For his namesake even though I walk through the valley of the shadows of death I will fear no evil for you are with me'. Moments later there were two more enormous blasts, discharging these mammoth balls of flames that shot up into the sky with a deafening screeching sound, black smoke and debris hurtled into the air. Fall out from the battle rained down splashing perilously near me at the foot of the river. 'Your rod and your staff they comfort me and you prepare a table before me'. The other side returned fire with a heavy duty machine guns and light arms, cranking off thousands off rounds at the incoming Israeli fighter jets, now screaming low over my head with a thunderous roar. 'In the presence of my enemies you anoint my head with oil and my cup overflows'. Then the jets unloaded missile after missile on top of them, this bedlam continued for about ten minutes and then two Apache attack helicopters joined in. 'Surely goodness and love will follow me all the days of my life and I will dwell in the house of the Lord forever'. Shell after shell rained down on the mountains before me, this was riveting to watch and I saw masses of foot soldiers leg it over the brim of the hill, some unfortunately died where they fell. I saw one poor guy get his right arm blown off; he just picked it up with his other hand running off over the rise, probably the only survivor. After that, it all stopped as quickly as it started and a deafening silence took hold, too quiet, and not even the birds weren't singing and all that was left was the sound of the trickling river. To be safe, I stay under cover for a while making sure it was all over. Returning with my fantastic true story and fish of the day, oh and it tasted really lovely. Indecently, I never went back there. I was told this was the hit and run tactic causing more psychological damage than anything else. Apparently the rockets missed the Kibbutz but ended up blowing up part of the Banana plantation. That night though they doubled the armed patrols and told us not to go fishing for a while.

As the wizard was a schoolteacher Judy agreed that he could be the treasurer/accountant for the pub, little did she know he was in on the free scam and couldn't get the beer down his throat quick enough either. The three of us never paid a penny so consequently the stock was always short. Each week on a Friday the four of us would count how much had been consumed and how much had actually been spent on the cards. One way round it for me was to keep the empty vodka or gin bottles, filling them back up with tap water and then counting them in as unsold stock. We had fifty crates of the stuff and it was getting bigger by the week; but I had more tricks up my sleeve than a wagonload of monkeys and by sheer chance was away for the weekend on a trip too Haifa, when there was a mysterious robbery. The mysterious Mr X was busy again and had nicked the entire lot. What the Israelis didn't know it was just bottles of water, so technically thousands of US dollars worth of booze went missing that cold fateful night. Returning from my short break I was absolutely aghast, shocked and even traumatised to learn about this fiasco? Honestly reader my dying swan act would have won me a double Oscar. Geoff said he saw a suspicious looking Arab guy hanging around in the middle of the night and he got the blame. What a laugh, Judy swallowed the lot in more ways than one, that's what Geoff said anyway, felt really sorry for me and wrote the debt off, allowing me to go to the store and get a load more booze, excellent.

For some weird mad unexplainable reason a week or so later I adopted a stray dog, it was brown with white spots, who strangely only had three legs, two at the front and one at the back; I suppose it must have trod on a land mine. Any case I called him Johnny but then I found out it was a girl dog, but it was too late and the name stuck. I don't know where Johnny slept, but this particular night I accidentally locked her in the pub overnight. The guards came and got me at 3 o'clock in the morning to open up, as Johnny was going mad trying to get out, barking and howling keeping half the people up all night. For the crac more than anything else, three of us, and Johnny went to the border to try and cross over to the Lebanon, just to see what the guards would do. With me was a nurse called Anna from America and a doctor called Steve from Australia, so if o did get injured I was in the right hands. We rode up to the checkpoint on our bikes waving our passports around. It was all very military looking, high fences and barbed wire and a couple of watch towers. Reaching the checkpoint I noticed the guards had their rifles pointing directly at us loaded. They could clearly see we were Europeans and posed no threat and with no luggage we were obviously not suicide bombers. Dismounting from our bikes, Johnny sat down and we stood at the gates stupidly asking one of them to open it. They picked up the phone and spoke to someone else and their captain came from a hut putting his cap on at the same time. He demanded to see our passports and asked what our business actually was here. We explained which Kibbutz we were from and we would like to visit the other side to find out what it was all about. He told us this was a restricted area and we weren't allowed, as he feared for our own lives. Under international law they could not actually stop us, I argued this point until I heard one of the solders fire a warning shot in the air. At this point Johnny lost her bottle and ran away howling and crying never to be seen again. They took the film out of Anna's camera and we were told in no uncertain terms to go away very quickly. Actually I was quite glad because at the time they were kidnapping all the Europeans, the journalist John McCarthy was one and I think a few American diplomats. In conjunction with that they would be reporting us to the officers at the Kibbutz, which they did. Arriving back at the Kibbutz later that afternoon they already knew about it and we were hauled in front of Judy, the elders and the Army.

The stock in the pub had gone wobbly again and this time even with the Wizards creative accounting couldn't help me, or Geoff's penis for that matter. Having no choice but to depart company very quickly, moreover I particularly didn't like been told what to do and where to go, especially by some jumped up Israeli. Geoff and I planed our escape to Elait on the Egyptian border to perfection and like some military manoeuvre and took the remainder of the Vodka, Gin Whisky and cigarettes with us, in fact we had two suitcases each full of the stuff. The first bus of the day was at five o'clock in the morning so we sneaked away at dawn while everyone was still asleep, plus we knew we wouldn't be missed until 12 o'clock when the pub was due to open. It was a bit sad saying good bye to my buddy the Wizard, as we knew we would never see each other again, I remember he said he was flying out of the country that morning to Canada, apparently it quite easy to get work with the Lumberjacks so that's what he did. Tracy on the other hand had two weeks before she had to return to England and asked if I could take her as well, so I did, in fact it ended up being a life long journey.

The trip took about five hours and I stopped off at Jerusalem, sight seeing. Did you know the Israeli government has designated Jerusalem as the capital, although this is not recognised by the United Nations, in fact we say its Haifa, another bit of useless information or is it? We booked into a cheap youth hostel and dropped off the rucksacks and suitcases. Like an Aborigine I went walk about; listening to the Rolling Stones on my little Walkman and honestly reader, the sounds smells and sights were all imposing. The old part of the city was surrounded by high stonewalls and you entered through these huge gates which were locked every night by the armed guards. Strolling through the tight narrow cobbled streets, Bedouins rode donkeys, and one even looked like Dougal. Strangely all the men had black moustaches and looked like Saddam Hussein. Sitting around all day with nothing better to do apart from smoking pot through a water pipe they called a Hubley bub-ley, talking a load of bullocks. There were a variety of small shops either side selling leather goods, copper and brass wear, spices and a collection of hand woven carpets. Readily available on the street corner was an Arab guy selling tea brewed from the locally grown pot. He served it up from an elaborate looking silver vase strapped to his back. Pouring it into a plastic cup it flowed freely from a long narrow curved spout pro-truding from under his right arm. No one took any notice and this was quite normal behaviour, routine in fact, it just goes to how one culture will accept things and others won't. I remember hearing the Jimmy Hendrix all time classic 'all along the watch tower' blasting out from one of the cafes nearby. I sat down outside on a wall listening to all this and had a cup of his tea, it was absolutely delicious and I started that mad spinning off thing that I do. Two or three poorly shod Arab children came up to me with their hands out begging, please Sir, have you anything to eat Sir. It was all very sad because I was in the same boat as them, probably worse off, although I did give them one of my last dollar bills. The highlight of my imposing magnificent all embracing tour was seeing the 'Wailing Wall,' properly the most Sacred holy place in the whole world. It was so impressive, bordering on absolutely awesome and if you get a chance go and see it. The colossal massive gigantic wall is about one hundred metres high and two hundred metres wide. Each individual stone block was about the same size of a family car. What baffled, puzzled and intrigued me the most was the fact this was over two thousand years old. How did they manage to construct it without heavy lifting machinery, cranes and bulldozers and the like? One theory was it was constructed by Aliens from Mars; whoever came up with that story had properly being drinking the locally brewed tea like me. My supposition was it might have been carved out of one solid rock face and then made to look like separate blocks, when in fact it is one fixed piece of natural stone, maybe. The Rabbi' dressed in all his gear ran around blowing a ram's horn and the little ones followed and chased him around like Father Christmas. The Jews prayed there, swaying back wards and forwards wearing black hats with their long curls dangling from the side. They also believe that in the closing stages of the world if you happen to be standing under the wall, you will survive whilst the rest will perish. I also heard that the Orthodox men never shake hands with the women simply because they may be having their periods, making them unclean, bizarre. To boot, apparently when the orthodox Jews make love they do so with a sheet between them, presumably with a whole cut out at the most decisive point. There was a sense of spiritual stimulation and I thought Jesus was here, so much so I sensed his presence holding my hand. I plucked up the courage and joined all these guys at the face of the wall. They made me take my shoes off and wear a skull cap, I remember thinking 'does this make me Jewish, although it doesn't matter anyway because Jesus was Jewish. Actually I knew I looked out of place and thought I hope they don't think I am taking the Mickey', but no one battered an eye lid. Traditionally they wrote a prayer on a piece of paper and stuffed it between the cracks in the blocks. I decided to write one myself for Gu-Gu and wrote the Lords prayer in memory of her, I felt really proud because I knew Mammy would have like that. Afoot, I saw a Roman Catholic priest and wanted to talk to him about all this, I asked 'Father, please can you help me' he must have thought I was beggar because he didn't even acknowledge me. As I continued to have a good look around I noticed a group of about twenty Muslims girls heading my way. All dressed in black wearing the veil, passing us one of them spat at Tracy for no apparent reason. This annoyed me even more, so I said to them in Arabic 'Legist Dian' translated means 'Feck you and your mother too', the bitch new exactly what I said and glared back at me through her veil. After that abuse and fearing for Tracy's safety I went touring outside the city to an old Castle ruin. Huge stone boulders and debris was laying about everywhere, honestly I thought another bomb had gone off. There I asked one of the armed guards what it was all about, he responded 'Jericho'. My mind flashed back to my Sunday school days when I read about it in class, recollecting an old story from the bible relating to these guys who blew trumpets and the walls came tumbling down and here was the proof and evidence in front of my eyes. Later on that afternoon I caught a local bus just up the road to Bethlehem passing through Nazareth. It was a lot smaller than I expected and I managed to visit the stable where Jesus was bourn; it was just like the Christmas card scene but without the Tanks armed guards.

The next morning after a light breakfast of cigarettes larger and donuts I caught the Greyhound express bus going south too Elait. It took about four hours and as we passed through the Negev dessert and the climate really started to warm up. I was expecting sand dunes and camels like a scene out of the Arabian Knights, but it wasn't a bit like that. It was full of canyons and mountains all barren and sterile. Not even one Joshua tree all alienated more like the surface of mars, in fact no life at all. I managed to get one of the back seats and crashed out listening to the classic guitar rock guitarist Peter Frampton, a favourite of mine was 'Do you feel like I do' Half way in the middle of nowhere we stopped off at this roadside café for a break. It really was an oasis and not a mirrarche and I enjoyed a cold glass of Guinness munching on a packet of cheese and onion crisps, another one of my favourites. I had heard through the worldwide traveller's unwritten guidebook that it was easy to get work in the bars and hotels and was really keyed up about my new escapade.

So inward bound I retrieved my luggage from the bus holdall heading down the hill past the airport towards the Red Sea. It was a relatively new resort and I believe it was only about forty years old, before just wilderness and home to a few camels' snakes and a few stoned Bedouins, simply because they had no fresh water. They were solving this problem by pumping and then piping the water directly from the River Jordan too the most southerly point here in Elait. Someone told me they got a grant from the Americans which wouldn't surprise me as the Americans bankrolled the whole country. Actually if it wasn't for their money: the State of Israel would go bankrupt. Outside its borders, the shekel wasn't and still isn't worth the paper it was printed on. In fact I remember we used to light our cigarettes with the stuff. I suppose it's the Americans way of keeping a foothold in the Middle East.

Officially I had to be back on the hospital ward by 8.30 pm, if I wasn't they would call the Police and send out a search party for me, although if it wasn't dark Vera would let me stay out a little longer, she was kind like that, in fact she became like a second mum to me and we would often walk the grounds together until dusk. We had a favourite wooden bench we used too sit on and discuss my problems and read my manuscript. She suggested I mingle more with the other patients so the readers could have a better understanding of mental health issues and the terrible stigma that goes with it. I took her advice and sat down with a girl called Robin who had a few visitors. They were drinking tea and coffee, smoking cigarettes quietly listening to the radio and reading girly magazines. As I sat down one of them nudged Robin and asked 'is he a patient nurse or visitor? I remember saying 'I'm not deaf you know, why don't you ask me yourself'. Dartanian was with me and he went back on the ward to fetch the coffee and chocolate biscuits. Robin turned down the radio and introduced me to her daughter Andrea and her friend Jackie. Jackie was a bit nosy and asked how long I had been here, and was I sectioned or voluntary? As I was telling her Dartanian brought out the drinks and a plate of biscuits, between dipping them in my coffee we started chatting.

'Who fancies a game of snap then', Jackie asked? Before anyone had a chance to even answer she dived into her bag pulling out a brand new pack of cards. For a joke I suggested strip poker, everyone smiled but no one responded, so I guessed that was off. Over the radio came the sound of the Irish band, The Corrs—Summer Sunshine—listening in I told a few more my jokes. Doctor, I keep thinking I'm God. When did this start? Well at first I created the Sun, then the moon and finally the Earth! Doctor, can I have a second opinion, of course you can come back tomorrow and last but not least Doctor, I keep thinking there are two of me, one at a time please! We all roared with laughter and it was difficult to distinguish who was who between the patients, the visitors even the staff joined in. It was like that old proverb; the lunatics have taken over the asylum, I remember making that comment which made things even worse. There was an empty Cola bottle on the table and I suggested we play the game spin the bottle. When it stops spinning, wherever the neck is pointing too means you either truthfully have to answer a question or complete some sort of mad dare. Just my luck it stopped at me first, so I choose to answer a question any question on any subject, honestly and truthfully. Jackie went straight for the jugular asking me if I ever had sex with a man. What a probe. Wearing my heart on my sleeve I whispered 'unfortunately once I had sex with a Transvestite but didn't know it was man until years later, I was duped he even had the operation to remove his penis and some how grew large breast. Although, I have contemplated was I raped, as if I had known it was man I wouldn't have consented, what do you think reader? Indecently, he called himself Sonia, so the men all over the world beware; he's out there on the louse. At the time I had my suspicions though and refused to kiss. It all went quiet when Vera inadvertently blurted out 'you never mentioned that before Bob, oops sorry Darling.' I remember saying 'don't worry about it and with my confession out of the way, I set the tone for the rest of the game and now it was my turn to spin the bottle and get my revenge. Slowly wobbling it eventually stopped pointing at Dartanian. He pondered for a moment or so and then said with smirk on his face 'oh go on then, I'll go for a truth, if I must.' This time Andréa wouldn't let him off the hook and asked him the same question. He went bright red and I guessed the answer was also yes but surprisingly he eventually replying crossing his legs in the way he did 'no, but I have thought about it quite a lot, anyways I would have to divorce my wife first, but she wouldn't mind anyway as she bisexual herself, but also thinking about what Robert just said, I suppose I could live with a transsexual, I imagine we would all get on rather well, I think I'll put that point to my wife and see what's she got to say on the affair.' To break the foreboding silence I started clapping and everyone else automatically joined in, another one of my old school tricks, it's called Auto suggestion, a bit like when you yawn.

We spun again only this time it stopped at Jackie. So for the crac I had to ask her 'have you ever kissed another woman'. Her mum instantly straightened herself up in the chair glaring at me, declaring 'I knew you would ask her that', what's this fascination men have about lesbians? She then looked at her daughter continuing 'you don't have to answer that if you don't want to honey'. Well honey wasn't that sweet and clasped her face in her hands and started to blush uncontrollably, actually I felt sorry for her. I suppose there must have been about ten people standing around waiting on with bated breath for her reply. To be honest from her body language, I wasn't at all surprised when she said 'yes it was nice Mum and I enjoyed it', I thought she's brave; I like that in a woman. We were all prepared to leave this well alone but her mum was insisting to know who it was, where and what the girl's name was. She was very persistent, bordering on demanding and relentlessly kept on. 'I'm your mum I've brought you up and I've got a rite to know who this slap-per is'. Eventually after a lot of huffing and puffing and stamping of the feet she had to tell her. And guess what? Her mum knew who the other girl was, saying 'that whore is not allowed in your bedroom anymore, in fact you wait till I see her'. One of the patients mischievously responded by saying 'I suppose that makes you a Lesbian then, hmm? I couldn't think of any thing to say so just said the first thing that came to my mind. 'Doctor, doctor I feel like an electric eel, that's shocking. Doctor, doctor I'm so ugly what can I do about it? Hire yourself out at Halloween parties'. After a few more coffees and idle chitchat it was dusk and time to go in for the evening. Back on the ward, things returned to normal and after my light supper of jam on toast I went for a smoke and watched a bit of TV. As usual at 10 pm we all queued up for smarty time and then I said my prayers and eventually fell asleep listening to Pink Floyds Dark Side of the Moon on my personnel Stereo.

Eventually we arrived at Elait and honestly reader it was like something from one of the posh Thomas Cook holiday brochure and I just couldn't believe my good fortune. Golden sandy beaches and palm trees, hot looking girls and white washed hotels that silhouetted the deep blue skies. Actually it was more like a scene from the American TV programme 'Bay Watch', sun sea sand and slow motion running.

Robert Charles Scanlan

Surprise, surprise near the beach I found a bar, trading some of my booze and cigarettes with the barman 'Liam' for a fist full of dollars, in reality not in my dreams free Guinness and food all day, excellent, what's next on my amazing agenda I thought. This was the best of the best, the sea was crystal clear and I couldn't resist the temptation trying out my new snorkelling gear. It was exceptional underwater vision; the fish must have been use to seeing the divers because they became quite familiar and darted in and out of the coral-reefs as if it was a game. The dolphins made funny squeaking noises and appeared to be smiling at me so I smiled back; one of them even showed of her baby, I held onto mum's dorsal fin and smiling we all went for a swim together. It was properly one of the highlights of my life, Mother Nature at its very best. Anyway as I starred out of my binoculars in front of me was the Red Sea and across this vast expanse of indigo blue and green I could just make out the coast line of Saudi Arabia. To my left was a huge moun-tain range and tourist would travel the world to get a shufti of the Sun setting in the west then beyond that lay Jordan. Egypt was to my east and so close it only took twenty minutes on the bus, departing every morning from outside the post office.

That opening day felt like I had won the national lottery, looking at all these people on their two-week holidays, paying thousand of dollars for the experience? On the other hand, there was myself having the crac, staying for the whole season with them having to pay me thousands of dollars. My life reached a peak an all time high and I felt incredibly lucky to be here. I did wonder what they would be doing this time back in England and wasn't at all sad I had made this Expedition. Didn't last though and I ended up being public enemy number one, I tell you about later! We crashed on the beach that night and the following morning after my little swim I went looking for work. Geoff and I got a start straight away in a hotel called the 'Queen of Sheba' I was the bell-boy whilst Geoff helped clean the rooms. The hotel had three floors and could cater for well over three hundred guests, it was high season February 3rd 1984 and everything was in full swing. The Hotel people helped me find accommodation giving me a letter of recommendation, instructing me to take it to a letting agency they suggested. I had to surrender my passport to my new landlord 'Fagan' and then pay him when I got my first month wages, simple. He liked the deal and gave me the keys to a three-bed roomed apartment, five minutes from the beach opposite the so-called civilian airport, which I will tell you about later. The rent was only one hundred US dollars a month and well within my scope so we agreed. I didn't bother paying the house taxes or the water rates and they got knocked, actually I found them all rather inconvenient and so did everyone else.

Inside my new accommodation I had a small kitchen complete with cooker and fridge, in the dining area was a round table and four chairs and in each of the bedrooms were two mattresses. Actually it reminded me of a squat in Bayswater I once stayed in for a couple of months, that didn't have a stick of furniture either. Tracy was due to fly back to London in two weeks but changed her mind and moved in as well, not bothering to do much lying around and getting a nice tan.

The very next day at 7.30 I had to start work, but first they gave me breakfast, cornflakes and hot milk, cup of tea and jam on toast. After breakfast I got measured for my new uniform but until it arrived, I was to help out in the laundry. Out the back in the courtyard the dirty linen was stored in green wheelie bins. My task was to unload that lot into one of the five industrial washing machines, put the powder in, press the big green buttons and hey- presto we were off. They also had three big tumble dryers, confidently I can say it was a state of the art fully equipped modern laundrette, all mine to play with, I even had time for a crafty smoke of the local brand. Morning time went quickly and dinner was at 1 o'clock. The food was excellent, the same as the guests and during the day I could have as many teas and coffees as I fancied, properly the best job I ever had in my life. Home time was 3 o'clock unless I wasn't working overtime at the heated swimming pool as the lifeguard; the pay was equivalent to 400 US dollars a month, plus they would feed me, so much so I never once used the cooker at home, I didn't even know how to turn it on, besides I didn't even have any cutlery. Everything was disposable including all the clean sheets and towels I nicked from the hotel. To keep up with inflation my wages went up 25% every month, with everyone desperate to get the hands on the US dollar, dubbed the green back. Most of the bills were in low denotation ones and fives that meant they only had to change up as little as possible on anyone purchase. My uniform took about two weeks to arrive and my Supervisor 'Amelia' a nice lady in her mid fifties was pleased as punch when the man delivered it. We both became great friends and later on she helped me out big time, properly saving my life and Tracy's too. Looking really smart and professional in my light grey suit, the jacket resembled a school blazer with the 'Queen of Sheba' logo as the badge. I had a sky blue shirt a dark blue tie with the same matching logo, and topping that a grey matching cap. All I had to do was greet the guest at the front entrance, get their keys and carry the luggage to their room. Too get a bigger tip I used to make them laugh a dollar a joke was the going rate. One they partially enjoyed was about this girl I used to go out with, her name was Helen Back. 'Her dads name was Left who a brother had called 'Right' they played in the same soccer team and the Coaches' name her uncle was 'Never-look'. Furthermore the two weeks I went out with her was 'Hell and Back!'

Amelia asked me to work a couple of hour's overtime in the laundry every so often and I gladly agreed. Little did she know? I was working my own laundry scam, washing all my friends' dirty laundry at 2 dollars a load, my beer money. Word soon got round about my new service and my customers were queuing up at the back door. If an official asked whose washing was that, I just replied one of the guests and they walked away mystified, and I made a small fortune from the racket. Whilst I was there, I picked up some of the local lingo, things like 'the Mop' was pronounced 'Gummee,' and 'Lam-a-low' meant 'why not'. Strangely after a while I found I could understand what they were saying but had problems pronouncing the words. Payday was great fun and once a month by cheque, only problem was I needed my passport to cash it at the bank. The landlord 'Fagan' who had a nose to match didn't trust me one iota and escorted me right to the bank teller, standing by my side as I got the cash, then he retained my passport for another month or so. Indecently all the taxis were all brand new Mercedes, I heard donated by the German government and quite rightly so. They were cheap and plentiful using them all the time, going to and fro; in fact I got so lazy I hardly walked anywhere. Tracy decided to stay and moved in with me into my room, we went out together and I got her a job in the hotel with me as a chamber maid.

On my days off I would I pretend I was on holiday like the rest of them, regularly going diving with the aqua-lungs doing underwater spins, what an experience and highly recommended if you ever get the chance, indecently I went on to pass my International Divers Licence, thanks Mr Williams you were rite! Most evenings were spent touring the bars or just strolling around like everyone else. Some days I would dress smart, all in white including my white leather shoes, others days looking more like a right free-loading hippie and proud of it.

Mad barmy unexplainable things happened all the time and it wasn't all the beer and the pot I was smoking either. Coming out of the post office early one sunny morning I was reading my mail from mammy, when I noticed the bus from Egypt arriving. It had to stop at the pedestrian crossing to let me cross the road. Engrossed in my letter I looked up briefly and lifted my hand slightly to thank the driver for stopping. Not taking any more notice when I heard from an unwound window at the back of the bus some one shouting 'Scanlan, you old tosser' it was a couple of my old school mates Ian and Richard. They had been travelling around Egypt checking out the Pyramids and sailing down the Nile for a few months, heard through the worldwide grapevine I was here, and came to find me, what a crac. I hadn't seen them since we done that runner from the Indian in Southampton, I suppose it was fate working its hand again. They told me all about their recent expedition, it sounded really fascinating and exciting, real exploring and I was dead interested in what they said, right up my street. Day dreaming I thought 'I am going to do that one day.' They were a nice set of lads and I invited them back to my flat. They hadn't had a proper hot shower in days and whilst they washed and shaved I made the tea. Later on that morning I gave them a guided tour. We spent the next week or so reliving the old times back at school and so on, talking, drinking, eating, laughing, a bit of telephony and finally, smoking vast amounts of pot again. Before they left we couldn't resist doing another runner for old time's sake. I was in disguise and wore my dark glasses and baseball cap. Tucking into scampi chips and salad, I got thirsty and washed it down with a bottle of chilled Mateo's Rose, delicious! Luckily we didn't get caught, thoroughly enjoying the meal; it always seems to taste better when you are not paying. Years later we met up in a pub in Hampshire, reliving the experience making some of our other mate's unintentionally jealous, tuff luck boys no one was stopping you, although they say it's never to late.

Months ticked slowly and enjoyably by and by, and now it was May. My birthday passed so quickly I didn't even have time to think. The night before we had been a wild sand storm that blew up from the Sinai desert in Egypt. Perchance when I woke up that morning glanced through my little bedroom window. It was incredible and I remember rubbing my eyes to make sure I wasn't actually dreaming this or seeing things. It looked like it had been snowing, you know when everything covered in white, only difference was this wasn't white, but a yellow golden colour, like something from Alice and wonderland, it was absolutely spectacular. That morning Tracy and I went shopping, I bought a white t-shirt with an illustration of a green Cannabis plant on the front, with the words Lebanon printed in red on top of that, real hippie gear. That unimportant trivial purchase later on changed my life forever. I only had been wearing it for about five minutes just enjoying my pint, sitting in a relaxed posture like Eddie reading the paper, in fact the article reported that they had just discovered the AIDS virus, and the sexual revolution was over, indecently shares in the Durex Company quadrupled overnight. Anyway two armed soldiers approached me demanding to know where I got my t-shirt from. Bizarrely playing on the duke box was David Bowie's smash hit 'Life on Mars' and we had now come to the lyrics 'take a look at the law man, leaning on the wrong guy'. I thought how amusing especially sitting here in this alien looking yellow location. Pointing to the shop not saying much apart from 'over there', they went over to the shop returning about five minutes later, only this time with my money from the shopkeeper wanting to buy the shirt back. I refused point blank saying 'it's not for sale at any price', unrelenting they even offered me more money than I paid for it, now that's a first for any Jewish businessman! Bowie continued in the background and they continued to point out it could be dangerous for my health to wear it; I could even be shot! I thought what planet were these guys on, furthermore they can't dictate to me, and now started demanding I take it off immediately saying 'we are not messing about, don't you no we are at war with them.' This time I sarcastically held back my reply 'Look, you may be, but I'm not, additionally, where you both off school when they were teaching communication skills, and exactly what part of No, don't you compredy.' They said something to each other in Hebrew and walked away with the heads stuck up their arses, constantly turning around staring at me, so I returned their unwelcome gesture. Probably trying to work out what I actually meant, in the meantime Tracy inquisitively asked 'what was all that about Bob?

Unbeknown to me sitting on the next table was a very important person. He had European features and was casually dressed with a rolled up towel and beach mat and I guessed he was off down the beach. Actually I did notice him in the background becoming interested; he smiled and waved, I called over and said 'why don't you come and join us'. He sat down and introduced himself and I just couldn't believe I was hearing this strong Irish accent. 'Mehal O'Sulivan' is what they call me, amongst other things'. I stood up and we shook hands 'Bob Scanlan and this is my friend Tracy, Please to meet you I'm sure' His handshake was firm and I knew there was sincerity behind it, little did I know this would also turn out to be yet another life long friendship? He asked can I buy you both a drink'. Never one to turn down a free drink, I replied back in my Dublin accent 'yeah that will be grand, it's my birthday, and lets get hammered'. Summoning the barman over I ordered three cold beers with three Irish Jameson whiskeys as chasers. The sun was shinning brightly, the sea looked blue calm and cool, my whisky was chilled and life was couldn't have been better, happy 24th birthday.

Mehal became engrossed in my life style, asking me all about my job where I lived, and how long I had been doing all this carry-on. I felt confident because of his accent and told him the lot, including all that trouble at the Kibbutz and that dodgy business with the stolen Majors uniform. He asked if I still had it? We drank some more Irish and he confided in me about his mad life. He was a captain in the United Nations presently serving in the Lebanon. Far out and the t-shirt had brought us together. For the crac we sent Tracy over the shop to get him one. Not surprisingly she returned empty-handed saying the Israeli Secret Police had confiscated all the remaining shirts. Furthermore they were now getting pulled in every shop in Israeli; moreover I had the only one in the world, another first. Mehal and I couldn't believe it, so we both marched over to the shop-keeper and he again he offered me double my money back, it was that controversial, I snubbed his offer saying 'go and take a run and jump pal' he didn't have a clue what I meant and looked some what bewildered, making us all laugh as we left.

We moved on to another bar it was called 'The Old Kent Road' and everyone kept asking me where I got the shirt. Out of devilment I told them 'Ah sure there's loads left' and sent them back to the same shopkeeper. This went on for months and the guy at the shop was pulling his hair out with all these lost sales, what a wind up! Settling down I introduced Mehal to all my friends overlooking his military status as he asked. The bar was set back north away from all the posh hotels and palm trees but we still ordered the finest champagne. Most of my neighbours were Arabs and this was my manner, and my little flat was just a stones throw away. Mehal loved it and we started singing Irish songs as the day progressed into night and then back into day again. We got so paralytic he couldn't make it back to his posh hotel, bobbling back to my flat having to crash on one of the mattresses. That morning I didn't bother going to work, probably because I didn't open my eyes until 2 o'clock the following afternoon. I remember everyone had gone to work and I had the flat to myself. Whilst drinking a cup of tea and lighting my cigarette I read a note left on the table from Mehal, explaining he would be back Wednesday with a few of his UN mates and good luck. Shaving with my cut-throat razor in the mirror, I thought about the crac and how funny it all was and couldn't wait until next Wednesday. What a birthday, properly the best birthday in my life. Presently though I had a few dollars left and was going to smoke yet another joint and go for a livener and see my hippie friends. Life was great fun and I wasn't at all sad about leaving my past behind. One sobering thought was the fact I had no medical insurance and this was a predicament for us all, but I coped and lucky didn't get sick.

Although one lad called Mad Mat from Leeds wasn't so lucky and nearly lost his life after being glassed in a pub brawl, just my luck I happened to be in the wrong place at the wrong time, why me again I thought! Anyway, it was at a bar called 'The Better Day's Night Club.' I suppose there must have been about thirty regulars in that afternoon and I was standing by the bar with Tracy, when abruptly a gang of around twenty Arab guy's gate crashed our bar looking for this particular German guy called 'Wolfgang'. Apparently he scored a load of drugs off them and done a runner with all the proceeds. They were absolutely fuming and stormed in wearing red and white chequered scarf's, carrying baseball bats, screaming and shouting in Arabic, I did recognise one word 'Ale-Baba' which means 'Thief' High on something probably heroin or Cocaine demanding him, the drugs or their money back or both. The thing is 'Wolfgang' had planned the whole thing and used their money to pay for his return flight home. I admit I was scared and

I remember thinking someone's going to get hurt here, this is every man and women for himself. Indecently dotted around the bar were eight television screens blasting out the Irish Band U2, live at Red rock, singing 'Sunday Bloody Sunday' and perchance this was a Sunday afternoon. The military or police were nowhere to seen and as a result the place erupted into a frenzy of violence. At one point literally exploding, even the girls joined in, handbags at dawn you might say. Like a scene from one of them old black and white Wild West cowboy films where it all kicks off in the Last Chance saloon. One of them made a lunge for me and Tracy so I had no choice but to take him straight out with a punch to the throat. He couldn't breath and collapsed in a big heap and for one terrible moment I actually thought 'Oh Jesus, I've killed him', but it was either me or him. Amongst all this commotion I noticed Bono was waving his white flag singing 'no more, no more'. In time with the music one of the Americans bravely stood on a table and hit out at the Arabs with the butt end of a chair, he took loads of them out. Funny thing was reader, the chair didn't disintegrate like in the Cowboy film, but the expression on their faces was the same. All hell was breaking louse, like one of those mad nightmares and I couldn't wake up from. One of the Arabs smashed a Gin bottle across the bar, turning round holding it by the neck swiping out wildly at Mad Mat. Like in slow motion the blow catching him on the left side his of his face. Half of his cheek and eye practically fell out and blood was spurting out all over the place. Then if that wasn't enough a live petrol bomb was thrown across the bar. On impacting the toilet door it exploded in a ball of flames, luckily no one was in there. Someone blew a whistle and all the Arabs ran out in a 'bomb shell pattern' basically all in different directions. The Barman a Dutch guy managed to put the fire out with distinguisher and we evacuated the building to a small green out the front. I did my best wrapping clean bar mats to his wound and apart from a few black eyes everyone else was fine. Then all tooled up with their Uzis sub machine guns and ferocious looking dogs the Israeli Army arrived on the scene and not surprisingly surrounded us at gun point. Their medic was quite friendly though and spoke fluent English; he was a brilliant doctor and I helped him on the scene with one of the nurses. Eventually they took him away in the ambulance. After that I was delegated to explain exactly what happened, but I wasn't prepared to talk about anything at gun point. They lowered there weapons and I spoke to the Colonel and told him what 'Wolfgang' had done, and the fact we were innocent. He wasn't too impressed but said, if we cleared up the mess, repainted the toilet door and paid a fine he was prepared to leave it at that and take no further action, we agreed. They were really crafty though and incarcerated Mad Mat in one of their military hospital, refusing to let him go until they got some money, they were actually holding him hostage. We had a whip-a-round to pay the fine and raised over 500 US dollars and he was officially medically discharged. Comrades over adversity you might say, but believe me if I ever see that Wolfgang again, sparks will fly.

The weeks passed into months and I was having the life of Riley. Mehal and his mates came and went on a regular basis and we all became great buddies. Over a cup of tea sitting round the table we talked about the War in Lebanon and what the Israelis were really up too. I found out all sort of secrets, one was that all the public telephones were bugged, and they opened the mail, what a nerve. Unbelievably one afternoon he asked me to be a Special Agent for the United Nations and Tracy as well. They gave me the rank of Major and Tracy became my Left Tenant. Well this was the opportunity I had been waiting for and couldn't wait to get officially involved, actually I was hoping he would ask me for weeks now. It was really exciting and it took a bit of time to sink in that I was a real life spy with life long 'Diplomatic Immunity.' Furthermore I was now in charge of my own Platoon of three hundred men and our names where officially added to the regiment's role of honours list. What's more Mehal introduced me to a guy from the C. I. A. who had access to secret military equipment; this gave me a lot more confidence as now it became a joint operation between the United Nations and Americans; he's still in it so we will call him Steve.

The job as the bellboy already gave me the perfect cover for the mission we were about too pull off. Around that time Nelson Mandela was being held captive by the South Africans and they wouldn't let him go, for neither love nor money, it was called Apatite. The world responded by slapping an International trade embargo on the lot of them, economically it was starting too bite crippling their Nation. Their currency the 'Rand' like the 'Shekel' became worthless over night. Although they still had their diamonds and gold reserves in tact, so in theory could trade to a renegade state if it could find one. Our intelligence led us to be believe Israel was one and Russia was another, I heard there was a few that where never got caught.

The Airport in Elait was meant to be for civilian use only. We thought: If that was the case why was it patrolled 24 hours a day by arm guards, with their fierce looking dogs with sharp teeth? They where up to a load of hanky-panky and we made it our business to find out exactly what it was? We gave the mission a code name 'British Bulldog' and set about planning our objectives and back up exit strategies in case it all went wrong. The target was surrounded by a high ten-foot perimeter wire meshed fence and rolled on top was barbed wire and at each end was a look out tower. We noticed Military planes with the South African markings arriving, properly from Johannesburg and flying out the same day with the illegal cargo. The Israelis were up too their necks in it, exchanging arms for the gold and uncut diamonds and then secretly stashing the Bullion in some Swiss bank account and to make matters worse double-crossing the Americans by denying it. More importantly thousands of black people where loosing their lives with these illegal arms, something had to be done. At the west end of the runway they had a garden the size of half-a-football pitch. Sign posted everywhere telling you to 'keep of the grass' and 'no entry' skull and cross warning you to keep away. Effectively with the clever use of warning signs, high shrubbery and tall palm tress they made it impossible to take photographs from a distance, but we planned a way round all that lot.

Mehal had to return to the regiment and my mission while he was away was to monitor the situation, recording the planes numbers and start to build a case against them. What's more if I had any South Africans booked in my hotel, I would thoroughly search their rooms going through all their personnel details taking photographs of the identification papers and so on, especially if they were pilots. Reels of film later we started to build up a pattern of the illegal activities. After collecting all this covert information, Mehal, Steve, Tracy and I agreed to meet outside a cigarette kiosk opposite the airport posing as holiday makers. Sounding like John Wayne whilst shaking my hand firmly said, 'hi Bob 'I've been looking forward to meeting you. I'm Steve, stand there whilst I take some photos to send home to Mammy'. This was the code for me too positioned myself with my back to the terminal, getting it in the background. We managed to shoot a few but the guards took the film out of the comer and hushed us away. Undeterred we set off too a three story shopping complex, slightly to the east of the airport with a good view over looking the runway. Up there was a bar with a veranda and from that vantage point photographs could be taken. Sitting down I ordered four large Irish whiskies and a bowl of chips with cheese on top, yum-yum! This time Tracy would act as the tourist and again stood with the air base in the background. I had only taken a few when I was spotted from the lookout tower. Within minutes the guards arrived on the veranda, confiscating the film out of the camera. The thing was we were expecting that and swapped the film just before they swooped; the file was getting bigger by the hour but still not enough though.

The following Shabbat I wore the stolen Israeli Majors uniform and marched inside the terminal, it was like our Sunday afternoon and they only had a skeleton staff on duty. The uniform looked the dogs under carriage. Tracy used her sewing skills to tailor it, measure in fact you might say, additionally I was visible armed with my Israeli gun in its holster supplied by Mehal. Wearing dark glasses and an Israeli Paratroopers cap I causally strolled in having a good look around, actually I was bricking it. My Hebrew wasn't up to scratch, as I said I could understand them but couldn't pronouns the words, so instead put on a stern face occasionally saluting saying 'Shabbat Shalom'. No one asked to see my I.D. just as well I didn't have any; my only defence was declaring my Diplomatic Status. Furthermore I didn't' see one civilian aircraft or passenger. It was definitely all military personnel and Police unloading heavy crates with a forklift truck, probably the Gold. Other crates were stacked up in the corner ready to be shipped out; they had the words Uzi written on the side, the guns and explosives. As causally as I walked in I walked out, got into a stolen white Mercedes Taxi and driven away at high speed, changing into my hippie gear in the back as we drove along. The whole operation took less than three minutes and they didn't have a clue, until now that is. Later on that afternoon I met up with Mehal and Steve at the pub and made a full written report, more evidence. After business we got absolutely rat arsed smoked vast amounts of pot going for a midnight swim naked, reminding me of the forty foot. Apparently the white Mercedes was later found burnt out some where in the Negev desert along with the uniform, that's a shame because I liked that.

Now we were starting to catalogue an astonishing case against this lot, but unfortunately still not enough concrete in your face proof. Again having more tricks than them wagon load of monkeys we moved onto the master plan. This was the most dangerous of them all but we had no choice, it had to be done, there was no one else. It was decided the only place to take the best photos was in the west garden, but that meant getting in close to the fence. We noticed every morning at 11 o'clock the sprinkler system was switched on to water the garden and then we would play our ace. Steve said he could arrange a live satellite link to concede with the timing of the sprinklers. So he ordered one like you were asking for fish and chips or something, catching them red handed in the act. Mobile phones were still ten years in the future, in the meantime he would get a sate of the art camera, linking up and beaming the pictures direct to a Satellite, stopping the Army nicking the film at the scene if we got caught.

The night before the mission we stole all the warning signs to keep off, and keep out. Now we could pretend we didn't even know it was a restricted area. The four of us met up just before 11 o'clock and Steve handed me the camera and said 'just aim and press the red button good luck' In case this all went belly up Mehal was armed and also taking photographs of the whole manoeuvre as it unfolded, oh they hadn't noticed all the danger signs missing and hadn't been replaced yet. Bang on time the sprinklers sprung into action and we were on. Months of planning and meetings had culminated in this moment and it was now or never. Causally hand in hand we strolled onto the plot, laughing properly with nerves? Dressed as a free loading hippie I deliberately wore an old pair of old flip flops and cut down Levi jeans, whilst Tracy was practically naked apart from her black bikini bottoms, a nice smile and a pair of Ray Ban sunglasses. We deliberately choose to dress like this to prove we were not armed and anyone fool could see this. Not wanting to make Tracy nervous, I hid that fact I wished I hadn't got her involved and thought about aborting the whole mission there and then, but it was too late, she was very brave. Worse than on my driving test the water droplets were the size of marbles, bouncing of the neatly cut green lawn and tricking down Tracy's cleavage, for a laugh I took a photo of that and sent it to my mates in 'The Pentagon'. The downpour

Robert Charles Scanlan

did have its uses though, distracting everyone and seriously impairing the guard's vision from the watch towers, plus they wouldn't be expecting any trespasser at that precise time.

Tracy acted as if she was a model posing top less in front of the fence, whilst I actually aimed the lens directly at the aircraft unloading in the back ground, real James Bond stuff. Two minutes into the sting a suspicious guard appeared from my left hand side, pulling his gun from the holster and pointing it directly at me, I thought here we go. Out of the corner of my eye I saw Mehal undo the little clip securing his gun in the holster! Believe me with all this water surging upwards, downwards made it even more nerve-racking. By-now I must have taken about fifty brilliant shots, busting them wide open with the new evidence, what's more there was absolutely nothing he could do because I had already sent them to the final frontier, far out. We knew this could happen and trained for this event. Firstly we were not to run; if we did he would surely take aim and shoot us both dead in our stride. So as rehearsed we brass-end it out using the rules of engagement to our advantage. Kneeling down in front of him putting our hands on our head, shouting don't shoot, don't shoot, now if he did it, it would be first degree murder and he knew it. As by prior arrangement all our friends starting hanging around the perimeter watching this dead lock unfold, the witnesses. One of them Jackie Kennedy started shouting over 'leave them alone they are friendly,' some big shot Israeli yelled out 'shoot the spies' he sounded South African. This was a bizarre and an out of the ordinary situation for him to comprehend and he kept looking around nervously. By now he was soaking wet from the water lashing down, very edgy and probably wishing he hadn't bothered, really it was like being in an Asian monsoon and he was making a complete pratt of himself. It didn't matter about us as we were suitable addressed for the occasion, more deliberate confusion. Distracting him further was the fact Tracy was nearly naked and all the warning signs were missing. He didn't know his arse from his elbow so confused he took aim and pulled back the safety catch on his pistol. It was a Magnum and I was looking right down the barrel, I thought 'this is it Bobby boy', Still topless he then started pointing the thing at Tracy, this worried me, so I pleading with him 'if you must, point it at me Sir', he replied 'Felling lucky punk, stop talking or I blow your fecking head off', he wasn't bluffing. At that aim, I indicated with my eyes for Tracy too lower her head and stop looking at him. I followed resisting the Lords prayer and strangely thought about my Mammy, she must have been praying for me. By now we had caused quite a commotion and another guard arrived demanding to know what exactly our business was here. Replying as the water continued to pelt down in buckets 'I was just taking some holiday snaps for mammy and didn't realise this was a restricted area.' Then someone eventually managed to turn the water off, however they all looked laughable soaked to the skin with water dripping of their poin-ted peak caps, more deliberate tactics to confuse the real issue. Not believing a word the officer snatched the camera off me inspecting it thoroughly, demanding too know where I got it, 'I bought it in London, Sir' answering back, 'Ah, you are a British terrorist then?' Calling to mind and like a scene from a Benny Hill show I remember one guard idiotically looking in the air to see if he could spot the Satellite. Pratt. The situation was now starting to spiral completely out of their control and into mine. The guard asked for our passports and I explained trembling 'the landlord Fagan has them and you will have to ask him, also he could vouch for our identities and furthermore could guarantee we were definitely not spies'. One of them ran over to Fagan's house dead opposite and 'Fagan' innocently and inadvertently confirmed our cover story, deliberately puzzling and confusing the issue even further. Their captain arrived with a big black dog questioning us even more. Now there were three of them with pistol drawn at dawn you might say. Explaining yet again 'I'm sorry its all my fault and it was just a mistake Sir, please, we work in the Queen of Sheba Hotel, I'm just a mere bell-boy and Tracy is a chamber maid, what's more our supervisor Amelia would also vouch for us, not spies just stupid tourist, also how was I to know I can't see any signs saying 'keep out'? He wasn't sure what to do now but had no choice anyway but to check my story, radioing ahead for a squad car to pick her up at the hotel reception. Lights flashing sirens blaring amongst the crowd Amelia appeared on the scene, shouting in Hebrew as she got out of the back seat. Immediately the guards disarmed their weapons sliding them back into their holsters. Actually the expression on there faces said they were glad to see her as much as I. Almost instantaneously, Tracy jumped up embracing her and the cover story was well and truly worked to perfection. In any case I knew they wouldn't have fired because we were obviously European and there were too many witness, the international fall out would have been too much for them

Robert Charles Scanlan

to handle, proving the point the Israeli policy shoot first ask question later. Getting to my feet I stood up requesting my camera back, so there would be no evidence. Point blank they refused and immediately confiscated it. We knew later on they would examine it under a microscope uncovering what it really was, but by then it would have been too late and we would have got away. They followed us back to the flat and we waited patiently for the others to arrive safely home, which after a snail's pace thank God they did. Mehal and Steve had to go to the police station first and confirm we were both in fact under cover Diplomats, apparently they weren't too happy. As we toured the bars that night suited and booted I was also armed, I felt really hard like the Lone Ranger and Mehal was Tonto real hero's proud to be part of the posse, Yee-ha. Surprisingly most of the guards accepted we busted them and those that knew saluted me smiling. All accept one that is, a racist South African guy with a chip on his shoulder, properly the same one who yelled over. The thing is, if he had actually caught me, he would have pulled that trigger and asked questions later! He was a real pig always hassling me over my I. D. not liking the fact we had one over on him and his fellow white countrymen, plus he knew I was a higher rank than him, jealousy more than anything. To wind him up even further I use to smile sarcastically and salute him but he never retuned. Indecently we stopped the illegal trade and it cost both nations billions of dollars, apparently they weren't too happy either! In due course Nelson Mandela was finally released six years later 1990 and became the first democratically elected State President of South Africa. Looking back I like to think I played a part in his release and possible that was the highlight of my career.

Over the months we kept an eye on the situation, making sure they didn't resume trade, but the Israelis wanted me out of the country as soon as possible and started boycotting me giving me a hard time. First off the cigarette kiosks would serve me; I got barred from all the pubs and restaurants, the taxi drivers wouldn't turn up, my mail was opened and one woman spat in my face calling me a terrorist, they even stopped me diving with the aqua lungs. What made it worse for me was Fagan had a grand son called Kenny and over the months we got to know each other. He was around twelve years old and looked up too me. Everyday after work he would wait for me to pass by his house and have a chat. He loved practicing his English on me and in turn he taught me Hebrew. Anyway he didn't go to school so consequently I became his only friend; I felt sorry for him and was always buying him ice-cream sweets and pop, routine in fact. He loved my stories about London and his favourite football team Manchester United and George Best; I even managed to get a poster of the team sent from England directly to him. Believe me he was over the moon, a dog with two tails you might say. Anyway his granddad Fagan told him 'I was a spy' and tried to stop us talking. Kenny on the other hand had been watching too many James Bond movies and thought it was all very exiting and asked if he could help me. So cunningly we started to meet in the park and I recruited him as my double agent, he loved it! His mission should he decide to accept was too break into Fagan's safe and retrieve my passport and hand it back to me. Apparently he started hanging around while Fagan dialled the numbers on the safe and then in the middle of the night opened it wearing gloves and took the passport, and as a present an Israeli 'Star of David flag'. I was so proud of him, and as a reward I gave him my 'United Nations Blue Cap', complete with badge and told him to say that he found it in the bus station a week after I left. He put it on and we saluted each other, in fact there was a tear in my eye as well, and that was the last I saw of him, thanks Kenny! Fagan went mad because he couldn't work out how I did it and what was really winding him up was the fact he didn't get his final months rent. He went to the Police but they couldn't help and was running around Elait driving me mad for the money and flag, threatening me with all sorts of people and things and at one point even accused me of hypnotising him, far out!

Tracy was due to fly home the next day so I tried to get a ticket on the same flight; it was the Israeli airline E.l.l.A. They refused to let me travel on one of their planes booking me on an Olympic Airlines the following day, saying the Greeks fecking brought you here they can fecking well get you out. To be honest the novelty had worn off and I had had enough and wanted too leave as son as possible, so the flight was booked and paid for that very moment. It was a little sad saying cheerio to all my dear friends and leaving this extraordinary mad place behind, but I was looking forward to my new life, living by the sea in Essex England. Looking through the back windows of the bus as I departed company, I passed through the thought gate once more doing that mad spinning off thing that I do. Contemplating on a scale of one to ten Bobby Boy what you would give this? Well I gave it a nine, excellent!

Robert Charles Scanlan

Ben-Gurion international airport was next and yet more fun and games with the authorities. The Army were waiting for us at the arrivals desk. We got the third degree about what we had been up to since we got here, searching Tracy's luggage they found a brand new electrical iron I nicked from the hotel, taking it away to be x-rayed and then confiscating it saying it could be a bomb. They brought in the snuffer dogs and took Tracy behind the scenes to be stripped searched, I insisted on being there but they wouldn't have it. Additionally even though I wasn't flying until tomorrow they quickly searched my gear as well and strangely asked if I spoke Hebrew, I lied and said I didn't. Eventually they let her board the plane, we had a little cuddle and said our good byes, I remember saying 'don't worry I will see you in a few days love you'. It was now Sunday morning 11 am and as I watched from the viewing gallery I saw her plane take off. I was the last one out and it was a feeling of aloneness I will never forget, totally isolated and cut off, but at least I didn't have to worry about her safety now. In five hours she would be in London and within seven sitting in her own back garden properly sipping a glass of wine, whilst I was still ensnared in this God-for-sachem hell hole. That's when all the grief started, not surprising the Army wouldn't let me stay in the airport escorting me at gun point to a bus shelter on the outskirts, forcibly telling me 'don't come back until tomorrow, other wise there will be big trouble, compredy.' I had to keep positive frame of mind and tried not to get too paranoid, at least I had my little sleeping bag, my walkman and a small camping stove a little food something to drink and a full packet of cigarettes. Eventually I found a park which had a nice wooded area and made camp in the dense under-growth. What I can say, it wasn't the Hilton and nor could I sleep a wink, I kept thinking about all that mischief I got up too and how much bother I had caused these guys. During the night I listened to Phil Collins and said my little prayer.

Look God, I have never spoken to you, but now I want too say, 'how do you do.' You see God, they told me you didn't exist, and like I fool, I believed all this.

I wonder God, if you would shake my hand; somehow, I feel you will understand. Strange, I had to come to this hellish place, before I had time to see your face.

I guess the zero hour will soon be here, but I am not afraid since I know you are near. Well God, I will have to go, I love you lots and this I want you to know.

Looks like this will be a horrible flight, who knows, I may come to your house tonight. Though I wasn't friendly with you before, I wonder God, if you would wait at the door.

Look, I am crying, shedding my tears! I wish I known you these all these years. Well, I guess there isn't much more to say, but I am sure glad, God, I met you today.

Monday, dawn was breaking the birds were singing and my small bottle of calor gas had nearly run out, although there was just enough blue flame to heat my last tin of hot dogs. All wrapped up warm and cosy in my sleeping bag I also enjoyed an apple and drank some fresh orange juice from a carton and lit my last cigarette. That was it. All I had left to my name was a ten-dollar bill to pay the airport tax, no food or cigarettes and unless I get on that plane I was in serious jeopardy of loosing my freedom if not my life. The flight was the last one of the day due to take off at midnight, boarding at 10 pm, so I tried to check in then. One of the other Israeli passengers jumped the queue, deliberately causing a big row with me. It must have been staged because the Army clocked all this bollocks going on and started on me again. Saying I was a trouble-maker, making all sort of allegations, [which were all true] asking all sort of bullshit questions where I been, who I met, how did I support myself. I responded by saying 'Under the rules of the Geneva Convention I don't have to answering any more of your questions' They didn't like that one bit and started talking to each other in Hebrew about me, what they didn't know was I could understand most of what they were actually saying. One of them said that I was an enemy of the state of Israel and if it was up to him he would line me up against a wall and shoot me.' They started searching my gear only this time found my 'Star of David flag'. I had folded the flag up tightly and then squeezed it in a cigarette packet, resealing it in the original plastic sleeve; it looked and felt like an ordinary packet of unopened Marlborough cigarettes. They kept looking at it and me, when one of them asked if I would like a cigarette, the game was up because he opened the packet any way. Immediately confiscating it remarking, 'you're not taking any trophies home with you Mr, where's the uniform you nicked from Kibbutz Beit Zera and who open that safe in Elait, and who was my

Israeli contact, they new they had a double agent on there hands, but never sussed it was a twelve year old boy. I remember saying 'I don't know what you're talking about.' They strip-searched me next, making me walk naked through a metal detector with my hands on my head, a bit like that guy in the film midnight express. Then if that wasn't enough got a bendy metal rod with a camera and small light fitted to the end, I thought what the feck they were going to do with that. One of them started waving it around in my face, I thought 'oh no Dover Hover point all over again'. Fortunately for me he was having a laugh just peering down the metal tubes of my ruck-sack. Although I did have to bend over again and touch my toes as they looked up my anus, we all know why, perverts. They let me get dressed and then demanded that they took my fingerprints and photograph. Then they kept me with them until the very last moment just before take off, watching the clock on the wall it said 11.45. I was starting to get a bit nervous with all this and thought they weren't going to let me go, thinking 'jail again'. With only minutes left two armed soldiers entered the room and ordered me to stand up, one stood in front of me whilst the other stood slightly back on the right. Obeying the command they then marched me at gunpoint all the way up to the aircraft door. Affirming 'don't you ever dare come back here, got it,' and I slowly stepped on board the Boeing DC10. Moments later I heard the door close and a hissing sound as the pressurized locks of the aircraft door engaged. I remember thinking: thank feck for that.

Feeling at ease and relieved I remember said to the air hostess in Greek jokingly 'Yatzoo ferist-of' which in English means 'it's very hot today isn't it?, Laughing she showed me to my seat and guess what, next to me was same guy who gave me all that grief at the check in, I thought 'I'm going to fecking have you mate'. The flight took about five hours and we never said one word to each other, you could have cut the atmosphere with a knife and he knew I was up to something. In fact he had the widow seat and refused to make eye contact. After having a splendid traditional Greek lunch of stuffed tomatoes and salad I landed at London Heathrow airport around 5 am. I remember it was a crisp clean sunny Tuesday morning and the sky was that pale blue colour only broken up by the clouds that bunched together like cotton wool buds. Out of devilment going through British passport control I spoke to the Special Branch officer on duty, stating whilst pointing, 'see that guy over there, he was sitting next to me in the plane and kept taking about guns and explosive, I think he's a bit dodgy, I would have a word with him if I was you'. I waited till they led him away by the arm, looking back over his shoulder he saw me sarcastically smirking. He wasn't at all pleased especially when I pointed my index finger in the air, waving it around mouthing 'spin on that you fecker'.

The bus service from the airport dropped me off at Victoria coach station. Recollecting all the magic buses I caught from here and perchance fate had brought me to this place one more time, I did think never again. The old Victorian clock was still hanging from the roof on its steel rods and it was precisely 'five-thirty.' The first of the day's tourist were boarding the coach and its destination was clearly written in the front window 'Athens' reflecting been there, done that got the t-shirt and what a crac that was! It felt grand to be back in these familiar places and even better as I didn't have to return to them carrot crunchers in Andover. In fact apart from Tracy know one even knew I was back in the UK and that's how I wanted it. London was still asleep as I causally strolled along the Thames crossing Tower Bridge heading east. The tide was in and I smelled the sea as it lapped against the mossy green banks. I'd recognize that smell anywhere, one of dead fish diesel fuel and what seemed like boiled cabbage. There was a pair of barges heading downstream with their cargo of yesterday's unwanted rubbish and a man out walking his dog tipped his Bowler hat and said in that unmistakable English accent 'Good morning Sir'. Passing the Houses of Parliament I watched as Big Ben's hands slowly ticked away the new day, it was precisely 6 o'clock and the famous chimes rang out across Whitehall. I stood there for a moment or so taking in the scenery and thought about what Winston Churchill once said, 'History will be kind to me for I intend to write it'. There were a few red buses and black cabs floating about and the street cleaners in the orange jackets were busy from the night before. The hot-dog sellers were gathering nearby and the junkies were off getting their morning fix. Passing a few dossers swigging on the bottle of cider I sat down in a shop entrance, no one was around and the street was completely deserted, exhausted I must have fallen asleep. An English copper woke me saying 'Wakie Wakie' rubbing my eyes and yawning, I explained I wasn't a tramp, and that I just landed from Israel heading for Liverpool Street. If that's the case he remarked 'you don't mind me having a look at your passport then'.

Robert Charles Scanlan

Thinking he's on the ball, and after inspecting it became very interested in my travels, noticing all the foreign stamps that I had proudly accumulated. Then enquired in a friendly manner, 'what's your final destination, Robert' I told him 'Southend on Sea', he said I was in the wrong railway station, suggesting it would be better from Fenchurch Street. He had a kind smile so cheekily I asked him for a cigarette, instead of giving me one he gave me near enough a full pack of ten embassies and my faith in human nature was instantly restored, it just goes to show not all coppers are bad. Then if he hadn't done enough stopped a Royal mail van instructing the driver to drop this officer [me] off at the right station. As we drove through London's deserted streets the all time classic 'that's entertainment' by the Jam blasted out on the cab radio, and I knew I was home. The postman smiled and handed me the morning newspaper. Sadly the front page reported the death of one of my all time hero's, Sir Bobby Moore. For a split second I relived the moment twenty sevens previously, when Bobby kissed the World Cup and waved to me at Piccadilly Circus and perchance fate had also brought me here once more. Indecently did you know he played for England 108 times, scoring 24 goals and was voted the greatest player in the last fifty years?

Having to Dodge the rail fare again I got past the train guard by flashing around another bent ticket I picked up in the bin, travelling in the dodgy smelly third class again as usual. Tracy had given me a hand drawn map to get to her house and after boycotting the final inspector arrived at her doorstep within ten minutes. Seriously, my belly thought my throat had been cut, tucking into my first tradition English break-fast in months. Having the lot including black pudding plus three rashers of bacon, two sausages, red tomatoes slightly grilled, fried mush-rooms with fried eggs and hot toast, but not from the nightly bonfire these ones just popped up. Oh and it was so lovely, rinsing it all down with gallons of tea, yummy! Unshaven and exhausted plus having no sleep for days on end, I was the worse for weather, but at least now I had a full stomach. Only problem was unless I got to bed rapidly, I would probably collapse in a big heap on the floor having to be rushed away in another speeding ambulance, just like that woman at the school play!

Waking up some time later the sunlight was beaming through the net curtains that draped this unfamiliar half-opened window. There was a slight breeze and in the distance I could hear an ice-cream van and children laughing and playing. My opening thought was 'I must be near a school or a playground but where, what day is it, what time is it, and finally what country am I in?' Then I heard the 6 o 'clock BBC news on the TV coming from downstairs. It was muffled, but laying there with my eyes open staring at the ceiling I heard the man talking about Nelson Mandela- and all that rioting going on in South Africa. For a split second, I buried my head under the pillow and thought 'oh Jesus no'. Eventually after day dreaming and staring into space for awhile I realised were I was and I got here, said my prayers blessed myself and thanked God for coming out of it alive.

Venturing apprehensively downstairs, Tracy excitedly introduced me to her family. There was Jade the little one about five, Adrian the brother, and Colin the step-dad who strangely she called the Head! Ruby, Tracy's mum was on holiday in Spain with her lover 'Archie' and wouldn't be back until next week, so I would have that pleasure then, strange but true. The Head told me I had just missed Mehal the following week. He had come to England especially to see me and drop of my uniform, but had left his telephone number in Ireland. I thought maybe he wanted me to go on another mission, and I believe me I would have gone. Anyways the Head fetched a scrap of paper from the sideboard with the number and I immediately phoned him. He was worried for our safety and was checking to see if we got out OK. We spoke for a long time and he told me Ronald Regan himself tacked the Israelis with our photographic and written evidence. He went on to point out my Diplomatic Immunity was for life and the Regiment was really proud of us both. Unfortunately I lost contact with him and Vera suggested publishing my diary in the hope he might read it and come forward. So if anyone knows a Mehal O'Sulivan who was a Captain serving in the Lebanon as part of United Nations in 1984 contact my publishers, there is a reward.

The following morning I set off down to the Job Centre to sign the unemployment register. I showed the my passport and said that Tracy and I were both returning migrants and homeless having to live on the beach in a tent, needing at least a thousand pounds to put down as a deposit on a flat. They fell for it and that day I got the biggest fastest greenest Giro you have ever seen in your life. The guy at the post office instantaneously got insanely jealous, asking if I intended bringing any more in for this amount, I asked why, what's it to you, I'm entitled to it otherwise they wouldn't have given me it to me in the first place. He muttered something about having to the get the money ready, to wind him up further I said 'I was expecting another one soon and I would come back to him personally, now that he knew me and had checked my passport' He didn't like that one bit, his face seething at full capacity as I made him count the money in front of me, all in twenties. Whilst trying to cram it into my pockets I sarcastically finished him of by saying, 'till the next time then, get the money ready adios amigo!

Straight away and somewhat loaded I heading off to buy some new clobber. Coming out of the shop looking like a new pin, next on my agenda was haircut and then a few pints of the black stuff for lunch. Over my pint I studied the racing form in the Daily Mirror, feeling lucky I backed a horse called 'Gold Song' in the 3.30 at Newmarket, plus my old school friend Richard Rowe was riding. The price was 12 to 1, so I put one hundred pounds on its nose to win, and it romped home by furlongs thanks Dickey, indecently he went on to win the Derby. Winning over twelve hundred pounds plus my stake money back. Now I was really loaded, what a day, in fact this was bordering on one increasable week for me; lady luck must have been on my side yet again.

Back at the house that afternoon the 'Head' told me where there was a flat to rent and the grocer was the man to see. With no time to waste, I took a stroll down to see him, carrying some of my fat wedge with me. Getting there he was just packing up for the day, introducing myself I asked 'are you the chap who has the flat for rent'? He answered 'yes that right mate, my name is 'Barry'. Smiling I came back with 'pleased to meet you I m sure, my name is Bob, can I give you a hand.' As we loaded the oranges boxes back inside his shop he put in plain words. It was short term let, as he was selling the business and the flat went with it. What's more he would expect me to leave when he asked me too do so, a gentleman's agreement? Giving him my word we shook hands, and I paid him. Stretching my all ready incredible luck even further I asked him for a letter. Stating it was unfurnished and I would need a grant to get things like a bed, cooker and general household goods like bleach and bulbs, things everyone needs, he did it. Feeling rather pleased with myself I went for a pint, contemplating all what had happened to me since leaving Israel. Standing by the bar smoking a fat cigar next to the sea with my own flat, fine looking clothes and pockets full of money I thought 'what's next'. The next day was Thursday so I got up early to be first in the queue at the job centre and the doors opened bang on time at 9.15 am. Again, I explained to the same clerk as yesterday the predicament I now found myself in today. Basically I needed another Giro to buy furniture for my new flat otherwise I can't move in. He read my letter from Barry explaining it was unfurnished and approved my request, thanks a lot Maggie. At 10 o' clock I heard my name being called over the public announcement service and I walked out with yet another grand. For the crac back at the post office I went to the same guy from yesterday, I just couldn't resist it. This time he was really up in arms, enraged I thought he was going to have a rupture saying 'what's the point in going to work all your life, paying Taxes when I would be better of on the dole like you'. Smiling sarcastically whilst nodding like a Dougal I agreed saying, 'your probably right mate, in fact instead at moaning about it, why don't you do us all a favour and just do it.' 'Do what' he snarled back, 'do your job and count my money' was my on the spot instant response'.

Spoilt for choice with bundles of cash and smitten with my recent successes I went for breakfast in some posh restaurant, ordering a bottle of the finest pink champagne money could buy, then one of my all time favourites' fresh lobster. This one was really fresh, in fact it was swimming around in a fish tank and I remember peering through the glass rubbing my hands together saying 'I'm going to eat you'. Only difference was, this time I didn't have to do a runner. Actually I gave the waitress a 50.00 tip and told her jokingly here's another tip 'don't get off a moving bus', she laughed and slyly slipped me her telephone number, I never bothered though. Back at the flat Tracy was busy cleaning and putting up the curtains she just bought, and I sat down on the new furniture watching Charlie Chaplin on the television, counting all my free money. That weekend I just pottered around, putting up shelving taking it easy, thinking what a mad week I had just had rags to riches you might say.

It didn't take long before my flat got straight and I started work in the amusement arcade that Monday. Learning all the bingo slang like

Kellies eye number one, legs eleven, two little ducks quack-quack, key of the door twenty one, two fat ladies eighty eight, blind ninety and all that baloney. The prizes were crap and so was the job, only lasting one game saying balls to all this and walking out. Anyway I had more important issue to attend too like signing on the dole and eagerly awaited my big fat green giro to come through the post. Again at the post office and went and saw you know who! 'Not you again' he said as I passed the cheque underneath the security screen. This was really starting to wind him up the wrong way, but fare dues he started all this animosity, trying to get funny with me. A big mistake even I wouldn't like to get into an argument with me! He then asked to see my passport again, sarcastically replying 'but you have already checked it twice, can't you even remember that.' Like rubbing salt on into an open wound I continued the onslaught 'it was only the other day.' Looking back through the glass he remarked, 'you certainly get about a bit don't you' more jealously I thought. 'Yes, that right mate, I'm an international gypsy planning my next trip to South America, actually I'm going to see 'One Ball Ted and the Mexican Bum-bandits', if you're a really good boy I'll send you a post card, what do you think of that Pal! He must have thought I was talking about a rock band or something. Anyway, handing back my passport and the cash I heard him say under his breath 'arsehole'. Well actually I didn't care what he thought about me, I had the last laugh having all the money not him. That night Ruby returned from her holidays with Archie and I was introduced to this nutter. We had a mad party in the new flat that went on to the early hours of the morning; even the new neighbours turned up and joined in for the crac. Slowly taking each day as it came I settled into my new surroundings and the beach looked rather cool and the pubs even cooler. Most days I just dosed about basically, chilling out relaxing drinking beer listening to music spending the big fat green giros. I suppose 'reader' you might say it was 'a life style I was getting accustomed too'. Actually this was turning out better than I anticipated, like Elait cut downs Levis jeans and flip-flops. We got to hire the stripy deck chairs the same as Eddie and would pretend we were holidaymakers, even going for evening swims in the English Channel. What a summer, ice cream candy floss sunshine and sand castles. I even managed a cruise up the Thames one bank holiday Monday in August. She was called 'The Montgomery' a paddle steamer built in Belfast in the late thirties and was moored at the end of Southend Pier. After boarding the pleasure cruiser I had lovely lunch and I managed a few pints of the black stuff at the bar. Sailing up the Thames I told the captain it my birthday and asked if I could visit the wheel-house. Amazingly he fell for it and let me steer the ship for a while, a real pirate. When we got to Tower Bridge in London they opened it up and the tourist waved us through, another great day. Eventually all good things come to and end and so did that summer.

On one sunny evening Tracy told me excitedly she had taken a pregnancy test it was positive and was expecting my baby and I was about to be a Dad. We planned our wedding at Southend Registrar office, thinking about my mates in Andover I invited a few, booking them in a small hotel along the seafront. Another mistake, unbelievably they all done a runner from the hotel and I had to foot the bill, one of them accidentally urinated in the bed and I had to buy a new mattress. This time I got knocked, poetic justice you might say, on the bright side Tracy had a little girl, and we called her Scarlett. It also was around that time there was an economic boom and Maggie was encouraging every one to buy there own house. Inflation was under control and the interest rate was at an all time low, money was cheap to borrow and the building society's and banks were falling over backwards to give you a mortgages and loans. Still on the dole without any real income I even managed to buy and I became what was known as a 'Yuppie.' As for the rest of my life I just let it take its own path leaving it to fate once more and continued to sign on the dole. It was a colossal massive amount of money as it included the repayments on my new house. The clerk at the post office couldn't take much more and on one day said, 'that's it, I've had enough' and stormed off in a huff, presumably he took my advice and signed on the dole himself. Anyway with the new baby and one thing and another I didn't pay the mortgage and kept the entire Giro for myself. Things went from bad to worse so I thought if I am going too get hung for a lamb I might as well a sheep and then got a load of secures loans on the property, over thirty thousand and then not paying them either, I had money coming out of my ears and went to Butlins holiday camp for six solid weeks, it was excellent fun. The banks and building societies were hoping mad, trying to get the government to pay them direct, as everyone was spending their big fat green giros on themselves, like me. Technically thousands of people where squatting in the houses waiting for the eviction notices and then applying for a council

Robert Charles Scanlan

house. Repossessions, bankruptcies and county court judgements were the order of the day and I thought I just join in with the swarm and deal with it like that, hopefully very soon becoming another government static, not yuppie, yippee! At lest I wasn't the only one, which in turn made me feel a lot better? Tens of thousand were going down every week and the knock on effect was a glut of cheap properties for sale, they called it negative equity. My house was only worth thirty thousand but had mortgages owing over one hundred thousand, with no hope whatsoever in paying it back. Eventually parliament had to intervene and after a special sitting at the House of Commons changed the law, paying the big fat green giros directly to the lender, but a least I had some of the action. Never the less it was too late for me and as time went on I managed too acquire yet even more county court judgements. The building society started repossession proceedings and wanted all there money back. I had over six or seven overdue credit cards, store cards, four or five catalogues personnel loans and a substantial overdraft at the bank. Things got so bad though even the milkman wouldn't give me any more credit; I never liked his eggs anyway! Although things weren't all that bad and I was still an active member of the free bank, called the 'National Giro Bank'. They had branches in every street corner at the post office and gave away free money, now that is what I call customer service. Thanks again Maggie! Every day even more fan mail arrived by the sack load and to be honest reader I just gave up; burying my head in the sand hoping it would all go away on its own? Obviously it didn't and by now was spiralling completely out of control; I suppose you could say I had become comfortably numb with it all. Sarcastically even the postman commented

Eighteen months of this went by and eventually they sent a private detective around my house. On the night Scarlett accidentally went to the front door and let the man in. She thought it was just one of my friends and marched him straight in the front room. I was just sitting there in front of the fire watching Benny Hill on the TV eating Cod and Chips out of the bag, yummy! He stood above me introducing him self as Detective Dick Dastardly from London. Furthermore had come all this way especially to interview me, I thought I should be so lucky! To confuse the state of affairs I acted a bit daft and carried on watching TV and even offered him a chip from the bag. I remember being rather persistent saying 'go on Dick, have one their yummy'. It had just come too a really funny bit on TV and Benny was been chased around a tree by about ten girls, all dressed in black bras and stockings. I deliberately started laughing hysterically and my act would have won me another Oscar, even little Scarlett joined in the performance clapping. He declined a chip saying 'look forget the chips and Benny Hill, what about all this money you owe to all these financial institutions, it's now over One hundred thousand pounds and getting bigger by the day? I couldn't think of anything to say apart from 'is it really, I thought it was more that that'. Then he looked on his clip board and started asking me how I intended to pay all these banks back, the list was as long as your arm. Scarlett was sitting next to the open fire and innocently asked 'are you in trouble again dad'. I didn't feel guilty about not paying them back, I saw them all as a faceless so there was no victim too greave for, society not me calls it 'white collar stuff'. Thinking on my feet I said 'Ah, no problem, come with me and I'll show you' and then I bizarrely led him and her into my back garden. He wasn't quite sure what was going on and followed behind nervously with nosey Scarlett in toe. It was winter time cold and dark, November 5th Guy Fawkes night to be precise. The fireworks were surging and screeching into the air and massive explosions and blast filled the night sky, you could even smell the cordite and gun powder.

Perchance the main sewage drain in the backyard had collapsed and I was in the middle of fitting a brand new one. I had been at it for a couple of days and already dug the huge hole around the broken pipe. It was really deep and dangerous and actually looked like a real life bomb crater. To bamboozle him even further I offered him another chip. He was starting to get angry with me and didn't answer so I refused to break the silence. Whilst standing motionless next to this it gigantic hole and pile of wet mud, a rocket exploded above our heads. I took this opportunity to stare into space, remarking 'Cur, look Scarlett that was good one'. Rite on cue she replied 'Look Dad there goes another one' He just couldn't believe it and whilst scratching his head and blinking to make sure he wasn't seeing things and asked, 'why are you showing me all this'? What a laugh, maybe he thought I was about to kill him and then bury him in it! With all the explosions going on know one would have noticed and extra bang or two. Again he shook his head in disbelieve saying 'how is all this relevant Mr Scanlan.' My brain stopped but my mouth kept going, 'Well actually, I'm digging my own water well and then I'm going to bottle and sell it, paying off all my creditors including you, amazing init'. By now I was well into it and continued my Comaneci-ambush, 'as a matter of fact I'm marketing it as S. O. S, South-ends only spring, what you think? Stepping back from the hole he nervously enquired, 'have you got planning permission for all this'. Shrugging my shoulders I didn't say much apart from 'Ah sure, were not really worried about them lot, are we Scarlett'. Humorously she piped up saying 'will you be able to buy it at Marks and Spencer's dad.' With that he turned his back and swiftly marched back into the house and now I had him on the run. Still visibly shaking, he got me to sign something and left pretty sharpest, properly thinking we've got a right nut case here, just what I wanted him to think.

It was so funny and I couldn't wait to tell all my friends at the pub. Strange thing happened though, a few days later I got a visit from the Town planning department. Banging on the front door demanding to see what I was up too. I remember saying to him 'hold your horse's mate, what's your problem'. He was deadly serious, 'I've heard rumours that you're digging a ninety foot water well in your back garden'. I couldn't help roar with laughter as I invited him in to have a look around. By now I started to fit the new brown pipe work, so any fool could see what I was actually doing. Standing above the hole he became rather embarrassed and continued to remark 'oh, I'm very sorry for wasting your time Mr Scanlan', and then he left with his tail up his bum as quickly as he came, I remember saying as he left 'thanks for coming.' However, this confirmed the private detective was well and truly fooled and must have reported back this guy is insane and incapable of handling his own affairs. They were very reluctant to proceed; obviously they already had thousands of vacant properties on there hands and didn't want mine either and we had reached stale mate. Eventually I new I would be evicted and every day was a day closer to getting the keys to my new Council house. Eighteen months of this staging went by and nothing changed apart from me fathering a son Rory, Scarlett was ecstatic with her new little brother and wouldn't leave him alone.

D day arrived and bailiffs turned up at my front door. I was expecting them as they phoned me up and told me they where on their way, the posse. Landing at the front door they hand delivered the court ordering me to leave the premises fore-with, the personnel touch, I should be so lucky. Tracy and the children had already moved out too Nanny Ruby's and all my furniture had been put into storage. All I had to do was sweep the floor, have one more final cigarette and hand over the keys. Strangely I remember thinking about what Mr Love taught me by the stream, 'trust your instincts in life Bob and be confident with them'.

The council weren't at all impressed with my antics, saying it was all premeditated, furthermore I had made myself intentionally homeless, but they couldn't prove it. To be honest I thought I was the only clever dickey on the planet, little did I know the whole town had the same idea and they where inundated with housing applications. After completing the forms and being accepted on the waiting list I moved us all into a hotel along the seafront and the children thought they were on holiday, central heating and cooked breakfast thrown in. The state picked up the tab, it was a colossal amount bordering on what society may call an outrageous waste of public money, no problem thanks Maggie. Anyway it's no good calling me a free loading hippie even if I am one, I didn't make the rules I just stuck to the lettering of them. Personally I didn't do much apart from continuing cashing the Giros like before and take the children to school and then sunning my self on the beach every day. The council were brilliant and after my little break gave me the keys to a new house. Excellent, another free-bee and well worth waiting for, much appreciated thanks again Maggie.

Happy enough though living by the sea, I started working on the building sites as a painter and decorator. One particular Saturday afternoon I was working late finishing off a contract, when I took a terrible beating for absolutely nothing. It all occurred so fast I didn't have time to think and was knocked off my ladder and ended up in a big heap on the floor. This guy was a completely stranger and completely out of control, viciously embedding his steel toe-cap boots rite it into my face. Sincerely I thought if he doesn't stop he's going to kill me. It seemed to go on. He stood above me shaking and pointing his finger, shouting at the top of his voice, 'Derek had sent him and he would be back' the thing is I didn't even know any Derek and didn't have a clue what he was on about. Drifting in and out of consciousness I didn't feel pain it was more like numbness, I couldn't breathe properly, the teeth he had kicked out lodged in my throat, revoltingly I had to gulp hard and

Robert Charles Scanlan

swallow them. My nose was also broken and blood streamed out by the bucket load and two of my ribs were cracked. Laying there in this deserted house on these cold wooden floor boards, I felt knackered as if I had been swimming and thought; you better not fall asleep Bob otherwise you might not wake up. Heaving myself up from the floor I wondered around and found a piece of broken mirror lying next to the cement mixer. My right eye had completely closed up and the tissue around it looked like a raw piece of pigs liver, that dark purple colour, contemplating any second now it was going to burst wide open. Two teeth were missing and my nose now leaned to the left hand side. Looking like one of the monster munches or a traffic accident, again I thought 'this it Bobby Boy' The building site had an outside water tap in the back garden, for a minute or so I ducked my head under the cold water and washed away my blood. Again not sure what to do next I thought about the friendship I had struck up with the old lady who lived next door. Florence as she was called was always giving me tea and biscuits, having a chat with me over the wall becoming quite sociable, reminding me a bit of our Kitty. Like Kitty, I went to the shops for her and she also lived on her own. Her back door was open so I knew she was in, in any case there were no phone boxes and I couldn't walk through the streets looking like this. Although on the same token did-n't want to worry her, so fibbing said 'I had fallen from the ladder land-ing badly'. She was so kind and sympathetic bathing my wounds in salt water, wrapping a bandage around me, suggesting even at one point, insisting I go to hospital, furthermore she didn't believe me about the fall. Later on she rummaged around in the sideboards and found a pair of dark glasses. The taxi driver didn't ask too many questions as Florence begged him 'just take this man home please'. She even paid the fare for me. On arrival back at the house Tracy went mad not taking no for an answer, adamant I go to hospital otherwise she would phone the emergence services herself. Reassuring her I said 'I would go in the morning when I feel better. I didn't, treating myself with my old reme-dies and home made potions, Witch-hazel to take away the bruising, Aspirin to bring down my temperature, pot to kill the pain antiseptic swaps to stop infections and raw beef steaks to draw the dried blood, there wasn't much I could do about the teeth apart from making sure they came out the other end, Bob's your uncle. I couldn't go to work for a fortnight convalescing. I found out later it was a mistaken identity and had absolutely nothing to do with me; and again just happen to been in the wrong place at the wrong time, why me! The only thing I could think of was, I had borrowed a mate's van that week while he was on holiday and it was parked outside the site. I did mention this to him on his return but he denied any knowledge, although mysteriously he soon moved away to another area. Mulling it all over now that's when the headaches, loss of smell, paranoia and flash-backs started, additionally I never did go to the hospital to get checked out properly, I wish I had now. At our weekly sessions Vera and the Doctors asked why I never mentioned this before, as it could be critically important. To be honest reader I just plain forgot until I started writing about it. That afternoon I was taken to the x-ray department and entered the world of science fiction. Deciding to check me out with a brain scan and a barrage of X rays and tests, discovering I had a hair line fractures in my skull, above my left eye and this was causing the migraines, making me feel fed up. Reassuringly they told me not to worry as it could be treated. As for the rest of it they said I should get a medal. They agreed to discharge me, and sent me home with medication, encouraging me to publish my diary as I had addressed a lot of social issues which others wouldn't touch with a barge pole, especially mental health issues. Hopefully some of the subject matter will never be repeated again and resigned for the school history lessons. And to finish up, a quote by Winston Churchill, 'I am prepared to meet my Maker. Whether my Maker is prepared for the great ordeal of meeting me is another matter.

The End

Robert Charles Scanlan

A tribute to my late Dad

Robert James Scanlan

1936—2006

Aged 69 years

TOGETHERNESS

Death is nothing at all; I have only slipped away into the next room. Whatever we were to each other—that we still are. Call me by my old familiar name; speak to me in the easy way which you always use to. Laugh as we always laughed at the little jokes we enjoyed together. Play, smile, think of me, and pray for me. Let my name be the household name it always was and let it be spoken without effort. Life means all that it ever meant. It is the same as it ever was, there is absolutely unbroken continuity. Why should I be out of your mind because I am out of your sight? I am but waiting for you, for an interval, somewhere very near just around the corner. All is well. Nothing is past, nothing is lost. One brief moment and all will be as it was before—only better. Infinitely happier and forever—we will all be one together with Christ, Amen.

William Shakespeare once wrote, All the world is a stage and all the men and women merely players. They have there exists and entrances and one man in his life-time plays many parts' Well, Robert played many parts in his life, and I suppose you can say 'this is his final exit'. He was born in Dublin 1936 and led a colourful and interesting life, and was always the first to sing and old song or tell a funny story. He first met Josie when she was only fourteen. Robert sister Marie introduced them; apparently Josie didn't fancy him at first and thought 'Well he's full of himself, prancing around listening to Frankie Lane Records. Eventually Robert's charming manner good looks and fantastic sense of humour won her over and they started dating when Josie was seventeen. It wasn't long before they fell in love and were married in 1959 and had five children, Anthony, Robert, Edward, Olive and the late Francis. In 1967 he uprooted his family from Ireland and moved to rural Hampshire in England. Within a week or so he was employed at the local engineering factory M.D.H. and was unanimously voted in 'shop steward' by the entire factory. Through his hard work and dedication he was finally promoted to 'Transport Manager' organizing shipments all over the world. He loved his work and the challenges it brought and eventually retired after twenty five years service in 1992. After retiring he spent the last fourteen years travelling extensively throughout the world and eventually settled here in Stoke on Trent. Robert was a well liked and loved man, and never had a depressed bone in his body or a bad word to say about anyone, and always had the knack of finding the good in a person. This is born out here today with the mere fact his family and friends have travelled the globe to get here, and I'm sure he would like to thank everyone who has turned up today, especially those who have made long journeys from America, Canada, Australia and Ireland.

Do not stand at my grave and weep. I am not there. I do not sleep. I am a thousand winds that swiftly blow. I am the diamond glint on newly

Robert Charles Scanlan

fallen snow. I am the sunlight on ripened grain. I am the soft and gentle autumn rain. When you wake from sleep in the early morning hush, I am the swift uplifting rush of quiet birds in circling flight. I am the soft, starlight at night. Do not stand at my grave and weep. I am not there. I do not sleep.

Amen

Printed in the United States
78378LV00007BC/5

9 781421 899053